Post-traumatic Stress Disorder in Children and Adolescents

Post-traumatic Stress Disorder in Children and Adolescents

EDITED BY

KEDAR NATH DWIVEDI MD, DPM, FRCPSYCH

CONSULTANT CHILD, ADOLESCENT AND FAMILY PSYCHIATRIST
Northampton General Hospital NHS Trust

W

WHURR PUBLISHERS

LONDON AND PHILADELPHIA

© 2000 Whurr Publishers
First published 2000 by
Whurr Publishers Ltd
19b Compton Terrace, London N1 2UN, England and
325 Chestnut Street, Philadelphia PA 19106, USA.
Except Chapter 8 – © Tania Phillips,
Chapter 10 – © Claire
Frederick and Constance Sheltren.

Reprinted 2001 (twice)

British Library Cataloguing in Publication Data
A catalogue record for this book is available from the British
Library.

ISBN 1 86156 163 6

Printed and bound in the UK by Athenaeum Press Ltd,
Gateshead, Tyne & Wear

Contents

Dedication

With warm affection and esteem, the editor dedicates this book to David Clark, Surya Bhate, Mike Law, John Lambert and Patrick McGrath.

Contributors

Kedar Nath Dwivedi, MBBS, MD, DPM, FRCPsych, is Consultant in Child, Adolescent and Family Psychiatry at the Child, Adolescent and Family Services, Northampton and is also Clinical Teacher in the Faculty of Medicine, University of Leicester. He graduated in medicine from the Institute of Medical Sciences, Varanasi, India, and served as Assistant Professor in Preventive and Social Medicine in Simla before moving to the UK in 1974. Since then he has worked in psychiatry and has contributed extensively to the literature, including editing *Groupwork with Children and Adolescents* (Jessica Kingsley, 1993), *The Therapeutic Use of Stories* (Routledge, 1997), and *Enhancing Parenting Skills* (John Wiley, 1997) and co-editing *Meeting the Needs of Ethnic Minority Children* (Jessica Kingsley, 1996), *Management of Childhood Anxiety Disorders* (Arena, 1997) and *Depression in Children and Adolescents* (Whurr, 1997). He is also the editor of *Transcultural Mental Health On-Line* and the Course Director for the Midlands Course in Group Work with Children and Adolescents.

Claire Frederick is a psychiatrist in private practice in Tahoe City, California. She is a Fellow of the American Society of Clinical Hypnosis and of the International Society for the Study of Dissociation. She is the co-recipient of the Crasilneck Award for excellence in writing in the field of clinical hypnosis and of the Cornelia Wilbur award for outstanding clinical contributions in the field of dissociation. She is a recipient of the American Society of Clinical Hypnosis Award of Merit as an outstanding clinician, author, and teacher as well as the American Society of Clinical Hypnosis President's Award. She is an adjunct faculty member of the Pacifica School of Graduate Studies in Depth Psychology. She is the co-author of *Healing the Divided Self: Clinical and Ericksonian Hypnotherapy* *for Post-Traumatic and Dissociative Conditions* (W.W. Norton) and *Inner Strengths: Contemporary Psychotherapy and Hypnosis for Ego-Strengthening* (Lawrence Erlbaum Associates). She teaches, presents, and publishes nationally and internationally in areas of ego psychology and ego-strengthening, Ego State Therapy, and mind-body healing.

Deborah Glass, BSc (Hons), Dip COT, SROT, has worked as a senior occupational therapist with children and adolescents with emotional and behavioural difficulties since qualifying from Dorset House School of Occupational Therapy, Oxford (now part of Oxford Brookes University) in 1984. She spent seven years in Israel, working in health and education settings, including during the period of the Gulf War. She has worked in various mental health settings in Oxfordshire.

Ricky Greenwald, PsyD, is a clinical psychologist and Assistant Clinical Professor of Psychiatry, Divisions of Traumatology and Child and Adolescent Psychiatry, at the Mount Sinai Medical Center in New York, NY. He recently served as Senior Psychologist for the Mokihana Project, Kauai (Hawaii) Department of Education. He is a leading authority on EMDR for children and adolescents and the author of *Eye Movement Desensitization and Reprocessing (EMDR) in Child and Adolescent Psychotherapy* (1999, Jason Aronson). His newest book is *Trauma and Juvenile Delinquency: Theory, Research, and Interventions* (in press, Haworth). He is active in research on child/adolescent trauma assessment and on the role of truma in disruptive behavior disorders.

Santoshkumar Mudholkar, MBBS, MDPsych, DPM, DNBC, has worked in the Department of Psychiatry, Charing Cross Hospital, London, and was a lead member of community based psychiatric intervention in earthquake-affected villages of Marathawada, India (a project co-ordinated by Voluntary Health Association of India, New Delhi and Department of Psychiatry, L.T.M.G. Hospital, Mumbai).

Smita A. Pandit, MBBS, MRCPsych, DPM, MD, DNB, Studied medicine and trained in psychiatry at the Bombay University. She worked as a lecturer in psychiatry at the University and was part of a team involved in treating people affected by communal riots and earth-quakes in Maharashtra, India.

Tania Phillips, MB, ChB, MRCPsych, studied medicine at Liverpool University and worked as a general practice trainee in Bedford. She trained in psychiatry in Liverpool and Manchester before joining the Oxford training scheme as a specialist registrar in child and adolescent psychiatry.

Konasale M. R. Prasad, MBBS, MD, DNB, MRCPsych, graduated in medicine in India. He underwent postgraduate residency training in psychological medicine at the National Institute of Mental Health and Neurosciences (an apex institution for brain sciences in India involved in research, training, policy formulations and providing clinical services). He also worked as a research officer in psychiatry and in child and adolescent psychiatry. He has more than a dozen publications to his credit and has been awarded the Bhagwat Award (given by the Indian Psychiatric Society for Young Psychiatrists) and World Psychiatric Association Fellowship for Young Psychiatrists.

Lalit P. Shah, MBBS, DPM, FRCPsych, FIPS, FAPA(USA), has worked as the Professor and Head of Department of Psychiatry at Seth G.S. Medical College and K.E.M. Hospital, University of Bombay, India. He has written many papers and books in child psychiatry.

Nilesh Shah, MBBS, DPM, MD, DNB, Associate Professor of Psychiatry, LTMML College, Mumbai, has presented numerous papers to national and international conferences.

Constance Sheltren, MA, MFT, is a licensed marriage family therapist in private practice in Truckee, California and a doctoral student in clinical psychology at the Fielding Institute. She specialises in the treatment of children and their families. She also has a background in child development and has taught human development to college students. She is a member of the California Association of Marriage and Family Therapists, the International Society for the Study of Dissociation; and a student member of the American Psychological Association.

Rosie Shepperd, MBBS, BSc, MRCGP, MRCPsych, is a consultant in child and adolescent psychiatry for the community in South Oxfordshire. Her clinical practice involves psychiatric assessment, provision of therapeutic interventions including medication, individual therapy, family therapy, consultation to professionals, supervision and support to the multidisciplinary team. She has close links with the Park Hospital for Children, a psychiatric inpatient unit for children and the Highfield Adolescent Unit in Oxford.

Susie Thompson, BSc (Hons), SROT, is currently working as a children's occupational therapist for West Sussex County Council Social Services. Following qualification at the University College of Ripon and York St John in 1994, she worked in an orphanage in Romania for over a year. She then worked for two and a half years for the Department of Child and Adolescent Psychiatry, Oxfordshire Mental Healthcare NHS Trust.

Leonard Thornton is consultant child and adolescent psychiatrist at the Countess of Chester Hospital, Chester. He worked previously as a consultant adolescent psychiatrist to the regional adolescent units in Manchester. Dr Thornton has wide clinical experience in the assessment of children and adolescents with post-traumatic stress disorder. He was involved in the assessment of adolescent survivors of the Jupiter disaster and has acted in an advisory capacity to solicitors representing children who have been involved in high profile, traumatic events.

Andrew West, MRCPsych, followed general medical studies with psychiatry and now works in child and adolescent psychiatry. He has experience of a wide range of therapies, and is a member of the Child and Adolescent Groupwork Association.

Jeremy Woodcock is the principal family and marital therapist and co-ordinator of the group therapy programme at the Medical Foundation for the Care of Victims of Torture, a unique charity that offers medical, psychological and practical assistance to survivors of torture and organised violence. Jeremy also teaches at the Institute of Family Therapy and is an honorary lecturer in the Department of Psychology at Birkbeck College, University of London.

Foreword

This is a very topical and useful book for a range of professionals working with traumatised children and their families. It provides a comprehensive guide for the assessment, management and understanding of child post-traumatic stress reactions and disorders.

Child mental health and related agencies have worked with victims of childhood trauma for several decades. Most of the research knowledge and clinical experience emerged from working with sufferers of abuse and neglect. However, this was based on general psychotherapeutic techniques. There was little empirical evidence of the nature of child psychopathology, the aetiological mechanisms involved in its development, and the specific treatment modalities to be used.

Since the early 1990s our knowledge has increased substantially, for a variety of reasons:

- Society has become far more child-centred, i.e. there has been wider recognition through the media and the welfare sector that children can be adversely affected in a variety of ways.
- Public opinion has been largely influenced and backed up by research findings from both the general population and some service cohorts. During the same period, there have also been substantial advances in psychiatric classification.
- Post-traumatic stress disorder (PSTD) has been identified as a separate clinical entity in adults and, more recently, in children and young people. The development and standardisation of rating scales and diagnostic interviews has facilitated this process, as PSTD often presents with other types of mental health problems.

Following earlier studies on the impact of childhood abuse, research addressed the effects of a range of acute and chronic traumatic experiences across different cultural groups:

- natural catastrophes, such as earthquakes and hurricanes
- accidents involving children, e.g. road traffic, rail or ferry accidents
- community violence, often in school, such as shooting or kidnapping incidents
- domestic violence, which highlighted the mediating effect of maternal distress and parenting capacity
- war trauma and displacement of refugee children and their families.

Although research evidence on the specificity and efficacy of treatment has only recently begun to emerge, treatment programmes have been described for children exposed to all these categories of traumatic events. It is now apparent that children with post-traumatic stress reactions can be helped by agencies and professionals from the health, education, social and voluntary sector. As in all his previous editorial work, Dr Kedar Dwivedi has ensured that the book has a multidisciplinary and practical focus. His task has been greatly assisted by a nice balance of experienced authors from different professional backgrounds.

Panos Vostanis,
Professor of Child and Adolescent Psychiatry, Greenwood Institute of
Child Health, University of Leicester
May 2000

Preface

Currently there are a number of books on PTSD, but they deal mainly with adult issues. Many of us working in the field of child mental health have therefore felt a pressing need for a practical book on PTSD in children and adolescents, which at the same time is comprehensive, scholarly and multidisciplinary.

It is a real pleasure to be able to fill this gap with this volume. It has also been an extremely pleasant task to edit it. In fact, I have been very fortunate in receiving high quality contributions from the authors. It has been a privilege to put together the work of such an extraordinary international team of professionals from a variety of disciplines with expertise and experience of working with PTSD in children and adolescents. I am therefore most grateful to all the contributors. Ricky Greenwald, in addition, has also helped me immensely with his comments on various draft chapters. I am also thankful to Karen Salter for help with indexing.

For me, this venture has coincided with a number of special events, such as my second short-term ordination as a Buddhist monk, the sudden death of our esteemed colleague Dr Malwankar, the reorganisation of our services and the celebration of the second birthday of our delightful grandson, Siddharth.

I received my first short-term Higher Ordination in Bodh Gaya, India in 1987 with the privilege of my mother's auspicious presence. The second one was in Heddington, Wiltshire, UK in July 1999 and it was equally auspicious to be accompanied by my son, Amitabh, receiving ordination at the same time. I remain deeply indebted to my meditation teachers, Mother Sayamagyi and Sayagyi U Chit Tin, and to all the dhamma friends, including Roger Bischoff, Jenny Alpern, Peter Ammann, Walla and Kathy Bachler, David and Elizabeth Borrie, John Boughey, Jean Claude and Natasha Brutsch, Martin Chadwick, Teresa and Michael Connolly, Kevin and Arabella Delahunty, Peter and Anna

Denger, Theo Doppenberg, Michael and Annie Dowling, Jim and Kyoko Emery, Beryl and Des Entwisle, Michael and Lucy Fraser, Sara Freeman, Grazia Cantoreggi, Orin Hargraves, Therese Keller and Mark Hediger, Jo and Coos Joosten, Eugen Jung, Horst Jughard, Virginia Judkins, Graham and Sue King, Eduard Klima, Michael and Tomoko Kosman, Hubert Knaus, Erich and Ursula Kuchers, Shukla Dhingra, Roy and Ma Millman, Franz and Imegarde Neuner, Roger and Nicola Newton, Dieter and Iris Nowotzin, Peter and Noreen Nyunt, Larry and Patti Palmer, Loven Pather, Neil and Kalia Pavitt, Mark and Clare Peterson, Bill Pruitt, Jim and Margrit Shannon, Matthajs Shouten, Kaye Hulena and Ray Shrimpton, Douglas, Gregory and Lee Solomon, Martina Stemich, Cherry Stephenson, Craig and Charlotte Storti, John Chittin, Marco Tosi, Chris and Alsion Fixsen, Bas van Vliet, Janos von Morzsinay, Monica Uhlrich, Richard Walsh, Christian and Regine Wunschik, Dave and Deborah Young, and Franz and Evelyn Zelsacher, to name but only a few.

On the traumatic side, we were really shocked to hear of the sudden death of Dr Malwankar. He too had graduated from the Institute of Medical Sciences, Varanasi. Most graduates from the Institute and their families living in the UK have been like a large extended family and this has been a great loss for all of us. I am thankful to Rajendra Agrawal, Shobha Agrawal, Umesh Chandra, Mahendra and Gargi Chopra, Ishwar Kumar Jagasia, Vaneet Khanna, Deepak Kaura, K.M. Mishra, Prem Swaroop Mishra, Babu Bhai Mistry, Thomas Peters, Megh Nath Roy, Ashwini Kumar Singh, Ram Akbal Singh, Mahendra P. Singh, Anil Sriwastawa, Mahesh Sriwastawa, Kamal Kant Shukla, R.S. Sumra, Gajanand Trivedi, Kala Tiwari, Vinod Kumar Tiwari and their families, to name just a few, for their support.

Putting together this book has coincided with important events in our professional arena as well. Our service has undergone many changes of names during the last few years: from Child and Family Guidance Service to Child and Family Consultation Service, to Child Adolescent and Mental Health Service and now to Child, Adolescent and Family Services. It has also moved from working as a sectorised multidisciplinary structure to a structure based more on unidisciplinary lines. However, there seems to be optimism for improving resources, although the clinical demands still outstrip the available resources. I would like to take this opportunity to thank my colleagues in the service for their dedication and commitment, including Brenda Baldwin, Mary Battison, Sue Buckland, Susie Chapman, Sheila Catchpole, Emma Fergusson, Lynda Davies, Gina Der-Kevorkian, George Butler, Brenda Fletcher, Linda Flower, Nein Gardner, Peter Harper, Avril Hart, Sarah Hogan, Frances Jones, Tania Kiana, Anthony Maister, Sharon Mallon, Guru Nayani, Ruth Nissim, Carol Passingham, Jan Pawlikowski, Annie

Ramsdale, Sandra Roberts, Annette Schlosser, Paul Sellwood, Jay Sriniwas, Vyvienne Tippler, Peggy Treseder, Michael Van Der Eijk, Melanie Westley, Sean Whyte, Cazz Wilhare, Phillipa Williams and Margaret Wysling.

Similarly I am grateful for the support of our paediatric consultant colleagues: Fran Ackland, Peter Daish, Tracey Davis, Nick Griffin, John Hewertson, Cliona NiBhrolchain, Susan Price, Sheila Shribman, Fiona Thompson and Christine Walker; Psychiatric Consultant colleagues: Suheib Abu-Kmeil, Jim Beehan, David Berry, Amit Bhattacharyya, Mohan Bonthala, Gavin Hendricks, Harnek Masih, Aly Mokhtar, Ram Mudaliar, Dawid Oberholzer, Alex O'Neil Kerr and Julie Roberts; Public Health Consultant colleagues, such as Charlotte Gath, Jill Meara, John Rogers, Silas Sebugwawo and other colleagues from the Child Health Directorate such as Bob Butcher, Stephanie Cairns, Lesley Cockerill, Jackie Coles, Jane Coles, Sue Collier, Joy Dinnage, Vee Hales, Helen Jessop, David Moscrop, Martin Scofield, Linda Scott, Damienne Sinclair and George Wilkinson, to name just a few.

I am also thankful to Andrew Northall and Barry Day from the Health Authority, Peter Kaye, Consultant in Palliative Medicine, Paul Cook, Director, Rainsbrook Secure Training Centre, Dawn Bason, Director of Health Promotion and David Wilson, Chief Executive of the Northampton General Hospital NHS Trust.

My special thanks to Dorothy Stephen, Carol Weller, Angela Concannon and Jan Winterburn from the Princess Marina Hospital library. They have been most helpful in coping with my 'a.s.a.p. requests'. I am particularly thankful to Karen Amos and also to Naina Sadrani, my secretary, who has been a dynamic hub of our service.

The warmth and support from my wife Radha, my sons Amitabh and Rajaneesh, my daughter-in-law, Amrita, and my most delightful grandson Siddharth have been immensely invigorating for me in this project. Finally, I would like to thank you, the readers, for taking the trouble to read and make full use of this book, in spite of so many competing demands on your time.

Kedar Nath Dwivedi
April 2000

Introduction

KEDAR NATH DWIVEDI

When we are subjected to hurtful or insulting remarks we often find ourselves feeling hurt, upset or angry. Within seconds there are massive physiological changes in heart rate, blood pressure, breathing, skin conductance, biochemistry, and so on. This may happen without our conscious awareness and certainly without our permission, as if someone has pushed a button. With the passage of time the feeling and the physiological changes may subside. However, when we remember the incidence again afterwards, those feelings and the physiological changes are also evoked, although no one is actually insulting us then. The system can thus respond to memories, fantasies, ideas, constructs and images as if they were real, substantial, here and now. It is in human nature to mix the real with the unreal like mixing milk with water (Dwivedi 1990, 1997a). Even deaths have been known to occur in such a psychogenic manner, as in Voodoo. The Buddhist approach to dealing with such intense feelings is to focus one's attention on the physiological processes (such as breathing) which are here and now and changing rather than on the mental objects (e.g. the memory of the insulting phrase) that keep churning up the feelings.

The illusory mechanisms involved in mental processes are clearly highlighted in Buddhist teachings. In the Indian culture, as early as the sixth century BC a systematised and coherent theory of consciousness became available, something that did not begin to happen in western culture until the nineteenth century AD (Reat 1990). In the eastern way of thinking there is no state of emotionlessness, as there is no state of weatherlessness; however, these emotions are normally preconscious and we become aware of them only when they intensify and break through our consciousness. Eastern meditative practices of expanding one's consciousness aim to get in touch with otherwise preconscious emotions. These emotions play a very important role in all our mental

1

functions such as information processing, cognition, memory and motivation but their excessive intensity can trigger a chain of disastrous consequences.

A particularly intense emotion may be felt as if it is everlasting and one may forget the fact that all emotions are only transient. If we do not fight, indulge or actively avoid, they will just run their course. One can also learn to utilise them as signals for oneself. Some of the meditative practices involve harnessing their energy for creative and constructive purposes, analogous to taming a tiger (Rinpoche 1987) and many have achieved enlightenment working through emotions.

Even in a newborn baby it may be possible to discern some kind of an emotional response that gradually becomes more sophisticated with maturation. There are at least four aspects to this process of emotional maturation (Dwivedi 1993, 1996a): differentiation, tolerance, desomatisation and utilisation.

- It is through **differentiation** that a large variety of specific emotions such as love, joy, fear, anger, anxiety, shame, jealousy and so on evolve from the early infantile emotional states of delight and distress.
- In order to facilitate the development of **tolerance** parents allow their children to experience emotions but intervene to protect them from being overwhelmed by excessively intense or prolonged ones. This enables children to learn to use comforting or distracting strategies for themselves and thereby achieve self-regulation of affect. Children who are discouraged or punished for any self-soothing activity may not succeed in developing a sense of accessibility to their automatically controlled parts of themselves or to their affect regulatory functions. Such a developmental incapacity can lead to a variety of mental health problems such as psychosomatic illnesses, substance abuse, total dependence on one's partner for sexual arousal, and so on (Krystal 1988).
- **Desomatisation** involves greater utilisation of symbolic and linguistic behaviours instead of only somatic or bodily responses for emotional expressions.
- **Utilisation** means the development of a capacity to utilise emotions as helpful signals to oneself and also to utilise the energy available through emotions for constructive and creative purposes.

Just as the development of speech, sphincter control, walking and so on are greatly influenced by the quality of parenting, similarly different aspects of emotional development are also dependent on the quality of parenting (Dwivedi 1997b), cognitive maturation (Dwivedi 1997c) and the cultural context (Dwivedi 1996b). Various aspects of emotional development have important implications for mental health.

A state of psychic trauma can threaten to destroy all psychic functioning when a child is not protected from an overwhelmingly intense emotional experience. Such emotions are subsequently perceived as particularly dangerous. Whenever such an emotion, even in a mild form, arises in consciousness, the child feels the dread of being flooded with it and therefore various strategies are employed in order to avoid experiencing the dreaded emotion. Such strategies may include inducing altered states of consciousness, soothing or distracting rituals, violent or destructive behaviours, substance abuse and so on. It can thus lead to serious personality and mental disorders such as addictive disorder, anxiety disorder, depressive disorder and so on (Dwivedi and Varma 1997a, 1997b).

When one experiences a state of inescapable suffering, the natural defence mechanisms enable one to emotionally detach and dissociate from the otherwise unavoidable pain. These protective mechanisms can then be triggered more and more easily even by the subtle reminders of the past painful experience or by subsequent stressful experiences. One could even take on the feelings, attitudes and behaviours of the aggressor, a process known as 'identification with the aggressor', and look, sound, talk and attack like the perpetrator as if 'possessed' or 'bewitched' by the mental state belonging to the aggressor (Dwivedi 1997d).

Astronauts tend to be extremely capable of handling stress. This is probably because they have experienced gradually increasing amounts of stress but not overwhelmingly excessive or traumatic levels of it (Krystal 1988). There is an Indian story of a man who had no problem lifting his huge buffalo in his arms. When asked how he could achieve this, he explained that he dearly loved his buffalo and had been lifting her in his arms since she was only a little calf! It is thus the smooth, tolerable and gradual increase in exposure to stress that is so significant. Another key to success is the opportunity, facility and space for smooth processing of such experiences.

In Sanskrit, *sukha* and *duhkha* (pronounced sukh and dukh) mean happiness and misery. *Kha* means space, *su* means good and *duh* means bad. Thus, the essential difference between happiness and misery is in the quality of space or surface around the experiences (similar to the space or the surface around an axle in a cart). If the space is reflective and smooth, it leads to happiness; if it is gritty, rough and non-reflective, it leads to misery. A number of therapeutic approaches outlined in this book to process traumatic experiences are meant to create this healing space.

The book is intended to be a scholarly introduction to the field of post-traumatic stress disorder (PTSD) in children and adolescents, along with its clinical assessment and treatment. It is practically oriented, so that professionals will find it useful in their work with children, adolescents and their families, schools and other contexts. It is also aimed at a wide readership such as clinicians, teachers and researchers in child psychiatry, clinical child psychology, educational psychology, social work, paediatrics, occupational therapy, school nursing, child psychiatric nursing, health visiting, special needs co-ordination in schools and so on.

Following are the introductory chapters (1–5) followed by a chapter on assessment (Chapter 6) and several chapters on treatments (Chapters 7–12).

Chapter 1: 'The trauma orientation and child therapy' by Ricky Greenwald offers an overview of the field by briefly outlining the vulnerability to trauma, its prevalence, effects, assessment and recovery.

Chapter 2: 'Post-traumatic stress disorder: causes and aetiological factors' by Smita Pandit and Lalit Shah outlines the psychoanalytic, cognitive, behavioural, developmental and biological theoretical frameworks used to make sense of responses to trauma and also examines various contributory factors (the characteristics of trauma and that of individual and social factors) that influence the development of PTSD in children and adolescents.

Chapter 3: 'Biological basis of post-traumatic stress disorder' by Konasale Prasad looks at various neurochemical, neuroendocrinological, electrophysiological, neurodevelopmental and neuropsychological aspects and models of PTSD. It also offers a full summary for those readers who may not be very familiar with the technical terminology unavoidably used in the chapter.

Chapter 4: 'Post-traumatic stress and the space between: an interpersonal perspective' by Andrew West explores traumatisation, its responses, maintenance and treatment from a systemic and interpersonal perspective.

Chapter 5: 'Clinical aspects of post-traumatic stress disorder in children and adolescents' by Nilesh Shah and Santoshkumar Mudholkar describes various aspects of clinical presentation and its similarities and differences with other disorders.

Chapter 6: 'The assessment of post-traumatic stress reactions in children and adolescents' by Leonard Thornton outlines the principles and format for assessment and deals with clinical interviews, assessment instruments, assessments of pre-event functioning, traumatic event and post-event adjustment and diagnostic formulation.

Chapter 7: 'Individual treatments for children and adolescents with post-traumatic stress disorder: unlocking children's trauma' by Rosie Sheppard looks at the place of psychotherapies in helping traumatised children, debriefing, pharmacotherapy, art therapy, family therapy and behavioural therapy and also focuses on psychodynamic psychotherapies with comments on post-traumatic responses, cognitive distortions, post-traumatic play, revenge fantasies, and trauma and grief.

Chapter 8: 'Cognitive-behavioural therapy for post-traumatic stress disorder in children and adolescents' by Tania Phillips examines the CBT outcome research along with the indications for and limitations of CBT. It then describes different stages of individual treatment with CBT and comments on co-morbid conditions and group work with CBT.

Chapter 9: 'Therapeutic group work' by Deborah Glass and Susie Thompson includes the historical development of group work in mental health services, advantages and types of group work with young people, the logistics, practical details and content of group work in relation to traumatic experiences along with examples of tools and methods used for these purposes.

Chapter 10: 'All in the family: therapy for the families of traumatised children and adolescents' by Claire Frederick and Constance Sheltren outlines the historical perspectives and models of family therapy. It also provides practical details of therapy with the families of victims traumatised by forces external to the family and of therapy with the families of victims whose trauma has occurred within the family, along with case examples. It deals with family play therapy to address the developmental level of the child and offers a roadmap for phase-oriented therapy with families within which children and adolescents have been traumatised.

Chapter 11: 'Eye movement desensitisation and reprocessing' by Ricky Greenwald not only outlines the historical account and research evidence for the use of this treatment approach in children and adolescents but also gives an account of the method with case examples.

Chapter 12: 'Refugee children and their families: theoretical and clinical perspectives' by Jeremy Woodcock not only brings us in touch with the realities of the context (such as extreme events, war and atrocities, dislocation, racism and so on) but also integrates theoretical perspectives (e.g. attachment) and therapeutic approaches (including indigenous healing practices, narrative, social constructionist, systemic and psycho-analytic) for working with refugee children.

References

Dwivedi, K. N. (1990) Purification of mind by Vipassana meditation. In Crook, J. and Fontana, D. (eds), Space in Mind. Shaftesbury: Element.

Dwivedi, K. N.(1993) Emotional development. In Dwivedi, K. N. (ed.), Group Work with Children and Adolescents. London: Jessica Kingsley.

Dwivedi, K. N. (1996a) Facilitating the development of emotional management skills in childhood. In Trent, D. R. and Reed, C. A. (eds), Promotion of Mental Health, Vol. 6. Aldershot: Ashgate.

Dwivedi, K. N. (1996b) Culture and personality. In Dwivedi, K. N. and Varma, V. P. (eds), Meeting the Needs of Ethnic Minority Children. London: Jessica Kingsley Publishers.

Dwivedi, K. N.(1997a) Management of anger and some Eastern stories. In Dwivedi, K. N. (ed.), The Therapeutic Use of Stories. London: Routledge.

Dwivedi, K. N.(1997b) Enhancing Parenting Skills: A Guide for Professionals Working with Parents. Chichester: John Wiley.

Dwivedi, K. N.(1997c) Introduction. In Dwivedi, K. N. and Varma, V. P. (eds), Depression in Children and Adolescents. London: Whurr Publishers.

Dwivedi, K. N.(1997d) Groupwork with violent children and adolescents. In Varma, V. (ed.), Violence in Children and Adolescents. London: Jessica Kingsley Publishers.

Dwivedi, K. N. and Varma, V. P. (eds) (1997a) Depression in Children and Adolescents. London: Whurr Publishers.

Dwivedi, K. N. and Varma, V. P. (eds), (1997b) A Handbook of Childhood Anxiety Management. Aldershot: Arena.

Krystal, H. K. (1988) Integration and Self Healing: Affect, Trauma, Alexithymia. Hillsdale, NJ: Analytic Press.

Reat, N. R. (1990) Origins of Indian psychology. Berkeley, CA: Asian Humanities Press.

Rinpoche, D. A. (1987) Taming the Tiger. Eskdalemuir: Dzalendara Publishing.

Chapter 1
The trauma orientation and child therapy*

RICKY GREENWALD

The dynamics of trauma and principles of trauma treatment may apply to child therapy more broadly than solely in the treatment of post-traumatic stress disorder (PTSD). Child therapists familiar with trauma dynamics and treatment can use this as an organising principle for a generic comprehensive therapy approach (Greenwald 1999). This chapter addresses the empirical and theoretical bases of the trauma orientation to conducting therapy with children and adolescents. The focus is on how current knowledge about child trauma prevalence, effects, assessment and treatment may be relevant to a broad range of child problems. This is not to say that every child has been severely traumatised, nor that every child problem represents PTSD. However, the argument will be made that most children have been exposed to some upsetting experiences which are relevant to the presenting problem, and which resemble trauma sufficiently for principles of trauma treatment to apply.

Definition of trauma

Child trauma generally refers to an experience of overwhelming horror, fear or pain, along with helplessness (Krystal 1978). Typical examples include road traffic accidents, physical or sexual assault, a house fire or witnessing violence. Such extreme events often lead to PTSD, although many outcomes are possible.

Children may also be exposed to a variety of other upsetting events that do not meet the DSM criteria (APA 1994) for trauma. Such events may include the death of a family member, family break-up, serious

---

*Reprinted with modifications from *Eye Movement Desensitization and Reprocessing (EMDR) in Child and Adolescent Psychotherapy* by Ricky Greenwald, pp. 275–292. Copyright © 1999 by Jason Aronson Inc. Reprinted with permission of the publisher.

illness, geographical displacement and a range of other challenges. Traditionally, the child's symptomatic response to this class of event, when recognised as such, has been called an **adjustment disorder**.

The research on so-called adjustment disorders of childhood suggests that this is a misnomer in many instances. For example, children's symptoms following family breakup are suggestive of a post-traumatic reaction (Heatherington et al. 1989), although this may be complicated by ongoing family dynamics. As with PTSD, so-called adjustment disorder symptoms also frequently fail to resolve within the specified 6 month period, and may be sustained indefinitely (Newcorn and Strain 1992). Another similarity is that, even when acute symptoms diminish, the internal damage is often maintained.

For children, at least, there may be relatively little difference between an unexpected traumatic experience and an unavoidable major loss experience which has been anticipated. Although a loss experience does not typically lead to an increased state of arousal (Pynoos 1990), the overwhelming fear and helplessness may be present in either case. Furthermore, many children develop similar reactions to chronically occurring but relatively minor upsetting events, such as repeated verbal abuse or school-related frustration. Thus, virtual post-traumatic responses may arise from many types of events. The clinician's concern is not with 'how bad it was' according to some objective criteria, so much as, 'how is it affecting you now?'.

For present purposes, trauma is defined in the broadest sense, to include any upsetting experience which has been incompletely integrated. Certainly this definition would not be acceptable in a research context, and much of the following discussion does refer specifically to the more extreme types of traumatic events. This is not to suggest that one child's adjustment reaction is likely to represent the same degree of distress as another child's PTSD. However, this inclusive definition of child trauma is arguably the most clinically relevant, since recognising trauma's contribution to a child's problem may enrich the treatment plan, regardless of specific diagnosis.

Vulnerability to trauma

Severity of exposure

Since Terr's (1979) landmark study of a group of kidnapped children, there has been considerable interest in children's responses to traumatic incidents such as accidents, abuse, exposure to violence and natural disasters. It is widely recognised that virtually all children exposed to extremely traumatic events will retain post-traumatic reactions for over a year (if untreated), and perhaps indefinitely (Greening and Dollinger

1992, Holaday et al. 1992, Nader et al. 1990, Newman 1976, Terr 1979, van der Kolk 1987). Vulnerability is increased with severity of exposure (Lonigan et al. 1991, Nader et al. 1990, Pynoos et al. 1987). Post-traumatic sequelae phenomena such as hospitalisation or separation from parents may extend the exposure to trauma, constituting continued traumatisation (McFarlane 1987). Other associated loss or displacement experiences may function similarly (Cohen 1988). Lesser exposure may also entail post-traumatic response, but typically involving lower frequency and severity of symptoms.

The severity of exposure to a traumatic event is mediated by perception, personal meaning of the event (Milgram et al. 1988), and emotional reactivity (Schwarz and Kowalski 1991). Such mediation may reflect developmental level (see below), as well as prior traumatisation or psychopathology, which have also been found to increase risk (Burke et al. 1982, Earls et al. 1988).

Developmental level

Children may be particularly vulnerable in general, as they are in many cases truly more helpless and easier to frighten than adults, who have more fully developed physiques, knowledge, social status, emotional resources and perspectives on the situation. However, developmental level *per se* has not been found to differentiate children in their vulnerability to traumatisation (Newman 1976, Terr 1979). For example, the cognitive distortion and regression associated with traumatisation is found across developmental levels (Schwarz and Kowalski 1991, Terr 1979). However, the child's level of development may influence the nature of the traumatic experience. Coping efforts are affected by current developmental-phase-specific issues, capacities and influences. For example, the ability to regulate affect and to obtain extra-familial emotional support normally increases with age. Level of development may also have some effect on the way an experience is understood (Newman 1976). For example, very young children may not accurately perceive their lives as threatened in a dangerous situation (Green et al. 1991).

Personality styles

Personality styles which are more prone to avoidance, denial and external locus of control, as opposed to actively facing and integrating experience, may also increase vulnerability (Gibbs 1989, Hyman et al. 1988). This predisposition may lower the threshold at which an upsetting event constitutes a trauma rather than being effectively processed. Along with severity of exposure, peritraumatic dissociation (during and after the event) is now considered one of the best predictors of subsequent post-traumatic stress problems (Shalev et al. 1996, Michaels et al. 1998).

Although temperament undoubtedly makes some contribution to this tendency, early development involves a pattern of parent–child interactions through which the child learns the extent to which painful emotions are tolerable, or must be feared and avoided (Winnicott 1965, Mahler et al. 1975). Thus, an avoidant processing style may already represent a low-grade chronic post-traumatic reaction. Similarly, for reasons discussed below, prior discrete traumatic experiences also predispose to vulnerability to post-traumatic reactions.

Environmental factors

The child's social environment following a critical incident can also be influential in supporting or limiting expression of feelings and integration of the traumatic memory (Galante and Foa 1986, Cohen 1988, Jones 1991). The nature of family interaction may be particularly important. When one or both parents 'fall apart' or give the message that they cannot tolerate exposure to the traumatic memory (perhaps expressed as overprotection, avoidance or denial) this may confirm and reinforce the child's own defensive post-traumatic reaction. Furthermore, the child may move into an emotional caretaker role (parenting the parents), leading to loss of feeling cared for, reduced opportunity for processing and increased disturbance (Bloch et al. 1956, McFarlane 1987, Green et al. 1991).

Prevalence of trauma

Some of the data on the prevalence of traumatic events in childhood are indirect and suggestive, yet persuasive and alarming (e.g. Pynoos 1990). Recent research has found astonishingly high incidence rates for prior experience of at least one criterion A (extremely traumatic) stressor among young adults – most of which presumably occurred during childhood or adolescence. For example, Riise and colleagues (1994) found an 85% incidence among a young military population (only a minority of which were military trauma), and Vrana and Lauterbach (1994) found an 84% incidence among college students, presumably a relatively well-protected population (for more discussion, see Vrana and Lauterbach 1994). Among disadvantaged urban populations, exposure to criterion A events appears to be a regular occurrence (Campbell and Schwarz 1996, Jenkins 1995). Trauma during childhood and adolescence is now so common as to be normative.

When major loss experiences as well as chronic minor trauma are also taken into account, it becomes increasingly clear that child trauma, broadly defined, is ubiquitous. In clinical practice it is unusual to encounter a child who has not been touched by at least one significant adverse life event. Although the majority of children and adolescents do not develop the full PTSD syndrome, a high percentage may carry symptoms of post-traumatic stress (Cuffe et al. 1998, Greenwald and Rubin 1999), sometimes sufficient for the development of other mental disorders.

Effects of trauma

Trauma involves an intense experience of helplessness and fear, frequently including physical or emotional pain. If this becomes intolerable to the child, an extraordinary effort may be made to escape these feelings. The scope of this effort is represented in the variety of symptoms which a traumatised child may develop (described below). These symptoms provide partial relief from the intolerable feelings, but have the paradoxical effect of deferring true relief, since they prevent the child from fully facing and processing the traumatic memory. Failure of integration leaves the traumatic memory in a fresh, raw state – a constant threat.

In effect, the traumatic experience constitutes such a shock to the system that it is, in some way, rejected from the normal processing routine. Instead of facing and gradually working through the upsetting aspects of the memory, it is experienced as too overwhelming, and pushed aside. Avoidance, a hallmark of PTSD, can include many strategies such as repression, distraction, self-medication, emotional numbing, emotional withdrawal and behavioural avoidance of reminders.

Meanwhile, the traumatic experience persists in an active unprocessed state, constantly threatening to intrude, as if still happening. The memory is preserved, perpetually waiting for a chance to go through the normal processing system and join its mates in long-term memory storage. When something thematically similar arises, the traumatic memory may become stimulated and then re-emerge in part or whole, as if to say, 'I'm still here, can I finally come through the system?'. This may be experienced directly as an intrusion of imagery from the traumatic memory, or it may be experienced as an intrusion of belief and/or affect, in the form of an overreaction to the current stimulus. Because the person may be unaware of overreacting, the danger value of the current stimulus, or 'trigger', is experienced as being magnified. This unwanted intrusion of memory aspects is another hallmark of PTSD.

Not only does the unprocessed trauma contribute to overreaction and an experience of increased environmental threat, the memory itself is aversive. Indeed, some children find many aspects of their life threatening simply because they never know when the memory will intrude.

In other words, a traumatised child may develop a sense of the world as literally more dangerous, along with a sense of their own mind as being dangerous by, in essence, attacking them with the traumatic memory, often without warning. The child may become hyperalert to possible threat, developing symptoms such as anxiety, worry, tension, a 'hostile attribution bias' (misinterpreting neutral communication as threatening) and exaggerated startle response. This hyperarousal, or 'survival mode' state (Chemtob et al. 1988), is another hallmark of PTSD. The hyperarousal also contributes to reactivity, as the child is already in a state of tension.

Avoidance in many forms becomes a priority, driven by the urgency of survival instinct. Meanwhile, intrusions may continue to drive overreactivity and infect the child not only with general fear, but with specific thoughts and feelings arising from the unprocessed traumatic memory. For example, the child may come to feel more generally helpless and ineffective, and so become apathetic. Thus, the child's response to the trauma becomes a primary organising principle for personality, mood and behaviour.

This combination of avoidance, intrusion and hyperarousal creates an extremely unfortunate dynamic for the traumatised child. Whenever the traumatic memory is stimulated, it sets off a process resulting in the reinforcement of the avoidance response. Of course, the avoidance response precludes facing and working through the memory, which is required for recovery (see below). To the extent that the spectrum of avoidance symptoms is effective in providing a measure of relief, they are self-reinforcing and may be maintained indefinitely.

The effects of trauma in individuals may be concealed or expressed in a number of ways. Post-traumatic symptoms in children are often manifested quite differently than in the classic adult PTSD picture; for example, children's reactions may include somatic symptoms, regressive behaviour or acting out (Fletcher 1993). Trauma effects, broadly defined, arguably form the basis of most non-organically-based psychopathology (e.g. Green 1983, van der Kolk 1987, Conaway and Hansen 1989, Brom 1991, Terr 1991, Famularo et al. 1992, Kendall-Tackett et al. 1993, Malinosky-Rummell and Hansen 1993, Flisher et al. 1997). Traumatised children may better fit behavioural criteria for diagnostic categories other than PTSD, such as attention deficit hyperactive disorder, generalised anxiety disorder, depression or oppositional defiant disorder. Child trauma effects may frequently be mislabelled with a diagnosis which accurately describes behavioural attributes but does not address the root of the disturbance. Note that trauma may also lead to lasting symptoms in lieu of any formal diagnosis (e.g. Sullivan et al. 1991, Terr 1991, Fletcher 1996, Cuffe et al. 1998).

The special problem of chronic trauma frequently entails even more pervasive changes in personality organisation, including the classic PTSD denial, numbing and hyperarousal as well as dissociation, self-hypnosis and rage. This pervasive reaction has been implicated as the basis of such adult pathology as borderline personality disorder, dissociative identity disorder (van der Kolk 1987) and complex PTSD (Herman 1992).

The burden of traumatisation

Here is a conceptualisation of the process underlying the apparent cumulative effect of traumatisation (see Figley 1985, Peterson et al. 1991). Trauma increases reactivity to thematically similar stimuli, to the extent that the current reaction encompasses prior unprocessed painful emotions as well as those evoked by the new event. The non-integrative response style, used to avoid the painful emotions, increases in value at each successive trauma, as the amount of pain in the reaction accumulates with each additional traumatic experience. Thus, as the **trauma burden** increases, so also does thematically related reactivity and predisposition to a non-integrative response style.

This concept of the trauma burden may explain the 'sleeper effect' shown by those without apparent long-term effects from trauma, when challenged in a thematically related area (e.g. Kantor 1980, Wallerstein et al. 1988). Recent research has also shown increased vulnerability to post-traumatic reactions following a traumatic experience among those with prior trauma history (Riise et al. 1994, Scott and Gardin 1994). At some point of critical mass, the burden of reactivity may simply overwhelm the containment mechanisms (or competing schemas) and become more generalised and apparent, manifesting in symptoms of depression, anxiety or PTSD.

It has become increasingly clear that children mature in a healthy way from experiences, even upsetting ones, that they can truly integrate; but they become psychologically crippled, not strong, from traumatisation (Pynoos and Nader 1988, Terr 1991). That symptoms may eventually diminish in prominence is not in itself indicative of recovery; instead it may reflect the child's effectiveness in defensive containment (or keeping a secret). The underlying damage may remain, impairing the child's future coping capacity, and perhaps altering the nature of career goals, future relationships, mood or sense of self. The scope of the damage may be pervasive, or quite circumscribed, so that similar reactivity would only arise in thematically similar situations. Of course, as noted above, many traumatised children's symptoms do not subside.

Assessment of trauma

There are many appropriate approaches to trauma assessment, which vary according to the situational context. Rather than outlining a particular assessment protocol, this section reviews the issues to be considered more generally in conducting an assessment, in order to most effectively discover evidence of post-traumatic stress.

The time factor

Children assessed with intensive clinical methods soon after a traumatic event tend to show disturbance more consistently, whereas both non-clinical assessment methods and greater time lapse since the event are associated with a decline in detected disturbance rates (Sugar 1989). Clearly, for many children, acute symptoms are more intense and noticeable than long-term symptoms. Also, immediately following a traumatic event, it is easier for the child and others to identify new symptoms as related to the event. Later, the child's personality may to some extent be organised around the post-traumatic symptoms, making the symptoms stand out less. Nonetheless, the child's post-traumatic response can certainly contribute to symptoms long after the acute response has faded. Clinical observations in adult populations also suggest that apparent recovery from childhood trauma may not constitute true recovery, with the adult remaining vulnerable in thematically related areas (Greenwald 1997, Kantor 1980).

One of the best ways to ascertain the possible contribution of specific past events to current symptoms is simply to obtain a history including both upsetting events and symptom development. Of course, other factors should also be considered, including history of head trauma and other medical problems as well as environmental factors such as changes in neighbourhood, school and family membership or lifestyle. It is astonishing how frequently the presenting symptoms are found to have developed, or escalated, immediately following a major trauma or loss, without anyone in the family having previously made the connection.

Sources of information

Children are generally the best informants regarding their internal states, but tend to be poor observers of their own behaviour. Parents, on the other hand, often underestimate their child's internal distress, but they are fairly good observers of the child's behaviour (Burke et al. 1982, Handford et al. 1986, Earls et al. 1988, Loeber et al. 1990, Yule and Williams 1990, Belter et al. 1991). It is therefore necessary to obtain multiple sources of information.

Parent and child reports are generally correlated, but not always. Some traumatised children may maintain exemplary behaviour to keep their parents from worrying, or to keep from being singled out, and intentionally avoid displaying their ongoing distress (Bradburn 1991). With such children, self-disclosure of post-traumatic symptoms may be the best indicator. On the other hand, some children may deny, or simply lack awareness of, their post-traumatic status, and fail to endorse any post-traumatic symptomatology. With these children, the parent's report may be most useful.

An additional source of information may also be telling. For example, evidence is stronger when the teacher and parent describe the same cluster of problem behaviours across settings. On the other hand, when a traumatised child misbehaves at home, where the discipline is inconsistent, but behaves well in a highly structured classroom setting, this can be quite informative. The situation could also be reversed, for example, when a child does poorly in the classroom of an unduly harsh or lax teacher, as compared to at home.

The family context

The family environment may contribute to the development and persistence of post-traumatic symptoms, and can certainly contribute to recovery. Assessment of the family context is therefore critical. Although parent and child interviews can be helpful in this regard, nothing can replace direct observation of family interaction.

As noted above, when parents are reactive to trauma-related material, the child may experience further traumatisation, or at least get an unfortunate message regarding the trauma. For example, after reporting a rape, if the parents respond with avoidance and denial, the child may feel rejected and discounted. If, following a road traffic accident, the parents manage their own guilt by indulging the child and retreating on discipline, the child may feel that he or she is seen as damaged or less capable. Parents who discourage the child from talking about the event, ostensibly to keep the child from feeling bad, may actually be impeding resolution by giving the child the message that the event is too scary to bring up. Of course, following a major trauma or loss, many parents are so overwhelmed with their own reactions that they find it difficult to attend to their child's emotional needs. When this co-occurs with the traumatised child's increasingly difficult behaviour, a cycle of negative interactions can easily develop and become entrenched.

Ongoing family dynamics may also be contributing to the persistence of the child's post-traumatic symptoms. For example, a girl who had been raped by her babysitter was being regularly re-traumatised, in a minor but significant way, when her older brother bullied her. A father who no longer beat his children re-traumatised them with his yelling – they would actually cringe and bring an arm up in front of their face in self-defence. Probably the most common of the destructive family dynamics involve parental loss of control (yelling, angry physical discipline, unreasonable punishment) along with inconsistent discipline. Ongoing interactions like these give the traumatised child the message that things still are unsafe, meaning that the trauma could happen again any time. This makes recovery much more difficult.

Of course, supportive elements of the family context should also be evaluated. Most families do provide elements of routine, security, support and safety. It is generally not too difficult to discern concrete evidence of parental caring and concern as well. These strengths, elements conducive to healing, can be developed and built upon in the treatment plan.

Current safety issues

Assessment of current safety issues is critical to developing an appropriate treatment plan. Attempting to treat a child's post-traumatic reaction while the child is exposed to continued risk for trauma makes as much sense as repainting a ceiling without first fixing the leak in the roof that caused the damage. The goal of trauma treatment is achieved when the child can say, 'That's over, and now I'm safe'. Therefore, major safety issues must be identified and resolved as far as possible, before attempting trauma resolution work. More subtle safety issues such as parental consistency with discipline may be addressed either first or simultaneously, according to clinical judgement.

Objective measures

Until fairly recently, reliable identification of traumatised children has been cumbersome, involving extended clinical interviewing (McNally 1991). This was because assessment of trauma via instruments designed to detect anxiety, depression, or general psychopathology can be very sloppy. However, a number of trauma-focused objective measures are now available and can be very useful in efficiently screening for post-traumatic symptoms as well as tracking progress in treatment. Of course, objective measurement cannot replace clinical assessment, but it can make a real contribution. Resources in this area continue to develop; a few will be mentioned here.

There is no single 'best' child trauma measure. Rather, the purpose of the assessment, and the conditions under which it is conducted, guide selection of the most appropriate instrument for the situation. The various issues to consider are addressed below.

Trauma history

A number of trauma history instruments are available, ranging from check-lists to extended structured interviews. Some are keyed to assess qualification under criterion A, whereas others assess a broader range of adverse life events. The briefer questionnaires, although convenient to administer, are not generally scorable, and are best used as a guide for follow-up questions during a clinical interview. The structured interviews are much more detailed, but they are relatively tedious and generally most appropriate for research settings. Incidentally, children's and parents' reports of the child's trauma history may not be entirely consistent, either in the specific events reported, or regarding the child's response to the events.

Identified traumatic event

Sometimes a trauma assessment is conducted specifically to determine the child's response to an identified event, such as a hurricane, a school shooting or recently disclosed abuse. The Impact of Events Scale is the only really well-established instrument which assesses post-traumatic response to an identified event, and there is a subset of eight items (IES-8) which have been thoroughly validated for use with children and adolescents (Dyregrov and Yule 1995). Although the IES-8 can be useful in screening for post-traumatic stress and for tracking recovery, it does have limitations. The first is the same as its strength: it assesses response to the identified event only, and may fail to pick up post-traumatic symptoms associated with other, perhaps unidentified, trauma history. The other major limitation is that the IES-8 only taps two classic post-traumatic symptoms – avoidance and intrusion – and does not address the full spectrum of post-traumatic responses which may occur.

PTSD vs. post-traumatic symptoms

Some instruments may be keyed to DSM criteria for PTSD. Although this approach is certainly useful both for research purposes and to help determine PTSD diagnosis, the PTSD criteria in the DSM do not address the full range of children's actual post-traumatic responses (Fletcher 1993). For clinical purposes, a more comprehensive full-spectrum symptom assessment is preferable. At the time of writing, the Trauma Symptom Checklist for Children (Briere 1996) is preferred by many clinicians and researchers, as it features good psychometrics and includes a broad symptom coverage as well as relevant sub-scales. The Los Angeles Symptom Checklist – Adolescent (Foy et al. 1997) also has good psychometric properties, and has been used extensively with urban teens. Both of those instruments do also have PTSD sub-scales.

The Child Report of Post-traumatic Symptoms and the Parent Report of Post-traumatic Symptoms (Greenwald and Rubin 1999) feature brevity, full-spectrum symptom coverage, sensitivity to change in post-traumatic status and the perspectives of both parent and child. However, as a newer instrument it is not as well established as the others mentioned.

In sum, selection of objective measures, as well as the general assessment approach, will be determined by the purpose of the assessment, the age of the child, and availability of suitable resources. For example, a kindergartner is not likely to be able to complete any of the available trauma-focused self-report measures, but the parent will be able to complete a parent report form as well as providing relevant history and behavioural observations. Many clinicians prefer to combine various approaches, for example, by following a screening for trauma history and symptoms with a clinical interview.

It is impossible to overemphasise the importance of routinely assessing for trauma/loss history and post-traumatic symptoms, whether in an identified post-trauma context or as part of the initial assessment of mental health and behavioural problems (Greenwald 1997). Many traumatised children are currently not identified as such (Burke et al. 1982, Terr 1983, Handford et al. 1986, Earls et al. 1988, Kendall-Tackett et al. 1993). This tragic trend permits an immense amount of preventable impairment and suffering. Effective identification of traumatised children is a critical step in helping the children to recover.

Recovery from trauma

Factors favouring ease of recovery include an integrative processing style (Hyman et al. 1988, Gibbs 1989), coupled with opportunities to discuss the event and express the associated feelings with supportive family members, peers, and/or counsellors (Bloch et al. 1956, Galante and Foa 1986, Cohen 1988, Jones 1991). These findings imply that, for some period of time following an upsetting experience, the support or inhibition of processing may be quite influential in determining whether the memory will become integrated or remain problematic.

The urgency of self-protection which post-traumatic symptoms represent may render the traumatised child impervious to parents and others who try to help the child recover. Such children must often be treated by psychotherapists who are specially trained to facilitate the recovery process. Those children not treated will probably continue to suffer, and will be at higher risk for psychopathology, emotional distress, maladaptive life choices, and additional traumatisation (Krystal 1978, Terr 1979, 1991, Sugar 1989, Pynoos 1990). Although treatment of the traumatised child may be a gradual, arduous process, it can be essential to the child's continued healthy development.

The post-trauma treatment approach may entail a number of inter-vention modalities, taking into account the cultural, community, social, family, and developmental contexts of the child's life, before, during, and after the event (Cohen 1988, Pynoos and Nader 1988, Terr 1989). Interventions involving media (Terr 1989), school (Chemtob et al. in press; Jones 1991), family (Cohen 1988), and group (Galante and Foa 1986, Yule and Williams 1990, Chemtob and Nakashima 1996) continue to develop. Early intervention is most advantageous because the post-traumatic reactions are still readily apparent and clearly trauma-related, treatment may be more appealing, and recovery more rapid (Pynoos and Nader 1988). Later treatment is certainly possible, but over time the trauma effects become more integrated into personality and lifestyle (Horowitz 1986). Periodic treatment at transitional developmental phases may be necessary when the event creates a long-term develop-mental challenge, for example following the death of a parent (James 1989).

For many children, individual treatment is required, whether as the sole intervention or in conjunction with other approaches. The format typically includes talk, play/art and/or exposure modalities. Despite the many variations in form and timing, these treatments are nearly identical in underlying structure, including: re-experiencing the trauma in a safe, controlled setting; working through emotional reactions; restructuring cognitive appraisals; and enhancing the child's sense of efficacy (Pynoos and Eth 1986, James 1989, Peterson et al. 1991).

Although individual treatment may be essential to trauma recovery for some children, it may not be sufficient. In particular, environmental support may be required to help the child to legitimately feel more safe. This may involve a range of efforts, for example, to imprison a rapist, expel a perpetrator of abuse from the home or advocate for the child's school to crack down on bullying. As noted above, the family environ-ment is also potentially a primary source of support for the child's recovery, if the parents can convey that the child is truly safe at home. This may entail an exaggerated effort at conveying safety, in considera-tion of the child's trauma-related hypersensitivity. Safety is reinforced by fairness, predictability, and a sense of control. When parents understand the reasons for the therapist's suggestions regarding their behaviour, they are generally quite motivated to improve their own self-control and consistency in discipline.

The trauma orientation

Although much of this discussion has referred to extreme trauma, it has been suggested that the dynamics of traumatisation, as well as the princi-ples of treatment, apply to a wide range of children's experiences and presenting problems (e.g. Greenwald 1999). The data certainly support this contention, since many or most children in treatment do suffer from at least some post-traumatic symptoms. One of the advantages to the trauma orientation is that the experiential sources of children's problems are likely to be addressed. Another advantage is that trauma-based case formulations can be non-blaming and non-stigmatising, eliciting a sympathetic view of the child. Finally, such case formulations tend to be successful in engaging children as well as parents in productive treatment-related activities. The therapist can explain the child's problem in terms of a natural reaction to a bad experience, which can be resolved by following certain treatment principles; this presentation tends to reduce blame while enhancing hopefulness and motivation to act. The trauma orientation can assist the therapist in helping parents and children to understand the problem, to organise the range of interventions required, and to mobilise the clients.

References

APA (1994) Diagnostic and Statistical Manual of Mental Disorders, 4th edn (DSM-IV). Washington, D. C.: American Psychiatric Association.

Belter, R. W., Dunn, S. E. and Jeney, P. (1991) The psychological impact of Hurricane Hugo on children: a needs assessment. Advances in Behaviour Research and Therapy 13. 155–161.

Bloch, D. A., Silber, E. and Perry, S. E. (1956) Some factors in the emotional reaction of children to disaster. American Journal of Psychiatry 113, 416–422.

Bradburn, I. S. (1991) After the earth shook: children's stress symptoms 6–8 months after a disaster. Advances in Behaviour Research and Therapy 13, 173–179.

Briere, J. (1996) Trauma Symptom Checklist for Children (TSCC) Professional Manual. Odessa, F L: Psychological Assessment Resources.

Brom, D. (1991) The prevalence of posttraumatic psychopathology in the general and the clinical population. Israel Journal of Psychiatry and Related Sciences 28, 53–63.

Burke, J. D., Borus, J. F., Burns, B. J., Millstein, K. H. and Beasley, M. C. (1982) Changes in children's behavior after a natural disaster. American Journal of Psychiatry 139, 1010–1014.

Campbell, C. and Schwarz, D. (1996) Prevalence and impact of exposure to interpersonal violence among suburban and urban middle school students. Pediatrics 98, 396–402.

Chemtob, C.M., Nakashima, J., Hamada, R., and Carlson, J. (in press) Brief treatment for elementary school children with disaster-related PTSD: A fieldstudy. Journal of Clinical Psychology.

Chemtob, C. M., Roitblat, H. L., Hamada, R. S., Carlson, J. and Twentyman, C. (1988) A cognitive action theory of posttraumatic stress disorder. Journal of Anxiety Disorders 2, 253–275.

Cohen, R. E. (1988) Intervention programs for children. In Lystad, M. (ed.), Mental Health Response to Mass Emergencies: Theory and Practice, pp. 262–283. New York: Brunner/Mazel.

Conaway, L. P. and Hansen, D. J. (1989) Social behavior of physically abused and neglected children: a critical review. Clinical Psychology Review 9, 627–652.

Cuffe, S. P., Addy, C. L., Garrison, C. Z. et al.(1998) Prevalence of PTSD in a community sample of older adolescents. Journal of the American Academy of Child and Adolescent Psychiatry 37, 147–154.

Dyregrov, A. and Yule, W. (1995) Screening measures: the development of the UNICEF screening battery. Presented at the annual meeting of the International Society for Traumatic Stress Studies, Boston, November.

Earls, F., Smith, E., Reich, W. and Jung, K. G. (1988) Investigating psychopathological consequences of a disaster in children: a pilot study incorporating a structured diagnostic interview. Journal of the American Academy of Child and Adolescent Psychiatry 27, 90–95.

Famularo, R., Kinscherff, R. and Fenton, T. (1992) Psychiatric diagnoses of maltreated children: preliminary findings. Journal of the American Academy of Child and Adolescent Psychiatry 31, 863–867.

Figley, C. (ed.). (1985) Trauma and its Wake: The Study and Treatment of Post-traumatic Stress Disorder. New York: Brunner/Mazel.

Fletcher, K. E. (1993) The spectrum of post-traumatic responses in children. Presented at the annual meeting of the International Society for Traumatic Stress Studies, San Antonio.

Fletcher, K. E. (1996) Childhood posttraumatic stress disorder. In Mash, E. and Barkley, R (eds), Child Psychopathology, pp. 242–276. New York: Guilford.

Flisher, A. J., Kramer, R. A., Hoven, C. W. et al. (1997) Psychosocial characteristics of physically abused children and adolescents. Journal of the American Academy of Child and Adolescent Psychiatry 36, 123–131.

Foy, D. W., Wood, J. L., King, D. W., King, L. A. and Resnick, H. S. (1997) Los Angeles Symptom Checklist: psychometric evidence with an adolescent sample. Assessment 4, 377–384.

Galante, R. and Foa, D. (1986) An epidemiological study of psychic trauma and treatment effectiveness for children after a natural disaster. Journal of the American Academy of Child Psychiatry 25, 357–363.

Gibbs, M. S. (1989) Factors in the victim that mediate between disaster and psychopathology: a review. Journal of Traumatic Stress 2, 489–514.

Green, A. H. (1983) Child abuse: Dimension of psychological trauma in abused children. Journal of the American Academy of Child Psychiatry 22, 231–237.

Green, B. L., Korol, M., Grace, M. C. et al. (1991) Children and disaster: age, gender, and parental effects on PTSD symptoms. Journal of the American Academy of Child and Adolescent Psychiatry 30, 945–951.

Greening, L. and Dollinger, S. J. (1992) Illusions (and shattered illusions) of invulnerability: adolescents in natural disaster. Journal of Traumatic Stress 5, 63–75.

Greenwald, R. (1997) Children's mental health care in the 21st century: eliminating the trauma burden. Child and Adolescent Psychiatry On-Line. Internet address: http://www.Priory.com/psychild.htm.

Greenwald, R. (1999) Eye Movement Desensitization and Reprocessing (EMDR) in Child and Adolescent Psychotherapy. Northvale, NJ: Jason Aronson.

Greenwald, R. and Rubin, A. (1999) Brief assessment of children's post-traumatic symptoms: development and preliminary validation of parent and child scales. Research on Social Work Practice 9, 61–75.

Handford, H. A., Mayes, S. D., Mattison, R. E. et al. (1986) Child and parent reaction to the Three Mile Island nuclear accident. Journal of the American Academy of Child Psychiatry 25, 346–356.

Heatherington, E. M., Stanley-Hagan, M. and Anderson, E. R. (1989) Marital transitions: A child's perspective. American Psychologist 44, 303–312.

Herman, J. L. (1992) Complex PTSD: a syndrome in survivors of prolonged and repeated trauma. Journal of Traumatic Stress 5, 377–391.

Holaday, M., Armsworth, M. W., Swank, P. R. and Vincent, K. R. (1992) Rorschach responding in traumatized children and adolescents. Journal of Traumatic Stress 5, 119–129.

Horowitz, M. J. (1986) Stress Response Syndromes (2nd edn). Northvale, NJ: Jason Aronson.

Hyman, I. A., Zelikoff, W. and Clarke, J. (1988) Psychological and physical abuse in the schools: a paradigm for understanding post-traumatic stress disorder in children and youth. Journal of Traumatic Stress 1, 243–267.

James, B. (1989) Treating Traumatized Children: New Insights and Creative Interventions. Lexington, M. A.: Lexington Books.

Jenkins, E. J. (1995) Violence exposure, psychological distress and risk behaviors in a sample of inner-city youth. In Block, C. R. and Block, R. L. (eds), Trends, Risks, and Interventions in Lethal Violence: Proceedings of the Third Annual Spring Symposium of the Homicide Research Working Group, Atlanta, pp. 287–297. Washington, D. C.: U. S. Department of Justice, Office of Justice Programs, National Institute of Justice.

Jones, C. A. (1991) Who takes care of the caretakers? Advances in Behaviour Research and Therapy 13, 181–183.

Kantor, D. (1980) Critical identity image: A concept linking individual, couple, and family development. In Pearce, J. K. and Friedman, L. J. (eds), Family Therapy: Combining Psychodynamic and Systems Approaches, pp. 137–167. New York: Grune and Stratton.

Kendall-Tackett, K. A., Williams, L. M. and Finkelhor, D. (1993) Impact of sexual abuse on children: a review and synthesis of recent empirical studies. Psychological Bulletin 113, 164–180.

Krystal, H. (1978) Trauma and affects. Psychoanalytic Study of the Child 33, 81–116.

Loeber, R., Green, S. M. and Lahey, B. B. (1990) Mental health professionals' perception of the utility of children, mothers, and teachers as informants on childhood psychopathology. Journal of Clinical Child Psychology 19, (2), 136–143.

Lonigan, C. J., Shannon, M. P., Finch Jr., A. J., Daugherty, T. K. and Taylor, C. M. (1991) Children's reactions to a natural disaster: symptom severity and degree of exposure. Advances in Behaviour Research and Therapy 13, 135–154.

Mahler, M., Bergstrom, A. and Pine, F. (1975) The Psychological Birth of the Human Infant. New York: Basic Books.

Malinosky-Rummell, R. and Hansen, D. J. (1993) Long-term consequences of childhood physical abuse. Psychological Bulletin 114, 68–79.

McFarlane, A. C. (1987) Posttraumatic phenomena in a longitudinal study of children following a natural disaster. Journal of the American Academy of Child and Adolescent Psychiatry 26, 764–769.

McNally, R. J. (1991) Assessment of posttraumatic stress disorder in children. Psychological Assessment 3, 531–537.

Michaels, A. J., Michaels, C. E., Moon, C. H., Zimmerman, M. A., Peterson, C. and Rodriguez, J. L. (1998) Psychosocial factors limit outcomes after trauma. Journal of Trauma 44, 644–648.

Milgram, N. A., Toubiana, Y. H., Klingman, A., Raviv, A. and Goldstein, I. (1988) Situational exposure and personal loss in children's acute and chronic stress reactions to a school bus disaster. Journal of Traumatic Stress 1, 339–352.

Nader, K., Pynoos, R., Fairbanks, L. and Frederick, C. (1990) Children's PTSD reactions one year after a sniper attack at their school. American Journal of Psychiatry 147, 1526–1530.

Newcorn, J. H. and Strain, J. (1992) Adjustment disorder in children and adolescents. Journal of the American Academy of Child and Adolescent Psychiatry 31, 318–327.

Newman, C. J. (1976) Children of disaster: clinical observations at Buffalo Creek. American Journal of Psychiatry 133, 306–312.

Peterson, K. C., Prout, M. F. and Schwarz, R. A. (1991) Post-traumatic Stress Disorder: A Clinician's Guide. New York: Plenum Press.

Pynoos, R. S. (1990) Post-traumatic stress disorder in children and adolescents. In Garfinkel, D. B. Carlson, G. A. and Weller, E. B. (eds), Psychiatric Disorders in Children and Adolescents, pp. 48–63. Philadelphia: W. B. Saunders.

Pynoos, R. S. and Eth, S. (1986) Witness to violence: The child interview. Journal of the American Academy of Child Psychiatry 25, 306–319.

Pynoos, R. S., Frederick, C., Nader, K. et al. (1987) Life threat and posttraumatic stress in school-age children. Archives of General Psychiatry 44, 1057–1063.

Pynoos, R. S. and Nader, K. (1988) Psychological first aid and treatment approach to children exposed to community violence: Research implications. Journal of Traumatic Stress 1, 445–473.

Riise, K. S., Corrigan, S. A., Uddo, M. and Sutker, P. B. (1994) Multiple traumatic experiences: risk factors for PTSD. Presented at the annual meeting of the International Society for Traumatic Stress Studies, Chicago.

Schwarz, E. D. and Kowalski, J. M. (1991) Malignant memories: PTSD in children and adults after a school shooting. Journal of the American Academy of Child and Adolescent Psychiatry 30, 936–944.

Scott, S. T. and Gardin, M. (1994) Multiple traumas and the development of post-traumatic stress disorder. Poster session presented at the annual meeting of the International Society for Traumatic Stress Studies, Chicago.

Shalev, A. Y., Peri, T., Canetti, L. and Schreiber, S. (1996) Predictors of PTSD in injured trauma patients: a prospective study. American Journal of Psychiatry 153, 219–225.

Sugar, M. (1989) Children in a disaster: an overview. Child Psychiatry and Human Development 19, 163–179.

Sullivan, M. A., Saylor, C. F. and Foster, K. Y. (1991) Post-hurricane adjustment of preschoolers and their families. Advances in Behaviour Research and Therapy 13, 163–171.

Terr, L. (1979) Children of Chowchilla: a study of psychic trauma. Psychoanalytic Study of the Child 34, 547–623.

Terr, L. (1983) Life attitudes, dreams, and psychic trauma in a group of 'normal' children. Journal of the American Academy of Child Psychiatry 22, 221–230.

Terr, L.C. (1989) Treating psychic trauma in children: a preliminary discussion. Journal of Traumatic Stress 2, 3–20.

Terr, L. (1991) Childhood traumas: an outline and overview. American Journal of Psychiatry 148, 10–20.

van der Kolk, B. A. (1987) The psychological consequences of overwhelming life experiences. In van der Kolk, B. A. (ed.), Psychological Trauma, pp. 1–30. Washington, D. C.: American Psychiatric Press.

Vrana, S. and Lauterbach, D. (1994) Prevalence of traumatic events and post-traumatic psychological symptoms in a nonclinical sample of college students. Journal of Traumatic Stress 7, 289–302.

Wallerstein, J., Corbin, S. B. and Lewis, J. M. (1988) Children of divorce: A ten-year study. In Heatherington, E. M. and Arasteh J. (eds), Impact of Divorce, Single-parenting, and Step Parenting on Children, pp. 198–214. Hillsdale, NJ: Erlbaum.

Winnicott, D. W. (1965) The Maturational Processes and the Facilitating Environment. New York: International University Press.

Yule, W. and Williams, R. M. (1990) Post-traumatic stress reactions in children. Journal of Traumatic Stress 3, 279–295.

Chapter 2
Post-traumatic stress disorder: causes and aetiological factors

SMITA PANDIT AND LALIT SHAH

In the twentieth century, post-traumatic stress disorder (PTSD) has emerged as a formidable mental disorder, quite distinct from other stress reactions. This is perhaps a consequence of the numerous technological and industrial disasters, wars and natural disasters such as earthquakes and hurricanes, this century has seen. In addition, there has been an increase in the reporting of child physical and sexual abuse, the emergence of new diseases such as HIV, and new treatments of diseases such as cancer. The common characteristic of these events is that they are traumatic to people involved as well as to people who hear about them and see them. As a result, there has been an increased interest in finding out the causes, mechanisms of action and risk factors for PTSD.

It was suggested earlier that childhood trauma was a risk factor for some of the psychiatric disorders seen in adulthood. It is only in the past decade, however, that investigators have acknowledged that children may develop PTSD as an immediate effect of severe trauma in childhood (Shannon et al. 1994). Also, in addition to the symptoms seen in adults such as intrusive thoughts, nightmares and autonomic hyperactivity, children show a range of symptoms which are varied and complex such as enuresis or regressive or antisocial behaviour (Yule 1994). Since their understanding and concept of trauma are different from that in adults, children perceive certain events as traumatic which adults would not. As a result, the various theories which explain symptoms and causes of PTSD in adults can be difficult to apply to children.

In order to understand PTSD, it is important to have some understanding of the different biological and psychological theories which try to explain the mechanism of action, aetiological factors and symptoms of PTSD in adults and to look at the factors which put children at risk. This chapter briefly outlines the main theories, but the reader can obtain an in-depth knowledge through the references provided.

Aetiological factors and mechanism of action

One of the earliest theories explaining PTSD was the psychodynamic theory formulated by Freud in the early 1900s. Following World War I, experimental studies showed that veterans exhibited intolerance of carbon dioxide. Concentration camp syndrome was described following World War II, when some investigators considered brain damage as a significant factor. These findings laid the basis for studying the role of biological factors in PTSD. Kardiner (1959) described PTSD as a 'physio-neurosis', emphasising the importance of both the physical and psychological factors in the causation of PTSD.

Psychodynamic theories

A number of psychodynamic theories have tried to explain the cause and symptomatology of PTSD. In his earlier stimulus–barrier definition of trauma, Freud stated that trauma occurred when the intensity of stimuli became so great that the stimulus barrier was overwhelmed, the organism was flooded with unmanageable impulses and its functioning was disrupted (Freud 1920, 1953). In his book *Introductory Lectures on Psychoanalysis* (1953) Freud talked about traumatic events like 'railway collisions and other alarming accidents involving fatal risks' producing 'traumatic neuroses' which he differentiated from 'spontaneous neuroses'. He also described some of the symptoms of PTSD (Wilson 1994).

Freud's original view of neuroses was a post-traumatic paradigm known as 'seduction theory'. He stated that, during childhood, there was a range of traumatic experiences or an emergency type of event that could be profoundly distressing to an individual. This was experienced as a threat to the ego. Repression was used as a defence in order to reduce the anxiety and remove from awareness unpleasant memories and emotions of the traumatic event, and led to the appearance of various neurotic symptoms and events (Wilson 1994). His initial theory regarded children as sexual beings from birth with basic libidinal forces, which led to intrapsychic conflict. He later abandoned this theory for an instinct-driven oedipal model with focus on intrapsychic mechanisms, in which he disavowed the consequence of external, event-based stressor experiences.

Freud also developed the 'repetition compulsion' principle specifically to account for the repetitive return of traumatic material in the nightmares of soldiers who fought in World War I. Following the overwhelming assault on the stimulus-barrier, regression occurs leading to the use of an early and primitive defence, **repetition compulsion**, which involves repeating a disturbing event in order to master it (Brett

1993). The aftermath of trauma in this model consists of the repeated return of traumatic material propelled by the repetition compulsion alternating with defences against remembering or repeating the trauma (Freud 1953) In *Beyond the Pleasure Principle* (1920) he considered traumatic events as external stressors which were 'powerful enough to break through the protective shield of the ego'. He further elaborated the concept of trauma as involving an external stressor, a reduction of ego-defensive and coping capacity, and secondary stressors, which take on traumatic proportions (Wilson 1994). A number of other models have been put forward since, by Fenichel (1945), Kardiner and Spiegel (1947), Parson (1984) and Krystal (1985).

Cognitive theories

A number of cognitive theories attempt to answer questions such as why some people experience PTSD whereas others, exposed to the same traumatic event, do not. The various theories also try to explain various symptoms of PTSD such as intrusive thoughts, avoidance and anxiety. Some of these are outlined below and are detailed in Dalgleish (1999).

Horrowitz (1986) formulated the **stress response syndromes** based on psychodynamic and cognitive theory. He hypothesised that there is a tendency towards 'completion' of any information presented to the mind. If any event is presented to the mind, there is a tendency to process the information in a way that matches the new information with models within the mind. This process involves revisions until the information is assimilated. In PTSD, there is an overload of traumatic information. This brings into play psychological defence mechanisms such as denial, which then try to keep this information out of consciousness. But a tendency towards 'completion' leads to the information breaking through the defences, leading to intrusive thoughts. The person initially has periods of intrusive thoughts alternating with periods of numbing and denial. The process of assimilation can be difficult and prolonged. If it remains incomplete, information is kept alive in active memory in the form of intrusive thoughts.

The **information-processing theory** of PTSD, postulated by Foa and her colleagues (Foa and Kozak 1986, Foa et al. 1989) tries to explain the basis of intrusive thoughts and avoidance phenomena seen in PTSD. Information related to the traumatic events such as the stimulus, cognitions, physiological responses of an individual are stored in the 'fear network' (Lang 1972, 1985) in the brain. Circuits in the fear network are activated by trauma-related stimuli, and the information threatens to enter into the individual's consciousness, which they actively try to suppress. This leads to the avoidance symptoms seen in PTSD. Information in the fear network has to be integrated and assimilated into the pre-existing memory structure if the trauma is to be successfully resolved. The more unpredictable and uncontrollable the traumatic event, the more difficult it would be to assimilate it.

Following their research in Vietnam War veterans, Chemtob et al. (1988) hypothesised that individuals who suffer from PTSD function in a 'survival mode' which is an adaptive way of functioning during the traumatic event. The fear network is thus in a permanent state of activation leading to hyperarousability, autonomic hyperactivity and intrusive thoughts. Ongoing research in this field has led to a number of other hypotheses being postulated and tested (Creamer et al. 1992).

Behaviour theories

Behaviour theories try to explain PTSD symptoms based on the two-factor learning theory (Mowrer 1947), which involves **classical and instrumental learning**. In the first phase, the traumatic event, which acts as the unconditioned stimulus, leads to an unconditioned response of fear and being upset. Neutral stimuli such as sights, sounds, thoughts, images and situations are paired with the trauma and lead to anxiety, arousal and fear response. These then become conditioned stimuli, which evoke similar responses even in the absence of the trauma. Higher-order conditioning and stimulus generalisation can occur and these can account for the response to additional stimuli. In the second phase, instrumental learning leads to avoidance of both the unconditioned and conditioned stimuli, which leads to a reduction in stress, unpleasant thoughts and anxiety (Charney et al. 1993, Redd et al. 1993, Dykman et al. 1997). Furthermore, there may be a **failure of extinction** in PTSD, which may relate to the recalling of traumatic memories. Sensitisation may explain the increased responsiveness of patients with PTSD to stress both related and unrelated to original trauma (Charney et al. 1993).

Biological theories

Studies based on biological theories have postulated a role of the various **neurotransmitter systems**, **structural abnormalities** and **endocrine dysfunctions** in explaining the causes and symptoms of PTSD. Noradrenergic dysfunction is related to anxiety, fear and hypervigilance whereas NMDA (N-Methyl-D-Aspartate) receptors and dopaminergic receptors play a role in the recall of memories and sensitisation. The amygdala and the hippocampus have been involved in studies related to the encoding and recall of painful memories. The hypothalamo–pituitary–adrenal (HPA) axis and the corticosteroids play a role in the stress response. The opiate system is involved in the analgesia, numbness and emotional blunting seen in PTSD (Charney et al. 1993,

Grillon et al. 1996, van der Kolk 1997). Krystal et al. (1989) suggested that the locus coerulus, a noradrenergic 'alarm centre', plays a pivotal role in the genesis of PTSD. A role for genetic susceptibility in PTSD is supported by preliminary studies using animal models. Studies show that there are significant genetic influences on symptom liability in PTSD (True et al. 1993).

Other models which correlate psychological and biological theories are the **learned helplessness** and the **kindling and sensitisation** models. Van der Kolk et al. (1997) applied the model of inescapable shock and learned helplessness to PTSD. Animals who are repeatedly exposed to acute stress (electric shock, loud noise and cold water) and prevented from escaping, develop a syndrome of learned helplessness that correlates with the symptoms of constricted affect and decreased motivation seen in patients who suffer from PTSD. This could explain the PTSD symptoms seen in people who are chronically abused. Animals exposed to inescapable shock show evidence of increased norepinephrine, initially followed by subsequent depletion (Anisman and Sklar 1979) which points towards a possible catecholaminergic mediation of PTSD symptoms, in particular, intrusive and avoidance symptoms. Drugs effective in PTSD, such as tricyclics, monoamine oxidase inhibitors and clonidine prevent the development of learned helplessness in animals exposed to inescapable shock and have an effect on the noradrenergic system.

Sensitisation (Antelman 1988) is a process by which animals exposed to either single or repeated stimuli at a particular threshold respond to further stimuli at a lower threshold. Kindling, a related phenomenon, occurs as a result of repeated sub-threshold stimuli, which lead to a lowered firing threshold. Post and Kopanda (1976) suggested that this phenomenon occurs in limbic circuits in people who suffer from PTSD. This model may apply to individuals experiencing repeated exposure to trauma such as child abuse, incest and combat or even to intrusive re-experiencing from a single trauma (Van der Kolk et al. 1984). This may explain why a past history of childhood sexual abuse or other traumatic event poses a risk factor for developing PTSD in later life.

Developmental model

The developmental model of childhood traumatic stress was described by Pynoos et al. (1993) and incorporates a tripartite model of the aetiology of PTSD deriving from the nature of the traumatic experience(s) and from the subsequent traumatic reminders and secondary stressors. The model incorporates a conceptualisation of stress proposed by Steinberg and Ritzmann (1990) based on **living systems theory** (Miller 1978). The model recognises the role of environment and evolving familial and societal expectations on the developing child.

It assigns a prominent role to the trauma-related formation of expectations as these are expressed in thoughts, emotions, behaviour and biology of the developing child. It takes into account the child's resilience and adjustment during development. After the traumatic experience, altered expectation places the child at risk for proximal and distal developmental disturbances. The model provides a framework for integrating the interactions involved in the aetiology, course and outcome of PTSD in children and adolescents.

Contributing factors

Although all the above theories and models try to explain the mechanism of action, aetiological factors and symptoms of PTSD, none has been able to do so satisfactorily. Trauma-related, individual and social factors act as important contributory factors in the development of PTSD.

Trauma-related factors

Concept of trauma

The concept of trauma that causes PTSD has been difficult to define and has undergone a number of revisions. For example, in one of its earlier definitions, trauma was defined in DSM-III-R, an international classification system for psychiatric disorders, as 'something outside the range of human experience' (APA 1987). Later, DSM-IV described trauma as 'an event that involved actual or threatened death or serious injury or a threat to the physical integrity of self or others' (APA 1994). ICD-10, another major classification system, describes trauma as a 'stressful event or situation either short or long lasting of an exceptionally threatening or catastrophic nature which is likely to cause pervasive distress in almost anyone' (WHO 1992). These descriptions apply mainly to adults. For children, an admission to hospital for an operation or seeing their parents in the same situation could mean threatened death or serious injury. Pynoos and Eth (1986) suggested a wider definition of PTSD to include those children who have indirectly experienced trauma, for example by witnessing violent acts. Terr (1991) has described two types of trauma that may lead to the development of PTSD in children:

- **Type I trauma** involves single traumatic events that are sudden and unexpected, for example witnessing a homicide or being the victim of a violent crime.
- **Type II trauma** entails the repeated occurrence of a traumatic event, which is often expected or predictable: for example, sexual abuse, ritualistic abuses or repeated physical abuse of a child.

These definitions of trauma, which are more applicable to children, have to be included in the classification systems.

Some of the trauma-related factors which influence development of PTSD are discussed below.

- **Dose of exposure, magnitude and amount of exposure, frequency and severity of stress**: There is a consistent and direct relationship between these and development of PTSD reactions and they affect the PTSD symptom profile, pattern of symptom accrual and improvement (Pynoos et al. 1987, Nader et al. 1990). This relationship holds across time and several kinds of trauma.
- **Proximity to the traumatic event**: This is related to the severity of traumatic symptoms. Pynoos et al. (1993), who studied the PTSD in children and adolescents following the Armenian earthquake, reported severe symptoms in those who were closer to the epicentre of the earthquake.
- **The traumatic event itself**: Various events which cause PTSD in adults can cause PTSD in young children too, such as earthquakes, hurricanes, etc. Widespread death, injury and destruction associated with natural disasters often occur in developing countries with larger numbers of affected child survivors (Pynoos et al. 1993, Weisaeth 1993). In developed countries, technological advances expose children to intrusive medical procedures, and to violence (Pynoos et al. 1993). The characteristics of some of the traumatic events which have an impact on the development of PTSD in children are discussed below:
  - Survivors of road traffic accidents commonly have PTSD symptoms. Children and adolescents showed serious traffic-related fears and parents reported increased mood disturbances compared to the period before the accident (Stallard and Law 1993, Di Gallo et al. 1997). Di Gallo et al. (1997) reported that high levels of distress during and immediately after an accident were associated with severe PTSD symptoms. Post-traumatic amnesia following head injuries may protect against recurring memories and the development of PTSD. Some patients with neurogenic amnesia may develop a form of PTSD without re-experiencing the symptoms (Warden et al. 1997). Gregg et al. (1996), who studied PTSD in the Kegworth air disaster, reported that those who saw injured or dead people at the scene or had sustained less severe head injury were significantly more likely to develop PTSD.
  - PTSD is found in children who have had respiratory arrest and required subsequent intubation, and is seen in young children as well as their family members (Gavin and Roesler 1997).

- PTSD is well recognised in survivors of cancer. Stuber et al. (1994) reported PTSD not only in paediatric leukaemia survivors aged 7–19 years, but also in their mothers and fathers. They suggested follow-up care for cancer survivors as well as preventive steps to lessen the traumatic aspects of paediatric cancer treatment. Severity and intensity of treatment were used to predict symptoms in survivors of childhood cancer though these were not found to relate to symptoms in adults. Duration of treatment has also been shown to predict stress symptoms in survivors of childhood cancer (Stuber et al. 1994). Interventions and treatments are carried out in children with their parents' consent and this may have an effect on the child's feelings of safety and security.

- Because of their age, children are more vulnerable to other traumatic events such as physical, emotional and sexual abuse. PTSD is known to occur in children who have suffered severe child maltreatment. Famularo et al. (1996) followed up children for 2 years who were removed from their parents' custody subsequent to a finding of maltreatment. The PTSD diagnosis was retained in 32% of the children, 2 years after the traumatic events. Interestingly, childhood sexual abuse is a well-known high risk factor for development of PTSD in adults and there is a large amount of literature on the effects of childhood sexual abuse on adults. It has, however, only recently been acknowledged that children can suffer PTSD symptoms, as its immediate after-effects.

Some of the other factors which require further studies as potential causes of childhood PTSD are bullying or severe punishment by parents and teachers in the presence of peers; incidents which can pose a threat to a child's integrity. Issues such as litigation, which influence symptom accrual and maintenance in PTSD, have been studied in adults but not in children.

Individual and social factors

In adults, it is well known that an individual's personality, ways of coping in the past, social supportive network and present circumstances influence the development of PTSD. In children there are various other factors, which influence its development, only some of which have been well studied.

- **Age**: Traumatic exposures vary with age and gender of the child. The level of a child's cognitive development reflects the ability to interpret traumatic events, symptom formation and ability to report symptoms. Very young children are protected from the effects of traumatic experiences by their limited ability to understand the concept of trauma (Yule 1994). Their interpretation of the trauma would depend on the levels of anxiety shown by their parents and adults. Young children may not be able to remove themselves from repeated exposure to domestic violence, whereas an adolescent may become injured by or injure a family member by intervention. Adolescents are perhaps more at risk of developing PTSD now than in the past, especially with the exposure to drugs and alcohol and teenage pregnancies on the increase. The death of a friend due to an accidental overdose can be traumatic. Reynolds (1997) described PTSD following childbirth in adults and called it a 'traumatic birth experience'. Teenage mothers may find the experience of childbirth or abortions especially traumatic.

- **Gender**: Some studies have reported a difference in reporting of symptoms by girls and boys, with girls reporting more anxiety and severity of symptoms (Pynoos et al. 1993, Khoury et al. 1997, Rossman et al. 1997).

- **Cognitive appraisal factors**: Besides the events involving actual or threatened trauma, cognitive appraisal factors are important. The victim's perception of being in a safe place at the time of assault predicted high levels of symptoms. Extreme shame or guilt, the experience of being extremely afraid, helpless or horrified is a likely risk factor. Being a participant in a brutal atrocity and acts of commission or omission resulting in manufactured disasters are likely risk factors (Pynoos et al. 1987, Yule and Williams 1990, Pynoos et al. 1993).

- **Political circumstances**: War and political persecution can have devastating effects on child survivors. Adolescent girls may be made victim to rape or abduction during civil war or military action; older boys may be targeted for elimination or imprisonment. PTSD has been reported in refugee children (Lavik et al. 1996, Almquist and Brandell-Forsberg 1997) and in children who were exposed to catastrophic community violence (Pynoos et al. 1987, Nader et al. 1990). Almquist and Brandell-Forsberg (1997) studied the influence of organised violence on Iranian pre-school children exposed to war and political persecution. The amount of traumatic exposure was strongly related to the prevalence of PTSD.

- **Social factors**: Exposure to violence and subsequent development of PTSD are related to social factors. Sociological findings have indicated that increased access to firearms is associated with children increasingly being victims, witnesses and perpetrators of violent acts and accidental shooting involving guns (Cotton 1992). Firearms and weapons are easily available and accessible. Personal disputes between children are being increasingly resolved through the use of knives or handguns. In the modern world, children and adolescents are at risk of kidnapping, individually and in a group. There is a potential risk of developing PTSD with all these incidents.

- **Role of the family**: Poor social support from the primary family caregiver, other relatives and friends increase the risk of psychiatric disorders, whereas good family support can have a protective role. This particularly applies to a child, as parental reactions to trauma have been reported to be the best predictor of a child or adolescent's adjustment to stressors (McFarlane 1989). Though none of these factors have been studied in PTSD in particular, they could be potential contributory factors in the development of PTSD.

    - Family factors associated with increased risk of intrafamilial violence include parental psychopathology, lack of supervision, marital discord, recent unemployment and abuse of alcohol or other substances by adult caretakers (Daly and Wilson 1981, Cicchettie and Lynch 1993). Changing family patterns also influence the rate of intrafamilial sexual abuse, such as increased risk of sexual molestation by stepfathers (Russell 1986). There is significant evidence of special risk of children witnessing violence to a family member or peer, such as rape, murder or suicidal behaviour and interspousal violence or abuse of a sibling (Carlson 1984, Malmquist 1984, Rosenberg 1987, Black and Kaplan 1988, Pynoos and Nader 1988).

    - Certain factors play a protective role. The broader and deeper the network of social support, the greater the chance of ameliorating the negative effects of stressful life events (Cohen and Wills 1985). Rossman et al. (1997) have reported that there are fewer symptoms and better adaptive functioning associated with a positive parental relationship after both single and repetitive adverse events. Richters and Martines (1993) have reported on the protective role of grandparents' involvement in the upbringing of grandchildren.

- **Role of the media**: The media play an important role in covering disasters, making people aware of the extent of the destructiveness of the traumatic event and the loss and suffering of people involved. However, extensive coverage of disasters and detailed reporting of events on anniversaries of the disasters with graphic pictures and sometimes inflammatory comments can invoke images and thoughts about the actual disaster itself. Kiser et al. (1993) reports on the post-traumatic symptoms experienced by children not from an exposure to a predicted earthquake, which did not happen, but from their exposures to the television programme and the surrounding talk in their communities. Opinion polls and chat-shows encourage victims to talk about their experiences, sometimes without providing adequate support and counselling. The media can thus serve as a constant, powerful and often uncontrolled reminder of trauma. The role of the media in maintaining the chronicity of PTSD requires further study.

Conclusion

Although various theories have tried to explain the aetiology and pathophysiology of PTSD, none has been entirely successful in doing so. Research has, however, led to a shift of focus from treatment of individuals following the trauma to prevention of the trauma itself, as well as viewing the family and the community as a whole as a target for intervention.

Childhood PTSD is emerging as a distinct entity, but so far it has only been acknowledged that children could show symptoms that are different from those in adults. Even today, PTSD studies concentrate mainly on adults. A change in focus is vital, with emphasis on further research into the various causes, forms and presentation of childhood PTSD and the role of the family, society and cultural issues. Research into the protective factors and risk factors in childhood would play a major role in the prevention and treatment of PTSD, not only in children, but also in adults.

References

Almquist, K. and Brandell-Forsberg, M. (1997) Refugee children in Sweden: Post-traumatic stress disorder in Iranian pre-school children exposed to organised violence. Child Abuse and Neglect 21, 351–366.

Anisman, H. L. and Sklar, L. S. (1979) Catecholamine depletion in mice upon exposure to stress: mediation of the escape deficits produced by inescapable shock. Journal of Comprehensive Physiological Psychology 93, 610–625.

Antelman, S. M. (1988) Time-dependent sensitisation as the cornerstone for a new approach to pharmacotherapy: drugs as foreign/stressful stimuli. Drug Developmental Research 14, 1–30.

APA (1987) Diagnostic and Statistical Manual of Mental Disorders, 3rd edn, revised (DSM-III-R). Washington, D. C.: American Psychiatric Association.

APA (1994) Diagnostic and Statistical Manual of Mental Disorders, 4th edn (DSM-IV). Washington, D. C.: American Psychiatric Association.

Black, D. and Kaplan, T. (1988) Father kills mother: issues and problems encountered by a child psychiatric team. British Journal of Psychiatry 153, 624–630.

Brett, B. (1993) Psychoanalytic contributions to a theory of traumatic stress. In Wilson, J. P., Raphael, B. (eds), International Handbook of Traumatic Stress Syndromes. New York: Plenum Press.

Carlson, B. E. (1984) Children's observations of interparental violence. In Roberts, A. R. (ed.), Battered Women and their Families: Intervention Strategies and Treatment Programmes, pp. 147–167. New York: Springer-Verlag.

Charney, D. S., Deutch, A. Y., Krystal, J. H. and Southwick, S. M. (1993) Psychobiologic mechanisms of post-traumatic stress disorder. Archives of General Psychiatry 50(4), 294–305.

Chemtob, C., Roitblat, H. L., Manadra, R. S. et al. (1988) A cognitive action theory of post-traumatic stress disorder. Journal of Anxiety Disorders 2, 253–275.

Cicchetti, D. and Lynch, M. (1993) Toward an ecological/transactional model of community violence and child maltreatment: consequences for children's development. Psychiatry 56, 96–118.

Cohen, S. and Wills, T. A. (1985) Stress, social support and buffering hypothesis. Psychological Bulletin 98(2), 310–357.

Cotton, P. (1992) Gun associated violence increasingly viewed as public health challenge. Journal of the American Medical Association 267(9), 1171–1174.

Creamer, M., Burgess, P. and Pattison, P. (1992) Reaction to trauma: a cognitive processing model. Journal of Abnormal Psychology 101, 452–459.

Daly, M. and Wilson, J. (1981) Child maltreatment from a socio-biological perspective. New Directions for Child Development 11, 93–112.

Di Gallo, A., Barton, J. and Parry-Jones, W. L. (1997) Road traffic accidents: early psychological consequences in children and adolescents. British Journal of Psychiatry 170, 358–362.

Dykman, R. A., Ackerman, P. T. and Newton, J. E. (1997) Post-traumatic stress disorder: a sensitisation reaction. Integrative Physiological and Behavioural Science 32(1), 9–18.

Famularo, R., Fenton, T., Augustyn, M., Zuckerman, B. (1996) Persistence of paediatric post-traumatic stress disorder after two years. Child Abuse and Neglect 20(12), 1245–1248.

Fenichel, O. (1945) The Psychoanalytic Theory of Neurosis. New York: W. W. Norton.

Foa, E. B. and Kozak, M. J. (1986) Emotional processing of fear: exposure to corrective information. Psychological Bulletin 99, 20–25.

Foa, E. B., Steketee, G. and Rothbaum, B. O. (1989) Behavioural/cognitive conceptualisation of post-traumatic stress disorder. Behaviour Therapy 20, 155–176.

Freud, S. (1920) Beyond the Pleasure Principle (Standard edn, vol. 18). London: Hogarth Press.

Freud, S. (1953) Introductory Lectures on Psychoanalysis (Standard edn, vol. 18, pp. 7–64). London: Hogarth Press.

Gavin, L. A. and Roesler, T. A. (1997) Post-traumatic distress in children and families after intubation. Paediatric Emergency Care 13 (3), 222–224.

Gregg, W., Medley, I., Fowler-Dixon, R. et al. (1996) Psychological consequences of the Kegworth air disaster. British Journal of Psychiatry 168(2), 254.

Grillon, C., Southwick, S. M. and Charney, D. S. (1996) The psychobiological basis of post-traumatic stress disorder. Molecular Psychiatry 278–297.

Horrowitz, M. J. (1986) Stress Response Syndromes, 2nd edn. Northvale, NJ: Jason Aronson.

Kardiner, A. (1959) The traumatic memories of war. In Arleti (ed.), American Handbook of Psychiatry. New York: Basic Books.

Kardiner, A. and Spiegel, H. (1947) War Stress and Neurotic Illness. New York: Paul B. Hoeber.

Khoury, E. L., Warheit, G. J., Hargrove, M. C., Zimmermas, R. S., Vega, W. A. and Gil, A. G. (1997) The impact of Hurricane Andrew on deviant behaviour among a multiracial/ethnic sample of adolescents in Dade Country, Florida: a longitudinal analysis. Journal of Traumatic Stress 71–91.

Kiser, L., Heston, J., Hickerson, S. and Mills, A. P. (1993) Anticipatory stress in children and adolescents. American Journal of Psychiatry 150, 87–92.

Krystal, H. (1985) Trauma and stimulus barrier. Psychoanalytic Inquiry 5, 131–161.

Krystal, J. H., Kosten, T. R., Perry, B. D. and Giller, E. L., Jr. (1989) Neurobiological aspects of PTSD. Review of clinical and preclinical studies. Behaviour Research and Therapy 20, 177.

Lang, P. J. (1972) Fear imagery: an information processing analysis. Behaviour Therapy 8, 862–886.

Lang, P. J. (1985) The cognitive psychophysiology of emotion: fear and anxiety. In Tuma, A. H. and Maser, J. D. (eds), Anxiety and the Anxiety Disorders. Hillsdale, NJ: Erlbaum.

Lavik, N. J., Hauff, E., Skrondal, A. and Solberg, O. (1996) Mental disorder among refugees and the impact of persecution and exile: some findings from an outpatient population. British Journal of Psychiatry 169(6), 726–732.

Malmquist, C. P. (1984) Children who witness parental murder: post-traumatic and legal issues. Journal of the American Academy of Child and Adolescent Psychiatry 25, 320–325.

Mcfarlane, A. C. (1989) The aetiology of post-traumatic morbidity. Predisposing, precipitating and perpetuating factors. British Journal of Psychiatry 154, 221–228.

Mcfarlane, A. C., Policansky, S. K. and Irwin, C. (1987) A longitudinal study of the psychological morbidity in children due to natural disaster. Psychological Medicine 17, 727–738.

Miller, J. G. (1978) Living Systems. New York: McGraw-Hill.

Mowrer, O. H. (1947) On the dual nature of learning: a reinterpretation 'of conditioning' and 'problem-solving'. Harvard Educational Review 17, 102–148.

Nader, K., Pynoos, R. S., Fairbanks, L. and Fredrick, C. (1990) Children's PTSD reactions one year after a sniper attack at their school. American Journal of Psychiatry 147.

Parson, E. R. (1984) The separation of the self: clinical and theoretical dimensions in the treatment of Vietnam combat veterans. In Wilson, J. P., Hazel, Z. and Kahana, B. (eds), Human Adaptation to Extreme Stress: From the Holocaust to Vietnam, pp. 245–279. New York: Plenum Press.

Post, R. M. and Kopanda, R. T. (1976) Cocaine kindling psychosis. American Journal of Psychiatry 133, 627–634.

Pynoos, R. and Eth, S. (1986) Witness to violence: the child interview. Journal of the American Academy of Child Psychiatry 25(3), 306–319.

Pynoos, R. and Nader, K. (1993) Issues in the treatment of post-traumatic stress in children and adolescents. In Wilson J. P. and Raphael B. (eds), International Handbook of Traumatic Stress Syndromes. New York: Plenum Press.

Pynoos, R. S. and Nader, K. (1988) Psychological first aid and treatment approach to children exposed to violence: research implications. Journal of Traumatic Stress 1, 445–473.

Pynoos, R. S., Frederick, C., Nader, K. et al. (1987) Life threat and post-traumatic stress in school age children. Archives of General Psychiatry 44, 1057–1063.

Pynoos, R. S., Goenjian, A., Tashjian, M. et al. (1993) Post-traumatic stress reactions in children after the 1988 Armenian earthquake. British Journal of Psychiatry 163, 239–247.

Redd, W. H., Dadds, M. R., Futterman, A. D. et al. (1993) Nausea induced by mental images of chemotherapy. Cancer 72(2), 629–636.

Reynolds, J. L. K. (1997) Post-traumatic stress disorder after childbirth: the phenomenon of traumatic birth. Canadian Medical Association Journal 156(6), 83–105.

Richters, J. and Martinez, P. (1993) NIMH Community Project I. Children as victims of and witnesses to violence. Psychiatry 56, 7–21.

Rosenberg, M. S. (1987) New directions for research on the psychological maltreatment of children. American Psychologist 42, 166–171.

Rossman, B. R., Bingham, R. D. and Emde, R. N. (1997) Symptomatology and adaptive functioning for children exposed to normative stressors, dog attack and parental violence. Journal of American Academy of Child and Adolescent Psychiatry 36(8), 1089–1097.

Russell, D. (1986) The Secret Trauma. New York: Basic Books.

Shannon, M. P., Lonigan C. J., Finch A. J. and Taylor, C. M. (1994) Children exposed to disaster I: epidemiology of post-traumatic systems and symptom profiles. Journal of American Academy of Child and Adolescent Psychiatry 33(1), 80–93.

Stallard, P. and Law, F. (1993) Screening and psychological debriefing of adolescent survivors of life threatening events. British Journal of Psychiatry, 165.

Steinberg, A. M. and Ritzman, R. F. (1990) A living systems approach to understanding the concept of stress. Behavioural Science 35, 138–146.

Stuber, M. L., Meeske, K., Gonzalez, S. et al. (1994) Post-traumatic stress after childhood cancer I: the role of appraisal; II: a family model. Psycho-Onchology 3, 305–312; 313–319.

Stuber, M. L., Christakis, D. A., Houskam, B. and Kazat, A. E. (1996) Post-trauma symptoms in childhood leukaemia survivors and their parents. Psychosomatics. 37(3), 254–261.

Terr, L. C. (1991) Childhood traumas – an outline and overview. American Journal of Psychiatry 148, 10–20.

True, W. R., Rice, J., Eisen, S. A. et al. (1993) A twin study of genetic and environmental contributions to liability for post-traumatic stress symptoms. Archives of General Psychiatry 50 (4), 257–264.

Van der Kolk, B. A. (1997) The psychobiology of post-traumatic stress disorder. Journal of Clinical Psychiatry 58 (9), 16–24.

Van der Kolk, B., Boyd, H., Krystal, J. and Greenberg, M. (1985) Post-traumatic stress disorder as a biologically based disorder. Implications of the animal model of inescapable shock. In Van der Kolk, B. A. (ed.), Post-traumatic Stress Disorder: Psychological and Biological Sequel. Washington, D. C.: American Psychiatric Press.

Warden, D. L., Labbate, L. A., Salazar, A. M. et al. (1997) Post-traumatic stress disorder in patients with traumatic brain-injury and amnesia for the event. Journal of Neuropsychiatry and Clinical Neurosciences 18–22.

Weisaeth, L. (1993) Disasters: psychological and psychiatric aspects. In Goldberger, L. and Breznit, S. (eds) Handbook of stress: Theoretical and Clinical Aspects, 2nd edn, pp. 591–616. New York: Free Press.

WHO (1992) International Classification of Diseases, 10th edn (ICD-10). Geneva: World Health Organisation.

Wilson, J. P. (1994) The historical evolution of PTSD diagnostic criteria: from Freud to DSM-IV. Journal of Traumatic Stress 7(4), 681–698.

Yule, W. (1994) Post-traumatic stress disorders. in. Rutter, M., Taylor, E. and Hersov, L. (eds), Child and Adolescent Psychiatry. Modern Approaches, 3rd edn. Oxford: Blackwell Scientific.

Yule, W. and Williams, R. M. (1990) Post-traumatic stress reactions in children. Journal of Traumatic Stress 3, 279–295.

Chapter 3
Biological basis of post-traumatic stress disorder

KONASALE PRASAD

The impact of stress on the human mind has always been a subject of intense curiosity and inquiry. In physics, a clear association between stress and strain is worked out mathematically. We see a similar relationship in the human experience of stress. In terms of physics, **stress** is the force exerted on an object and **strain** is the change brought about by stress on the object on which it is exerted. Psychological stress similarly brings about changes in the mind or its physical counterpart, the brain. Sudden, unexpected and enormous stress can bring about colossal changes (strains) on the object (the human brain and mind), so that the impact can have enduring and immutable effects on the functioning of the mind. Setting aside the controversial nature of the mind–brain dichotomy, the footprints of stress must be left on the brain to be reflected in the functioning of the 'mind'. Explorations into the nature of such changes have revealed exciting findings giving a new perspective to the understanding of the nature of post-traumatic stress disorder (PTSD).

In biological research and clinical parlance, stress is something that threatens **homeostasis** of an organism. Homeostasis can be defined as the dynamic balance of the internal systemic environment. Walter Cannon coined the term 'wisdom of the body' to refer to the beneficial effects of homeostasis. Organisms have a built-in capacity to mount wide-ranging adaptive responses to stress by increasing or decreasing the activity of one or several systems. Equally importantly, organisms can restore their systems to the original state once the stress is removed. If adaptive responses remain even after their relevance ceases, they can manifest pathologically as symptoms (Holsboer 1995). PTSD may be a case in point. Therefore, restitutive mechanisms are very important in any organism to avoid persistence of post-traumatic changes. Further, the concept of **allostasis** is very important. It represents the ability of the body to mount adaptive responses within an operating range for each system. However, when the systems are maintained over a long period of time at the upper or lower limit of their normal functioning, the strain produced on the body can lead to 'wear and tear' of a number of systems. This can potentially predispose the body to develop stress-related diseases. This is called the allostatic load (reviewed in McEwen 1996). The allostatic load can also impair the restitutive mechanisms.

In this chapter, an attempt is made to describe the current understanding of the biological basis of PTSD. Instead of cataloguing the research evidence in different areas, such as neurophysiology, neurochemistry, neuroendocrinology, etc., I have tried to link the findings in basic science and preclinical research with the clinical presentation, which is very important for clinicians and professionals involved in the care of people with PTSD.

To review the literature for this chapter I employed a MEDLINE search with the terms 'PTSD', 'aetiology', 'human' and '0 to 18 years'. In addition, searches were also made using 'PTSD', 'biology', and 'aetiology' without specifying the age limits. The available journals were also searched manually using cross-references. Further, in order to provide a better understanding of the biological basis, I have attempted to review the research evidence from the perspective of different models.

I do not intend to argue in this chapter that PTSD is a purely biological condition. In fact, PTSD has been argued to be a 'biopsychosocial trap' (Shalev 1996) and its study has allowed scientific methods to systematically investigate human suffering (van der Kolk and McFarlane 1996). This highlights the importance of psychological vulnerability and contribution of social factors in the causation and perpetuation of this condition.

The technical terminology unavoidably used in this chapter may not be very familiar to some of the readers of the book. The salient pieces of information from each section have, therefore, been included in a full summary at the end of the chapter.

Neurochemical model of PTSD

Neurochemicals are the chemical messengers that transmit signals from one nerve cell (or neuron) to another. It is estimated that there are 100 billion neurons in the human brain. Neurochemicals may be broadly classified as neurotransmitters and neuromodulators.

- **Neurotransmitters** are usually either amines or amino acids. They exert their effect at a highly specialised point of contact, called a

synapse, where two or more nerve cells meet. They act on special proteins situated on the neuronal cell membranes in the synapse called **receptors**. Each neurotransmitter acts on a specific set or sets of receptors. The action of neurotransmitters is immediate and short lasting. Neurotransmitters secreted into the synapse are rapidly degraded or taken back into the secreted nerve cell.

- **Neuromodulators** are either peptides or small proteins whose actions are relatively delayed but more enduring than those of neurotransmitters. They bring about long-term changes in the receptors and nerve cell membranes at the synapse, making them either more or less sensitive to neurotransmitters.

Recent advances in neurophysiology have found that nerve cells contain more than one neurochemical messenger. Neurochemicals are released into the synapse when the nerve is stimulated and the signal, in the form of an electrical pulse, reaches the synapse. However, neurotransmitters and neuromodulators have different signals and mechanisms for the release. Neurotransmitters may be broadly classified as inhibitory or excitatory depending on their actions. For example, acetylcholine and glutamate are excitatory neurotransmitters irrespective of the subtype of receptors on which they act whereas gamma-aminobutyric acid (GABA) is inhibitory. Some neurotransmitters are both inhibitory and excitatory, depending on the receptors on which they act, e.g. noradrenaline and serotonin. Noradrenaline is excitatory when it acts on α_1 and β receptors but inhibitory at α_2 receptors. Similarly, serotonin is excitatory at 5-HT_{1C}, 5-HT_2 and 5-HT_3 receptors but inhibitory at 5-HT_{1A} receptors. Recently, gases such as nitric oxide and carbon monoxide have been demonstrated to be neurotransmitters. Gaseous neurotransmitters have been found to have considerable influence on learning and memory. Neurons containing different neurotransmitters interact among themselves to exercise various degrees of control over each other. This is crucial for information processing.

Noradrenaline (also known as epinephrine; grouped under the broad rubric of catecholamines, along with dopamine and adrenaline) is undoubtedly the most intensively investigated of the neurotransmitters in PTSD. Conceivably, noradrenaline is critical to an animal's fight-or-flight response under stressful conditions. Noradrenaline is also an important neurotransmitter for anxiety, selective attention, vigilance and consolidation of memory. Evidence for involvement of noradrenaline is available from peripheral receptor studies, assay of catecholamines and their metabolites in blood, cerebrospinal fluid and urine, and neuroendocrine studies.

Although it is reasonable to expect an overactive sympathetic nervous system and elevated catecholamines in PTSD, the empirical data are conflicting. The studies so far have reported increase (Kosten et al. 1987, Yehuda et al. 1992), decrease (Pitman et al., reviewed in Yehuda 1998) and no significant change (Perry et al. 1990, Mellman et al. 1995) in 24 hour catecholamine levels. De Bellis et al. (1994) found increase in 24 hour urinary catecholamines in sexually abused girls. The study of phasic release of catecholamine has also shown significantly elevated plasma noradrenaline levels in PTSD sufferers compared to control subjects (Yehuda et al. 1998). However, Marburg et al. (1995) reported reduced levels of arterialised noradrenaline – indicating lower noradrenaline clearance – in PTSD patients than in normal controls. Davidson et al. (1985) reported low platelet levels of monoamine oxidase (MAO) – the enzyme required for the metabolism of catecholamines. These findings suggest that the control of noradrenaline secretion is dysregulated.

Further, Perry et al. (1987) found a decrease in the number of platelet α_2 receptors. This decrease was more pronounced in high-affinity α_2 receptors coupled to the cyclic adenosine monophosphate (cAMP) system in people with PTSD. Interestingly, the study of cAMP signal transduction system showed that there was significant reduction of basal cAMP and adenylate cyclase in lymphocytes of individuals with PTSD (Lerer et al. 1987). These findings indicate that the noradrenergic receptor system is down-regulated. It may be in response to chronically altered sympathetic activity or, alternatively, receptor sensitivities may be the basis for catecholamine disturbances (Yehuda 1998).

Although the findings regarding noradrenaline levels are conflicting, the data on overresponsivity of the noradrenergic system is fairly robust. Children exposed to acute stress develop long-term changes in central noradrenergic system responses (Terr 1996). When the noradrenergic system is challenged chemically (Southwick et al. 1997) or by stress (McFall et al. 1990) overreactivity of the system has been demonstrated in people with PTSD. Children exposed to extreme stress had overresponsive noradrenergic and dopaminergic systems as evidenced by increased growth hormone release with clonidine and L-dihydroxyphenylalanine (L-DOPA) challenge (Jensen et al. 1991). Clonidine inhibits central α_2 adrenergic autoreceptors resulting in enhanced release of noradrenaline; and L-DOPA is dopaminergic, and so stimulates the release of dopamine. Noradrenaline and dopamine stimulate the secretion of growth hormone. An association between the overactive noradrenergic system and symptoms of PTSD is supported by the findings of Southwick et al. (1997). They could induce panic attacks and flashbacks with yohimbine injections in veterans with PTSD. Yohimbine stimulates the secretion of noradrenaline by inhibiting α_2 adrenergic autoreceptors. It therefore appears that noradrenaline mediates the symptoms of PTSD. Yehuda (1998) proposes that enhanced noradrenergic response to stress and difficulty in achieving a basal state may underlie the pathophysiology of PTSD. Interestingly, pre-existing sympathetic overdrive could not be demonstrated in people with PTSD. There was no significant difference in noradrenaline levels between the groups with and without PTSD before they were exposed to stressful stimulus, suggesting lack of pre-existing sympathetic overdrive (McFall et al. 1990, Blanchard et al. 1991, Marburg et al. 1995). This further suggests that the sympathetic system overreacts to combat-related stimuli. Similar findings were reported for the heart rates for this group.

In summary, the available data on the noradrenergic system shows that:

- there is no pre-existing sympathetic overdrive in people with PTSD before they are exposed to traumatic stimuli
- the regulation of noradrenaline secretion is impaired
- the adrenergic receptors on which noradrenaline acts are down-regulated
- the signal transduction system which translates the receptor signals to modify the cellular response is also down-regulated
- the system is overresponsive to stress
- the system does not return to its basal level of functioning (cf. allostatic load and the importance of restitutive mechanisms mentioned earlier).

These abnormalities may underlie the pathophysiology of PTSD.

Serotonin (5-hydroxytryptamine, abbreviated as 5-HT) has also been found to be abnormal in PTSD. 5-HT is important in the inhibition of behaviours motivated by emergencies and previous experience of reward (Soubrie 1986). In addition, it is involved in the modulation of noradrenergic system responsiveness and arousal. Thus, it is possible that stress-induced serotonin dysfunction results in the dysfunction of the behavioural inhibition system (discussed later in the chapter). There is ample evidence in the literature about the relationship between reduced 5-HT and aggression and impulsivity (Mann 1987, Coccaro et al. 1989). The importance of 5-HT in PTSD is clearly illustrated by Southwick et al. (1997). They could evoke PTSD symptoms by challenging people with PTSD with meta-chlorophenyl-piperazine (mCPP) – a serotonergic drug (although an oversimplification) with relatively low affinity for noradrenergic and dopaminergic receptors. Supersensitivity of 5-HT_{2C} has been suspected to be the basis for this. In the same study, the researchers used yohimbine challenge for the adrenergic system. They found that only 19% of the subjects had their symptoms evoked by both yohimbine and mCPP; and the rest responded to either yohimbine or mCPP. They proposed a possibility of two neurobiological subgroups characterised by a dysregulated noradrenergic system in one and a dysregulated serotonergic system in the other. The reciprocal regulation between 5-HT and the hypothalamo–pituitary–adrenal (HPA) axis is also important and is discussed later in the chapter.

The above findings clearly indicate that dysregulation of noradrenergic, serotonergic and dopaminergic systems occurs in PTSD. The locus coeruleus (LC) in the brainstem tegmentum and rostral pons (see Fig. 3.1) contains the greatest concentrations of noradrenergic neurons. Similarly, the raphe nucleus present throughout the brainstem (see Fig. 3.1) contains the largest population of serotonergic neurons. The neurons from these structures project widely throughout the brain. Krystal et al. (1989) postulated that the LC could be conceived as a 'trauma centre'. The LC influences many areas in the brain involved in higher abstract functions, such as processing and responding to fear, associative learning, memory formation, signal-to-noise discrimination of the environment and differentiating between interoceptive and the exteroceptive inputs. Further, it also helps in flexible monitoring of the environment to produce situation-appropriate behaviours without relying entirely on interoceptive cues that may be situationally irrelevant (van der Kolk 1997).

The areas concerned with the above functions are located mainly in the limbic system and cerebral cortex, especially the medial temporal lobe. Dysregulation of the noradrenergic system pathologically alters the above functions, resulting in behaviours such as inappropriate detection

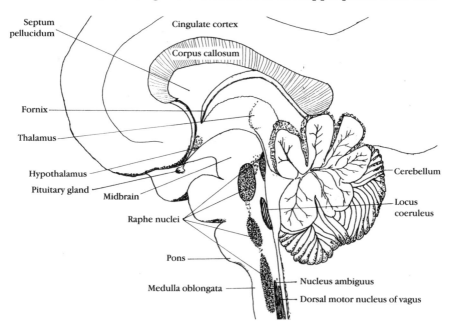

Figure 3.1. Sagittal section of brain with brainstem.

of dangers and anomalous response to perceived but unreal dangers. Evoked potential studies (discussed later) have supported this by demonstrating faulty information processing in PTSD. Such PTSD patients had problems in distinguishing between the actual stimulus and the distracter (Davidson 1995). The studies using chemical and electrical activation of the above areas of brain have produced behaviours akin to the clinical symptoms of PTSD. Psychopharmacologic interventions using propranolol (a β-adrenergic receptor blocker), clonidine (a central α_2-adrenergic autoreceptor blocker) and antidepressants support these findings (reviewed in Krystal et al. 1989). 5-HT is critical in modifying noradrenergic control of higher cognitive functions, as reviewed earlier. The serotonergic system functions as a 'braking system' for the noradrenergic system and, in addition, influences the behavioural inhibition system (discussed later in the chapter). Thus, an abnormal serotonergic system contributes further to the dysregulation of the noradrenergic system. It would certainly be interesting to see how dysregulated noradrenergic and serotonergic systems interact with the neuroendocrine and endogenous opioid systems in PTSD, as elaborated in the subsequent sections. This could throw further light on the links between clinical symptoms and pathophysiology.

Abnormalities in the endogenous opioid system

Three distinct endogenous opioid families have been described (Fig. 3.2). Interestingly, opiates such as morphine and codeine have been

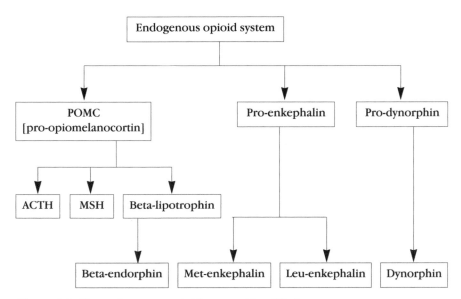

Figure 3.2. The endogenous opioid system (simplified).

found in the brain and adrenal glands of mammals. The natural cleavage products of ß-endorphin have opioid antagonist properties stronger than those of naloxone. Certain other endogenous opioid antagonists and weak agonists, such as neuropeptide FF, are not derived from these families (reviewed in Jaffe 1995). In PTSD, disturbance of the endogenous opioid system has been described which has multiple implications.

- Pitman et al. (1990) found naloxone-reversible analgesia in pain-resistant combat veterans. The degree of analgesia was equivalent to the administration of 8 mg of morphine sulphate. In addition, they also found that the emotional responses became more normal in those who received naloxone. They hypothesised that endogenous opioids produce psychic numbing when exposed to severe trauma. In such individuals, the endogenous opioid system was implicated in the failure to inhibit feelings, response to trauma and avoidance of the situation.
- Close links between the release of ACTH and ß-endorphin have been demonstrated (Fig. 3.2 and 3.6). This is especially important because a dysregulated HPA axis has been reported in many studies.
- Trauma-seeking behaviour may be enhanced by ß-endorphin (reviewed in Terr 1996).
- Alternative processing of propiomelanocortin (POMC), as seen in major depressive disorder (Holsboer 1995), may also underlie the pathophysiology.
- Finally, stress-induced analgesia is a component of the inescapable stress model of PTSD proposed by van der Kolk et al. (1985). Inescapable stress response is based on the learned helplessness model. When animals are exposed to inescapable stress they demonstrate an initial alarm response and subsequently fail to mount previously successful coping responses and develop impaired avoidance learning and behavioural depression. Inescapable stress leads to the development of opioid analgesia, noradrenergic overresponse and dysregulation in other neurotransmitter systems.

Endogenous opioids reduce the magnitude of startle response whereas antagonists enhance it. The role of endogenous opioid antagonists is not yet fully understood.

Neuroendocrine model of PTSD

The hypothalamo-pituitary-adrenal (HPA) axis is undoubtedly involved in responding to stress. In addition, neuroendocrine dysfunction in PTSD has also been demonstrated in the hypothalamo-pituitary–thyroid (HPT) and hypothalamo– pituitary–gonadal (HPG) axes. However, the emphasis in this chapter is mainly on the HPA axis with a brief reference to abnormalities in other endocrine axes.

Only a brief overview of the HPA can be given here. The hypothalamus (Fig. 3.1) secretes various releasing and inhibiting hormones to control the pituitary gland (Fig. 3.1), which has been termed the 'bandmaster of the endocrine orchestra'. For example, corticotrophin-releasing hormone (CRH) from the hypothalamus stimulates the secretion of corticotrophin or adrenocorticotrophic hormone (ACTH) from the pituitary, which in turn stimulates the adrenal gland resulting in the release of various adrenal hormones. The adrenal hormones may be broadly classified as adrenal steroid hormones and catecholamines. Steroid hormones may be further classified as glucocorticoids (GCs) and mineralocorticoids. The latter are important in the maintenance of the fluid and electrolyte balance in the body, whereas GCs affect various metabolic pathways and mediate stress. Cortisol is the most important of the GCs. ACTH stimulates the secretion of GCs. CRH, ACTH and cortisol exert negative feedback inhibition on each other. When cortisol level is low, it signals the hypothalamus to secrete CRH in order to maintain homeostasis. CRH stimulates the pituitary for the release of ACTH, resulting in the secretion of cortisol from the adrenals. When cortisol level is high, it inhibits ACTH and CRH until the cortisol level reverts to normal levels. This finely tuned control exists for other endocrine systems as well.

Exposure to stress brings about release of CRH from the hypothalamus through the mediation of noradrenaline. In the past, similarities in the HPA axis abnormalities and symptom overlap with major depression led several workers to conceptualise a very close relationship between major depression and PTSD. However, there are major differences in the HPA axis abnormalities, as shown in Fig. 3.3 (based on the review in Yehuda 1998).

CRH is not only present in the hypothalamus but also localised in extrahypothalamic regions, such as the amygdala (Fig. 3.4) and the LC. The amygdala is a part of the limbic system and has close anatomical connections with the hippocampal formation (Amaral and Insausti 1996) and thus with the Papez circuit. This is a neural circuit concerned with emotion and primarily consists of hypothalamus (Fig. 3.1), anterior thalamic nuclei, cingulate cortex (Figs 3.1 and 3.4) and hippocampus (Fig. 3.4). The importance of the LC was described earlier and will be further elaborated later in the chapter.

Bremner et al. (1997a) found increased CRH in the cerebrospinal fluid (CSF) of veterans with PTSD compared to normal controls. In fact, CSF CRH reflects both hypothalamic and extrahypothalamic secretion of CRH. Such hypersecretion from both these sites has been demonstrated in depression also (Nemeroff et al. 1984). Hypersecretion of CRH is also

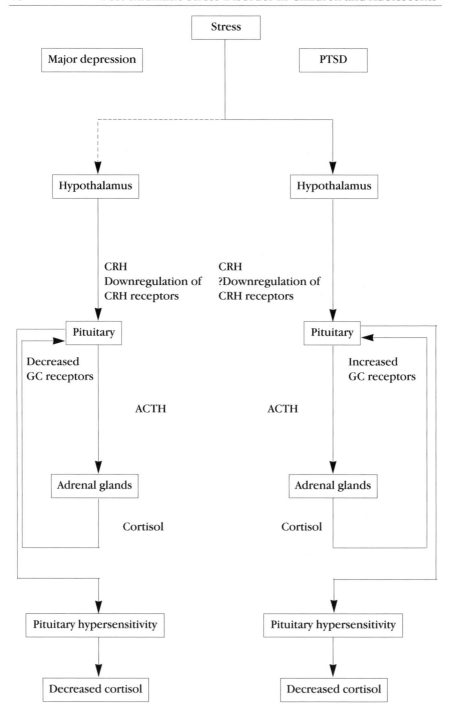

Figure 3.3. Comparison of the HPA axis in major depression and PTSD.

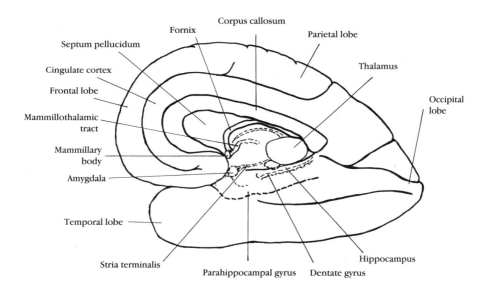

Figure 3.4. Sagittal section of brain.

demonstrated by metyrapone stimulation test. Metyrapone is a drug that inhibits the 11-β-hydroxylase, the enzyme that converts 11-deoxycortisol to cortisol. Metyrapone prevents the synthesis of cortisol in the adrenal glands. This test directly examines the pituitary secretion of ACTH eliminating the effects of circulating GC and the degree of pituitary sensitivity to GC (Yehuda et al. 1996a, Lisansky et al. 1989). Metyrapone administration elevates the CRH, ACTH and 11-deoxycortisol levels because of disruption in the negative feedback. A metyrapone stimulation test in PTSD has shown that the levels of ACTH and 11-deoxycortisol are substantially higher (over four times the normal) than normal controls, indicating that the pituitary is hypersensitive to CRH stimulation (reviewed in Yehuda et al. 1996a).

Research findings on cortisol levels in PTSD are also conflicting. However, most of the studies have shown low cortisol levels. This reduction has been demonstrated in 24 hour cortisol production (Mason et al. 1986, Yehuda et al. 1992, 1993, 1995b) and also in single samples of blood (Goenjian et al. 1996) and saliva (Kellner et al. 1997). Nevertheless, Pitman and Orr (1990) have reported an increase in cortisol. The variations in these findings may be because of variations in sample characteristics, storage and assay techniques, differences in the types of PTSD and the symptomatic state (Davidson 1995, Yehuda 1998). Women with a previous history of trauma had lower mean cortisol and greater odds (unadjusted odds 6.7 with a 95% confidence interval of

1.5–30.3) of developing PTSD compared to those who did not. This supports the epidemiological finding of increased susceptibility of women to develop PTSD following exposure to stress. In addition, exposure to severe stress is not sufficient to cause these changes in cortisol levels but the presence of PTSD is necessary. Yehuda et al. (1995b) demonstrated that urinary cortisol was significantly lower in those with PTSD following exposure to the Holocaust than in those who were exposed but did not develop PTSD. Exposure to trauma *per se* did not result in low cortisol but the presence of PTSD did.

In PTSD, cortisol level is low despite elevations in CRH. Elevated CRH with low cortisol indicates that the ACTH response to CRH is blunted. Normally, ACTH level increases with elevated CRH. Figure 3.3 shows complex interactions between adrenals and pituitary, resulting in heightened sensitivity of pituitary to cortisol, so that even with low circulating cortisol level ACTH secretion remains inhibited. Interestingly, low basal cortisol and blunted ACTH response to CRH challenge correlated with severity of PTSD symptoms (Davidson 1995). In addition to this, investigation of circadian rhythmic release has shown decrease in the overall level and a substantially different pattern of release of cortisol compared to normal controls. Chronobiological analysis revealed that the cortisol level was comparable to that of normal subjects during the daytime (when it is high), but was significantly higher when it is low in normal subjects. They suggest that this may be due to altered regulation of the HPA axis which can, as a corollary, potentially lead to altered response to stress (Yehuda et al. 1996b).

The low cortisol level in PTSD is suspected to be due to increased pituitary sensitivity resulting from increased number of or up-regulation of GC receptors. This implies that lower levels of cortisol can exert greater feedback inhibition of the pituitary, blocking the release of ACTH. Greater numbers of GC receptors have been demonstrated in PTSD (Yehuda et al. 1991, 1993, 1995a, 1996). However, the issue that has not yet been resolved is whether the up-regulation of GC receptors is a cause or consequence of low cortisol levels. Although it is reasonable to suspect increase in GC receptors to be secondary to low cortisol, some workers feel that it could be the primary abnormality in PTSD (reviewed in Yehuda 1998). Besides, low cortisol may also be due to down-regulation of pituitary CRH receptors, which may be the result of chronic hypersecretion of CRH. This is demonstrated by blunting of ACTH response to CRH challenge in PTSD (Smith et al. 1989). Owing to the increased number of pituitary GC receptors and consequent pituitary hyperresponsivity to cortisol, the increased CRH in PTSD is not associated with evening rise of plasma cortisol levels, as is encountered in major depression (Fig. 3.3).

Abnormalities in the HPA axis may be summarised as follows:

- CRH response from both hypothalamic and extrahypothalamic sites is increased
- ACTH response to CRH is blunted
- CRH receptors are down-regulated, making the pituitary less responsive to CRH so that ACTH levels are low despite elevated CRH.
- the presence of PTSD is necessary for low cortisol, not merely exposure to stress
- the pituitary is hypersensitive to cortisol
- GC receptors are up-regulated so that low levels of cortisol can exert negative feedback inhibition on the pituitary
- cortisol levels are low (but findings are conflicting)

It was pointed out earlier that the neurochemical systems and the endogenous opioid system closely interact with the HPA axis. The effect of this interaction is described further in the subsequent sections.

Other endocrine systems are also associated with certain abnormalities. Mason et al. (1994) reported persistently elevated tri-iodothyronine (T3) and thyroxine (T4) in PTSD. These are the major hormones of the thyroid gland. Kosten et al. (1990) found that the thyroid stimulating hormone (TSH) response to thyroid releasing hormone (TRH) is augmented. Serum testosterone has also been shown to be increased. A multidimensional interactional analysis of abnormalities in various neurochemicals and hormones has shown that a consistent pattern of low cortisol, increased norepinephrine and increased thyroid hormones could discriminate 100% of patients with PTSD (reviewed in Yehuda 1998). Therefore, it appears that a complex interaction among these systems underlies pathophysiology of PTSD.

Stress, HPA axis, neurotransmitters and brain

Corticosteroids affect the functioning of the brain in various ways. Through genomic action they alter the expression of steroid-related genes, and through non-genomic action they affect neural excitability. The HPA axis and the noradrenergic system influence each other reciprocally and affect the functioning of the brain. CRH infusion increased the activity of the LC in rats (Valentino et al. 1983), and adrenalectomy activated the central noradrenergic system (McEwen 1987). The cortisol/noradrenaline ratio has been found to be different in PTSD from other psychiatric disorders. This alteration has been suggested to cause brain changes through its influence on genomes. Thus, the reciprocal influence of the HPA axis and the noradrenergic system may bring about a gene–environment interaction which can result in enduring changes in the brain. It has been proposed that stimulatory effects of GCs on noradrenaline produce repetitive behaviours and startle responses whereas numbing of responses and avoidance could be due to the effects of GCs on genomes (Terr 1996). Such interactions affect gene expression, which in turn affects the activity of enzymes that synthesise neurotransmitters and other vital proteins for neuronal survival and sprouting. Consequently, altered gene action can affect neuronal connectivity, growth of neuronal processes (dendritic and axonal branching), and survival of neurons (Black 1996). These interactions can be extended to understand the way stress affects brain to make it increasingly vulnerable to developing the clinical symptoms.

A binary system of adrenal steroid receptors has been demonstrated in the hippocampus and amygdala. Type I receptors are mineralocorticoid receptors with low affinity for GCs. Type II receptors are high-affinity GC receptors. Such a receptor system ensures the response of brain tissues at varying levels of corticosteroids. The action of adrenal steroids has been described as biphasic. At moderate levels, it protects the brain from stress and anxiety, but when it is either excessive or insufficient it could cause structural damage to some areas of brain and bring about emotional instability and cognitive deficits. Chronic stress causes neuronal degeneration in the pyramidal cells of the CA3 region of the hippocampus through the mediation of type II receptors. In contrast, GC is required to mediate the survival and stabilisation of the population of the granule cells of the dentate gyrus (Fig 3.4, a component of the hippocampal formation) through type I receptors (McEwen et al. 1992, Holsboer 1995, McEwen 1996, Bremner 1999). The hippocampus, in turn, exerts inhibitory control over the HPA axis. Bremner (1999) proposes that the hippocampus may be the centre for integrating neuro-hormonal, neurochemical and cognitive response to stress.

Recent studies have shown that hippocampal volume is reduced in PTSD. Bremner et al. (1995) found 8% reduction in the volume of the right hippocampus in PTSD patients compared to controls. Other workers have found reductions varying from 12% (Bremner et al. 1997b) to 26% in PTSD patients (Gurvits et al. 1996). The former study was done on adults with a history of childhood abuse and ruled out depression as a confounding factor. The reduction in hippocampal formation is also seen in those exposed to prolonged stress, such as extended exposure to combat, as was found by Gurvits et al. (1996). In addition, the duration of exposure predicted the degree of atrophy. Many studies have demonstrated that the higher the plasma cortisol levels, the smaller the volume of the hippocampal formation. The severity of symptoms of PTSD directly correlated with the degree of reduction in hippocampal volume (reviewed in van der Kolk 1997 and Bremner 1999). Short-term exposure to excessive GC causes reversible atrophy of hippocampal dendrites whereas long-term exposure leads to permanent damage (Sapolsky 1996). Similar changes in hippocampus have been observed in abused children (reviewed in Perry and Pollard 1998).

Bremner et al. (1997b) found reductions in the volume of the amygdala in addition to hippocampal volume shrinkage. However, Gurvits et al. (1996) could not find any changes in amygdalar volume. Functional studies using positron emission tomography (PET) scan have shown abnormalities in blood flows compared to controls. Activation in the right amygdala was found by some (Rauch et al. 1996, Shin et al. 1997) and yet others have found it in the left amygdala (Liberzon et al. 1999) in response to emotion-arousing stimuli such as reading scripts or combat-related sounds. The latter workers also found that there was enhanced blood flow in the vicinity of the left amygdala and deactivation in control subjects. In addition, in functional neuroimaging studies other workers have found activation to emotionally arousing visual stimuli of the whole region of the amygdala, variously called the extended amygdala or amygdaloid region (Taylor et al. 1998, Reiman et al. 1997). There are several interpretations of these findings:

- They may indicate that the amygdala is abnormal in its structure and function in PTSD.
- They may indicate that smaller amygdala may have to overwork in order to maintain the level of functioning of a normal-sized amygdala. However, empirical data to support such conclusions are lacking. It is difficult to conclude that an overworking smaller amygdala leads to the development of PTSD symptoms.
- An overworking amygdala could, itself, bring about cellular damage accounting for a smaller volume of amygdala in PTSD.
- Supersensitive GC receptors might have brought about cellular death in the amygdala, as happens in the hippocampus.

Structural and functional abnormalities in the hippocampus and amygdala have wide-ranging implications, including:

- poor integration of traumatic experiences
- inadequate contextualisation of the interpretation of such stress
- inability to mount adequate and adaptive emotional response
- difficulty in proper verbalisation of the experience
- defects in preventing unnecessary overgeneralisation of the stimulus
- insufficiency in distinguishing the real from unreal threat to self.

Further aspects of abnormalities in the hippocampus and amygdala will be discussed later in the chapter.

In addition to their role in adaptation to stress, GCs affect memory and learning. Several studies have shown that higher GC levels produce memory deficits, and reduced levels are associated with improved memory function (reviewed in Bremner 1999). Starkman et al. (1992) found that patients with Cushing's disease (prolonged hypercortisolism) had deficits in declarative verbal memory, such as paired associate learning and verbal recall. Declarative memory is a memory of facts and events that is flexible and applicable to novel contexts. Wolkowitz et al. (1990) in their well-conducted study reported that significant cognitive dysfunction could be demonstrated in depressed patients with a dysregulated HPA axis and healthy volunteers who received significant doses of synthetic cortisol. Thus, it can be inferred that GCs affect memory and learning to a significant degree, which is reversible at least in the early stages. Owing to their effects on learning, GCs affect the learning of certain adaptive responses, too. Responding to inescapable extreme stress requires a normal response of the HPA axis. It has been found in animals that GC prevents the development of learned helplessness (see Gross 1996, p. 169, for a basic understanding of learned helplessness). At a molecular level, GCs reduce the noradrenaline-stimulated formation of cyclic adenosine monophosphate (cAMP) and calcium–calmodulin adenylate cyclase activity, reducing the effects of noradrenaline (McEwen 1996). Activation of this enzyme cascade and consequent protein synthesis is probably important for memory formation. Abnormalities in the control of GC could lead to the development of maladaptive responses to stress. In addition, some of the cognitive effects described above could be associated with hippocampal dysfunction.

Hippocampal formation is strongly suspected to have an important role in the regulation of the HPA axis. A dysregulated HPA axis can result in impaired feedback to the hippocampus. In addition, the hippocampus is important in memory, information processing etc., as will be discussed later. 5-HT mediates the interaction between the two systems. 5-HT and GCs regulate each other through rich serotonergic innervation of hippocampus. GCs increase the turnover of 5-HT through GC- or CRH-induced induction of tryptophan hydroxylase, the enzyme required for the biosynthesis of 5-HT. In turn, the 5-HT_{1A}, 5-HT_{1C} and 5-HT_2 receptors stimulate the release of cortisol. In major depressive disorder, chronic elevation of GCs alter the function of 5-HT_{1A} and up-regulates 5-HT_2 receptors. Furthermore, depletion of 5-HT in the hippocampus has been shown to reduce the expression of GC receptors and attenuate the negative feedback effects of cortisol (reviewed in Maes and Meltzer 1995). Excessive cortisol down-regulates hippocampal 5-

HT_{1A} receptors and up-regulates cerebral cortical 5-HT_2 receptors, as is seen in depression (McEwen 1996). From the above findings, it appears that a fine balance between 5-HT_2 receptors in the cerebral cortex and 5-HT_{1A} receptors in the hippocampus is essential for maintaining resilience in the affective state. It is not clear whether chronically low levels of cortisol alter the 5-HT receptors in the opposite direction, which may be relevant in PTSD, but reciprocal interaction between these two systems is essential for adaptive response to stress. However, many preclinical and clinical studies have shown supersensitive 5-HT_{2C} receptors in PTSD. Because 5-HT_2 receptors stimulate cortisol release, supersensitive 5-HT_{2C} receptors should lead to elevation of cortisol level in PTSD. All but a few of the studies have shown low basal cortisol level, as reviewed earlier. Bremner (1999) in a recent review hypothesised that the early stage of the illness may be characterised by a high cortisol level, whereas a decreased level appears in the chronic stages of the illness. This is suspected to be due to the effects of allostatic load leading to long-term changes in cortisol regulation.

PTSD can be conceptualised as a chronic stress syndrome heralded by an acute stress, probably owing to lack of restitution of stress-related alteration of bodily functions. A low cortisol response to acute stress (Resnick et al. 1995) could lead to prolonged high arousal that can make a person vulnerable to developing chronic stress syndrome. In the face of stress, it is essential to shut down some systems in order to make an adaptive fight-or-flight response. GCs mediate this through their anti-stress effect. A low cortisol response to stress prevents this from happening, leading to enduring undifferentiated fight-or-flight responses (Yehuda et al. 1990) that last beyond the point of relevance and thus become pathological. The importance of an adaptive fight-or-flight response and the neural circuits involved are discussed later in the chapter. Chronic stress leads to increased secretion of CRH (Bremner et al. 1997a) from both hypothalamic and extrahypothalamic regions, such as LC and amygdala. Over a period of time CRH receptors in the pituitary are down-regulated, making pituitary less responsive to CRH. Consequently, ACTH response to CRH is blunted. The increased GC receptors (either as a cause or as a consequence) result in the pituitary becoming hypersensitive to cortisol. With these changes the HPA axis cannot respond adaptively when exposed to stress. Further, ACTH and GC are essential in some aspects of memory and in altering the hippocampal susceptibility to long-term potentiation (LTP) (McEwen 1996) – an important cellular mechanism in memory and learning. In addition to the above changes, abnormalities in the structure and function of hippocampus and amygdala may result in inadequate integration of the experience of acute stress. This could lead to constant rumination of stress and symptoms of PTSD, as described later in the chapter. The disturbances in the endogenous opioid system can add further behavioural components to this, as discussed earlier.

Immunological abnormalities

Severe and/or chronic stress alters the immunological functions. Ironson et al. (1997) found in their study of hurricane victims that only the natural killer cell cytotoxicity (NKCC) was negatively related to both damage and PTSD. In addition, white blood cell (WBC) counts were significantly positively related with the degree of loss and PTSD. Both lower NKCC activity and WBC count were significantly related to the increase in retrospective self-report of somatic symptoms. Interestingly, the herd immunity showed that the victims had significantly lower NKCC, CD4 and CD8 lymphocyte number and higher NK cell number than controls (basic understanding of the interaction between stress and immunity is given in Prasad 1996). Animal studies have yielded similar findings. Stress lowered the NKCC activity so much that it resulted in metastasis of cancer in rats (reviewed in McEwen 1996). This could increase susceptibility to infection in such people. Figure 3.5 illustrates possible interactions between the neuroendocrine, neurochemical and immunological systems in PTSD.

Electrophysiological findings

This section gives a brief overview of electrophysiological methods and their findings in PTSD. Basically, specific electrical activities in certain areas of brain are measured by extrapolation from an electroencephalogram (EEG). The electrical potentials are generated through the transmission of nerve impulses while they communicate with each other. The movement of various ions between the interior and the exterior of the neurons generates the electrical signals. Such electrical activity can be recorded using special techniques by placing electrodes on appropriate sites on the scalp. EEG is a generalised representation of the brain activity, whereas in electrophysiological studies very discrete and specialised recordings, related to performance of a variety of cognitive and motor tasks, are derived from the EEG. They are called **event-related potentials** (ERPs). ERPs give a fairly good indication of the information processing in the brain and also the possible neurotransmitters that may be involved. Examples of commonly measured ERPs are P300 and contingent negative variation (CNV). P300 is the positive wave that occurs around the 300th millisecond in the ERP and is related to conscious thought and contextual updating. CNV is the negative deflection in anticipation of an event that reflects attention, motivation and motor preparation. Similar responses recorded following sensory

HPA axis

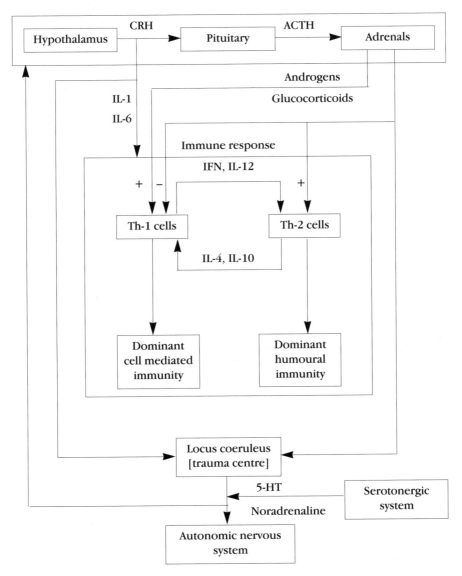

Figure 3.5. Interaction between the HPA axis, immune system, LC and automonic nervous system (simplified).

stimuli in different sensory modalities (visual, auditory etc.) are called **evoked potentials** (EP): examples are somatosensory evoked potential, brainstem auditory evoked response (BAER), etc. These potentials primarily reflect the integrity of the neural tract subserving the sensory modality.

Although the literature on schizophrenia and depression abounds with such studies, research in this area in PTSD is lagging behind. Paige et al. (1990) demonstrated that people with PTSD have enhanced sensitivity for sound and reduced wave amplitude. McFarlane et al. (1993) concluded that PTSD patients have difficulty in differentiating relevant from irrelevant stimuli and require more effort to react to current experience, especially when it is affectively neutral, as reflected in slowing of reaction time. Other researchers have replicated slowing of reaction time (Boudarene and Timsit-Berthier 1997) and reduction in amplitude (Boudarene and Timsit-Berthier 1997, Metzger et al. 1997) of P300 in PTSD. In addition, Kounios et al. (1997) reported different types of abnormalities in ERP suggestive of impaired perceptual input, altered tonicity of cortical excitability and exaggerated emotional importance attributed to the stimulus. These findings suggest that people with PTSD have perpetually activated inhibitory feedback loops and have difficulty in neutralising innocuous affective stimuli and attending to affectively neutral inputs, making it difficult to be involved in day to day life. The importance of these findings is briefly discussed in the next section.

Neurodevelopmental aspects of trauma and PTSD in children and adolescents

The growing brain is more vulnerable to environmental influences. Brain grows at an enormous pace and reaches 90% of its adult size by 3 years of age, when the body is still only about 20% of adult size. However, differentiation continues throughout life, especially during childhood and adolescence. Differentiation of the brain during childhood and adolescence occurs in three overlapping phases:

- formation of synapses
- stabilisation of essential synapses
- elimination of unwanted synapses.

Differentiation is also a sequential process that occurs initially in the areas regulating vital physiological functions (e.g. respiration, cardiovascular functions) and progresses to the evolutionarily most recent areas of the brain in the cerebral cortex. Any stress during this period may alter the pattern of synaptic connectivity in the brain which may in turn alter the way the child responds to the environment. These neural changes affect the later differentiation of the brain, patterns of learning and reacting to the external world, particularly to stress. It should also be emphasised that most cognitive development occurs in this age range, altering the way the young human views and imbibes the experiences in both the internal and external world.

How does a child learn fear? Fear has enormous survival value, especially in the evolutionary context. Some stimuli have a greater propensity to be recognised as dangers. This innate preparedness is crucial in acquiring and properly categorising the stimuli from the world, external or internal. The brain acquires huge amounts of information from the external and the internal worlds and stores this in a systematic way in order to use it for the future. As an individual grows, the amount of information that is stored in the brain also increases. When the brain receives any information that is not yet present there, it responds to this as a novel stimulus, increasing arousal and attention. The cortex analyses and interprets the stimuli before presenting it to the limbic system. If the novel stimulus proves to be safe, it is categorised as such. Otherwise, the cortex pulls the trigger for an alarm reaction that sets off the cascade of stress events. This information is also stored in the brain for future reference. Because of the adaptive nature of the fear response, any stimulus that matches the previously stored fear-inducing stimuli is viewed as a true danger and the response is mounted. The degree of danger posed to the child, real or perceived, determines the amount of stress experienced. Those stimuli that were previously perceived as extremely dangerous may have to be very quickly avoided or the stress response mounted immediately. Because of the survival value of this response, closely matching stimuli are also given the same degree of attention; however, the cerebral cortex exerts its inhibitory control when the stimulus does not threaten homeostasis. However, in PTSD such stimuli may bypass the cortical processing and reach the limbic system or amygdala. Such subcortical circuits may acquire greater importance as the child grows.

The time at which the growing brain is exposed to stress determines the clinical presentation. Children who experienced acute stress in the form of trauma before the age of 4 years manifested with pre-psychotic and psychotic symptoms, especially when they had a family history of schizophrenia. Those exposed after 4 years of age predominantly had anxiety and mood symptoms similar to adults, more so if they had a family history of mood disorder (reviewed in Perry 1994). Perry and Pollard (1998) in their review point out that the entire brain takes part in responding to stress in turn, ending up with difficult-to-erase memories in each of those areas. In fact memory can be conceived as internal representations of events. These representations contain various kinds of data, such as episodic, semantic, procedural, emotional etc. Of these the emotional memories are almost indelible. In terms of anatomical structures involved, cerebral cortical areas contain cognitive memory (mainly informational), limbic areas contain emotional aspects, midbrain contains the motor memories and the brainstem the physiological memory.

Children respond to stress in a different way from adults. The response is even more pronounced in infants, because of their restricted repertoire of behavioural responses. Infants and children respond in a very primitive way because they do not have a well-developed fight-or-flight reaction. Their response is restricted mainly to vocalisation that can attract the caregiver so that they can escape from the stressful situation. When they do not get the expected reaction from caregivers, these behaviours become extinct. Predictable caregiver responses lead to healthy development of stress response at a later age (reviewed in Perry and Pollard 1998). Perry (1994) described primarily two patterns of responses, hyperarousal and dissociative responses. Perry and Pollard (1998) argue that a balanced mixture of these two patterns is very adaptive in times of stress. In addition, the degree of development and the ability to mix these two patterns in an adaptive way reflect the degree of maturity of the neurobiological systems of infants and children.

The mechanism of behavioural hyperarousal is much the same as in adults, but the overt manifestations may be different. The child could be hyperactive, impulsive, and anxious with sleep problems and tachycardia. Nevertheless, hyperarousal is essential for an adaptive fight-or-flight reaction. As mentioned earlier, with poorly developed fight-or-flight and/or poor response of caregivers to such a reaction, a defeat reaction ensues leading to adaptation of dissociative mechanisms. Although the neurobiological mechanisms are not very clearly elucidated, physiological hyperarousal occurs similar to that seen in the fight-or-flight reaction. One important difference is increase in vagal tone accounting for a drop in blood pressure and bradycardia. The dopaminergic system is very important in the mediation of dissociative or defeat reaction because of its co-localisation with the opioid system. As discussed earlier, the opioid system mediates numbing and dissociation.

Freezing is also one of the reactions to severe stress. Children are more prone to freeze because of a poorly developed anxiety management system, which can be seen as defiance by adults. Freezing can be so severe that abused children can regress to a near-psychotic regressed situation (see Perry and Pollard 1998 for further details).

Neuropsychobiological model of PTSD

The phenomenological approach too has provided inroads into the pathophysiology of PTSD. Many workers have looked at intrusive imagery as a phenomenon in its own right in order to understand the phenomenology of PTSD. This is clinically very relevant because the DSM-IV (APA 1993) emphasises the presence of intrusive imagery as an essential requirement for the diagnosis of PTSD. The most important feature of intrusive imagery is its association with intense physiological response. The basic conceptualisation of intrusive imageries is founded on reactivation of traumatic memories. The intensity of reaction to the initial trauma leaves an indelible impression on the memory circuits of the brain. Their subsequent retrieval in various forms manifests phenomenologically as flashbacks, ideas, etc., and is dependent on various factors. Information-processing paradigms have been particularly useful in understanding this.

Some of the theories are now briefly discussed to provide a background to the possible ways in which we can relate the clinical symptoms with the findings from biological research. There are three main theories that attempt to explain the possible underlying mechanisms for the intrusive imageries and other symptoms of PTSD. Lang's (1993, 1994) bio-informational theory is the most important. Foa et al.'s (1989) associative memory network model and Chemtob et al.'s (1988) parallel distributed processing model extend it further.

According to Lang's **bio-informational theory**, 'emotions are action dispositions'. Information about the emotional experiences is stored in propositional form, organised into associative networks called **emotion prototypes**. This information is contained in neural networks concerned with memory. These memory networks are organised as mutually activating informational units. The emotional network is proposed to be three layered with the semantic code in the highest layer, stimulus characteristic representation in the middle and the response output systems in the lowest layer. The top layer containing the semantic code consists of stimulus, meaning and response units that correspond to perception, declarative knowledge and outputs in terms of behaviour, physiological activation and verbal expression, respectively. Matching stimulus inputs activate the network. The closer the match, the stronger the activation and the greater the chances of outputting response. In addition, the processing can be internally modulated. When the network is well established owing to repeated activation and learning, the behavioural output becomes independent of internal modulation. The activation of the network is not controlled and intentional, but automatic and feed-forward. Sartory (1993) postulates that vicarious learning following an initial conditioning exposure may also strengthen the network. Such conditioning can give rise to a negative appraisal of a stimulus that in reality may be innocuous and neutral. The neurotransmitters that may be involved are noradrenaline and 5-HT, as described earlier.

The theory proposes that the amygdala, hypothalamus, central grey area in the midbrain and autonomic nervous system structures are central to emotional processing. Following exposure to traumatic stress, the emotional network involving these structures is activated. From a neurophysiological perspective, the threshold for neuronal firing is altered through the influence of neuromodulators making the network more sensitive. In other words, there is no need to establish an altogether new network; the change can be accomplished partly by finer modification of the existing network enhancing the chances of inducing either an excitatory post-synaptic potential (EPSP) or an inhibitory post-synaptic potential (IPSP). This step leads to learning an emotional reaction to a new stimulus. However, retaining the learnt emotional response in long-term memory requires repeated exposure to such stimuli resulting in repeated release of neuromodulators (as discussed earlier). This leads to altered gene expression and new protein synthesis and, consequently, establishment of new synaptic connections (Bailey and Kandel 1996). Owing to considerable neural plasticity in these subcortical structures, learning and stimulus generalisation occurs easily. The amygdaloid nucleus is said to be the centre of emotional learning. The afferent signals come mainly from the sensory cortex through the thalamus and the medial prefrontal cortex to the lateral nucleus of the amygdala (Figs 3.4 and 3.6). The signals are then transmitted to the central nucleus of the amygdala from where the efferent signals reach the hypothalamus and then the somatic nervous system through the central grey area, which form the subcortical primary motivational system (SPMS). This circuit is said to be the centre for mediating the general aversive motivational system. In addition, the efferents from the amygdala reach the sensory cortex, the association areas of the brain and the hippocampus from where the lateral amygdala receives reciprocal afferent inputs. The amygdala has close interactions with hippocampal formation (Amaral and Insausti 1990) which is important for long-term memory encoding, storage and retrieval. In addition, these structures are involved in conceptual processing and complex pattern recognition.

In PTSD, significant trauma is the primary stimulus, but we do not know what combination of factors makes this primary trauma leave its indelible imprint at the neuronal level (Ledoux 1998). This is crucial in deciding who develops PTSD and who does not after exposure to the same or similar primary stimulus. Cues matching the primary stimulus act as further stimuli to strengthen the network. As the network strengthens, the degree of match with the primary stimulus that is required to activate the network decreases. When the network becomes fully established, even innocuous stimuli with remote reference to the traumatic incident can activate the network. The meaning units that consist of the semantic knowledge associated with the experience of the stimulus determine the nature of response (which may be physiological, verbal or affective or a combination of these). The intrusive imageries may consist of one or more of these. Therefore, the response units are the most important part of the network for producing the intrusive imageries. Repetitive activation of the network by matching cues reinforces and elaborates the emotional memory network, further lowering the threshold for subsequent activation. This makes the likelihood of experiencing intrusive imageries more likely when a person is exposed to such matching cues. The person with intrusive imageries experiences lack of control because the network activation is mutual, feed-forward and automatic. The direct association of the emotional memory network with the SPMS and autonomic nuclei explains the intense autonomic response. These subcortical processing networks are so well established that such stimuli bypass cortical processing and inhibition to activate them. In other words, these networks directly activate the amygdala even before the cortex is aware of the stimuli so that the cortex does not have a chance to discriminate the stimulus and issue relevant commands to start or stop reacting. For these reasons these pathways are termed 'quick and dirty pathways' (Ledoux 1998). In fact, this neural circuitry is a high-priority network that mediates the sympathetic reactivity. The higher the emotional content of the arousing stimuli, the stronger its activation of the SPMS. Thus, activation of this subcortical network facilitates memory encoding and further storage. In summary, trauma or its reminiscences activate the SPMS, which is already primed by a previous exposure to the trauma, and this in turn activates the emotional memory circuit to produce the intrusive imageries.

Extending Lang's theory, Foa et al. (1989) suggest a structure of fear that broadly consists of affective, cognitive and interpretative components:

- the **cognitive** component consists of information about the situation
- the **affective** component consists of information about physiological and behavioural responses to the feared situation
- the **interpretative** component comprises of information about the meaning of the first two components.

In contrast to Lang, Foa et al. (1989) emphasise the meaning units because they distinguish between safety and danger. Thus, the theory conceives PTSD as a disorder that develops when one's concept of safety is pathologically altered, in effect leading to inadequate discrimination between real and perceived threats (cf. noradrenergic mechanisms and electrophysiological findings discussed earlier). According to this theory, there are three important features of the network that account for the persistence of the intrusive imageries:

- representation of trauma-induced intense reactivity in the response units

- large size of the network due to enhanced recruitment of elements
- ready accessibility of the network.

The reactivity is so intense that it prevents habituation and directs the person to avoid the situation rather than process the structure-inconsistent information. This can lead to modifications in the network that lead to maladaptive habituation to faulty interpretation of safety and danger. The large size of the network allows for greater likelihood of both full and partial activation.

Chemtob et al. (1988) present the **parallel distributed processing** (PDP) model that further extends Lang's theory. Two rather new and less well-known concepts need to be introduced here:

- **PDP** itself, an interesting, revolutionary and exciting concept, is borrowed from the field of advanced computing. The brain is likened to a network of computers where all information is not processed at a central point but distributed to various peripheral points. PDP involves distribution of central information processing over various networked peripheral points where concurrent information processing of relevant bits takes place.
- **Non-linear dynamics** implies that the relationship between two systems is not always proportional (Goerner 1995), in contrast to linear dynamics where they are predictably related. For example, when two systems, *a* and *b*, interact according to the principles of linear dynamics, changes in the activity of *a* lead to proportional changes in *b*, whereas in non-linear dynamics an increase in the activity of system *a* does not proportionally increase the activity in system *b*.

Chemtob et al. (1988) extend the PDP model by including non-linear dynamics as the basis for the interaction of various simple processing units. According to their theory, neuronal signals are processed in relatively simple neural network units that form part of a complex parallel distributed network. The processing units are hierarchically arranged and each unit represents various mental, physiological and behavioural components. Those representing higher abstract functions, such as motivations, expectations, etc., are at a higher level than those that control the neurophysiological responses. The nodes higher in the hierarchy affect those at the lower levels, as well as being affected by the external environment. The nodes exist in either an inhibited or a potentiated state. The mutual interaction of nodes follows principles of non-linear dynamics involving various combinations of inhibitory and stimulatory signals from other units and the environment. Processing of stimuli that match the components of memory activates the network, which depends not only on the closeness of the stimulus match but also on the previous state of the network. When the network is in an inhibited state, it requires a much closer match than when it is in a potentiated state. Thus, a person with a potentiated network can have intrusive imageries even with degraded cues.

Furthermore, Chemtob et al. emphasise the importance of a 'threat-arousal node' situated hierarchically at the highest level, which is counteracted by an inhibitory node. People with PTSD experience greater threat expectancy, so that innocuous information may be misinterpreted as the harbinger of real trauma. This leads to some degree of constant potentiation of the threat-arousal node, which is kept inhibited by the inhibitory node. Once the network is activated to a sufficient degree, the activation continues as a feed-forward process leading to further potentiation of the network until it can no longer be inhibited by the inhibitory node resulting in intrusive imageries. As mentioned earlier, the hierarchical arrangement of the nodes leads to activation spreading from higher to lower nodes resulting in the appearance of imageries associated with autonomic symptoms. These symptoms are interpreted as further evidence of threat, creating a positive feedback loop.

In summary, the above theories propose that exposure to a significant traumatic incident primes the emotional circuits in the brain making them more sensitive to further exposure to similar or matching stimuli. Such stimuli trigger intrusive imageries and autonomic symptoms associated with PTSD. The unfavourable outcomes reported by many workers following early use of critical incident debriefing where early re-exposure to traumatic incident is used (Hobbs et al. 1996; Mayou et al., submitted) could be explained on the basis of these theories. Mayou et al. (submitted) suspect that such early re-exposure could impair recovery by interfering with reparative cognitive processes. However, when the intervention was done 6–12 months after exposure to trauma the clinical outcomes were better. Chemtob et al. (1997) found that psychological debriefing either 6 or 12 months after Hurricane Iniki yielded significant reduction in Impact of Event Scale (IES) scores within groups, whereas there was no difference between groups. Passage of time alone could not account for these differences.

Gray (1994) posits a model for emotional processing consisting of three fundamental emotional systems in the central nervous system of mammals:

- the behavioural inhibition system (BIS)
- the fight-or-flight system (FFS)
- the behavioural approach system (BAS).

These systems are described at three different levels: behavioural, neural and cognitive. Table 3.1 summarises the inputs, outputs and neural circuits of each of these systems.

Table 3.1 Emotional systems proposed by Gray (1994)

Emotional system	Inputs	Neural system	Outputs
Behavioural inhibition system	Punishment, non-reward, fear, novel stimuli	Septohippocampal system	Behavioural inhibition, increased arousal, increased attention
Fight-or-flight system	Punishment, non-reward	Amygdala circuit	Unconditioned escape, defensive aggression
Behavioural approach system	Reward, non-punishment	Septohippocampal system, basal ganglia, cerebral cortex, brainstem structures	Approach

It is impossible (and unnecessary) to delve deeply into these circuits in this chapter; only those aspects that are relevant to PTSD will be considered. The details of these neural circuits may be obtained from Swerdlow and Koob (1987), Gray et al. (1991) and Gray (1994).

The septohippocampal circuitry consists mainly of:

- the Papez circuit (cingulate gyrus, mammillary body, fornix, and anterior nucleus of the thalamus)
- the septal areas (medial and lateral septal areas)
- the hippocampal formation (dentate gyrus, hippocampus, entorhinal cortex and subiculum).

The subiculum, situated at the interface between hippocampus and the parahippocampal gyrus, acts as a comparator. The septohippocampal circuit is important for the behavioural approach and inhibition systems, and the amygdala in fight-or-flight reactions. Several abnormalities that might affect these systems were elucidated earlier. For example, serotonergic system abnormalities are involved in impaired behavioural inhibition and those in HPA axis regulation are implicated in undifferentiated fight-or-flight response. The importance of the amygdala lies in its central integrative role in fear conditioning (Ledoux 1996). Fear conditioning, and the subsequent response to its real or perceived presence, are crucial in triggering the manifestation of clinical symptoms. Fear conditioning is thought by some to be a central concept in understanding many psychiatric disorders such as PTSD, phobia, anxiety and so forth. Conditioning is a form of associative learning where an animal learns to associate a neutral environmental stimulus with a natural trigger for a particular behaviour. Pavlov conditioned his dog to salivate at the sound of a bell (a neutral stimulus) after repeatedly associating it with meat. Here, meat is the natural or unconditioned stimulus (US), the sound of the bell is the conditioned stimulus (CS), salivation in response to meat is an unconditioned response (UR) and that to the sound of the bell is the conditioned response (CR). What is learnt is not the response (salivation, in this case, which is natural) but the association. Similarly, fear is a protective behaviour of immense evolutionary importance built into the constitution of every animal. Animals learn to detect fearful situations and respond appropriately. Unlike other conditioned learning, fear conditioning is quick (a single exposure may be sufficient) and enduring. Although the learning may be made extinct by not pairing CS with US, the emotional memories are almost for ever. An excellent account of this concept in very simple language is given in Ledoux (1998).

At the cellular level, fear conditioning has been proposed to involve a process called **receptive field plasticity**. The receptive field of a nerve cell is a sensory physiological construct defined by the set of sensory stimuli that affect that particular cell's activity. Conditioning produces general enhancement of reaction across the receptive field, which reflects associative learning. A highly specific change to the characteristic CS also occurs, reflecting the altered information processing. Fear conditioning produces a very rapid and highly specific plasticity in the receptive fields of the cells concerned, with specific effects on information processing (Weinberger 1996). Although the importance of this concept is not yet fully understood, these enduring changes in the brain could lead to learning to respond in ways that may no longer be relevant after the importance of the stress comes to a halt. This may underlie the pathophysiology of PTSD.

Abnormalities in many of these areas have been demonstrated in human beings with PTSD. Symptom provocation studies (Rauch et al. 1996, Shin et al. 1997) have found enhanced activity on the right side of the brain, especially in the medial temporal lobe, amygdala and the insula as measured on PET. The importance of these structures was discussed earlier. Laterality-specific changes have been reported, e.g. reduced activity of Broca's area (the motor speech area), which is in the left hemisphere in most of the population. This indicates that individuals with PTSD may have difficulty in verbalising the emotional content of their feelings. Furthermore, single photon emission computed tomography (SPECT) studies have shown increased activation of bilateral anterior cingulate cortex and left prefrontal cortex after treatment with eye movement desensitisation and re-processing (EMDR) (see Chapter 11). No such differences in the activation of anterior cingulate cortex could be found in PTSD patients before the interventions. Besides, the hippocampal shrinkage found in PTSD adds to difficulties in the discrimination of innocuous and threatening stimuli and can lead to irrelevant response to external stimuli (see van der Kolk 1997 for further details). In other words, a disturbance of BIS occurs. Similarly, some degree of lateral specificity is observed in hippocampal shrinkage also. Nevertheless, robust findings on differential affliction are yet to emerge.

From the above review, it is clear that PTSD is the result of multisystem abnormalities in the brain. From the available evidence, it appears that abnormal functioning of the amygdala has a central role in the mediation of abnormalities in various systems. The following discussion and Fig. 3.6 are based on the above review and an excellent discussion on emotional systems by Ledoux (1996). Figures 3.1 (p. 44) and 3.4 (p. 49) depict the approximate anatomical positions of some of these structures in the human brain.

The amygdala is an almond-shaped structure consisting of the central, lateral, baso-lateral and baso-medial nuclei. The central nucleus of the amygdala (CNA) has important efferent (exit fibres) connections with structures that control the emotional responses. The stria terminalis carries most of the efferent fibres. The lateral nucleus of the amygdala (LNA) receives the main afferent connections (entry fibres) from relevant sensory processing regions. They consist of noradrenergic, serotonergic and dopaminergic nerve terminals in addition to those from temporal and frontal association areas. Primary emotional stimulus is presented in many ways to the LNA depending on the structure that inputs the signal. Simple featural sensory inputs are provided by the sensory thalamus whereas association cortices and the hippocampal formation provide more processed inputs. Thus, unimodal and polymodal association cortices provide inputs of objects and concepts, respectively. The hippocampal formation, containing the subiculum as the comparator, provides contextual inputs. These inputs can be processed in parallel.

The LNA sends afferent fibres to the CNA through the baso-lateral (BLNA) and baso-medial (BMNA) nuclei of the amygdala. The CNA has main efferents to the lateral hypothalamus, bed nucleus of stria terminalis (BNST), parabrachial nucleus, dorsal motor nucleus of vagus, nucleus ambiguus and periaqueductal grey matter. Each of these efferent connections is important for emotional behaviour and its physiological manifestations. Needless to mention, efferent projections to the

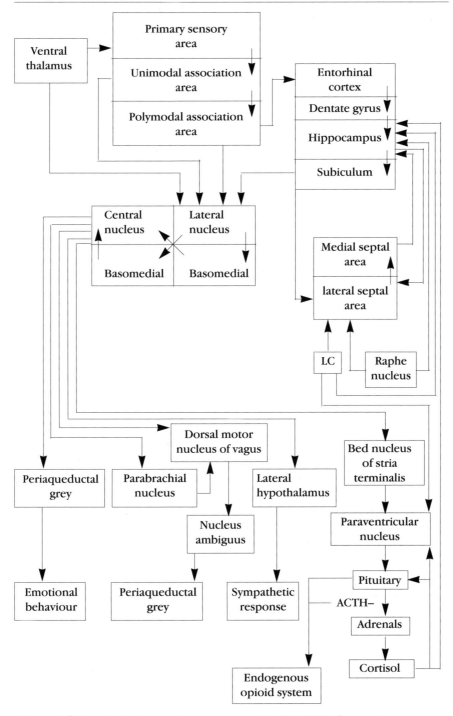

Figure 3.6. Neural circuitry and responses involved in PTSD (from various sources, see text).

lateral hypothalamus control the sympathetic responses. The BNST provides efferents to the paraventricular nucleus, which secretes CRH that stimulates ACTH secretion from the pituitary. Parasympathetic responses are controlled through the CNA's projections to the parabrachial nucleus, dorsal motor nucleus of vagus and nucleus ambiguus. Through its connections with the ventral medulla, the periaqueductal grey matter controls emotional behaviour. The LC and raphe nuclei (RN) have projections to the hippocampal formation, septal area and amygdala. In addition, the LC also influences the hypothalamus.

Conclusions

Life is dynamic. Dangers exist at every corner, and survival and life depend on the way we surmount them. They could lead to immense amounts of stress and suffering. The study of PTSD provides a unique opportunity to understand human suffering, fears and adaptational processes from an objective scientific perspective.

The brain is a rather conservative organ. Any input that surprises the brain would make it more active and demanding on its resources. Adaptation takes a long time, so any adaptive delay could prove very dear. The resultant anomalous information processing and the neural circuitry, along with dysregulation of neurochemical systems and the HPA axis, affect the way environmental stimuli are appraised and responded to. Significant stress with initial intense reactions conditions the emotional circuit, which is brought about by neural plasticity that involves formation of new connections, altering the probability of neuronal firing and transcription of relevant genes. Current evidence indicates that the amygdala, hippocampus and possibly the LC play crucial roles in the pathophysiology of PTSD.

The interest in the biology of PTSD is recent. Future work should focus on understanding the interrelationship between various abnormalities in neurochemical, endocrine, neuroanatomical and neurophysiological abnormalities.

Non-technical summary

The impact of stress on humans and animals is studied with great curiosity and concern. Stress is anything that alters the dynamic balance of the internal systemic environment (**homeostasis**). All organisms can adapt to stress by making certain changes within physiological limits, which is called **allostasis**. Once the stress is removed the body brings the systems back to their original level of functioning. Maintaining physiological functioning at an altered level (either higher or lower) for a long time in the face of chronic stress could lead to long-term changes in the functioning of these systems, referred to as allostatic load. This could lead to stress-related disorders, of which PTSD is an example. PTSD has been considered as a 'biopsychosocial trap', which emphasises the importance of psychological and social contributions to the aetiology in addition to biological causes.

Several underlying mechanisms have been found in PTSD. Neurochemical and endocrinal abnormalities are very widely studied. Dysregulation of several neurotransmitters, such as noradrenaline, 5-HT and dopamine, have been demonstrated to be important in PTSD. In addition, the respective receptor systems have also been found to be abnormal in terms of their number and/or sensitivity to neurotransmitters. The result of these abnormalities is the inability to monitor the environment flexibly, inappropriate detection of dangers and anomalous response to them. Abnormalities in the serotonergic system lead to the loss of the 'braking system' for the adrenergic transmission. An overresponsive dopaminergic system adds to the effects of the other neurotransmitter abnormalities. Electrophysiological studies have provided more direct evidence in support of these findings. Excessive activity of the endogenous opioid system in PTSD has been linked with psychic numbing and failure to respond to trauma in an adaptive way. Besides, one of the endogenous opioids (ß-endorphin) has close links with the release of ACTH that regulates the secretion of cortisol, also known as stress hormone. The above abnormalities result in abnormal fight-or-flight response and an impaired behavioural inhibition system.

In PTSD, the finely balanced interaction between the neurotransmitters and endogenous opioid system on the one hand and the endocrine system on the other is lost. Basal cortisol is low and ACTH response to CRH is blunted; these findings correlate with symptom severity. In addition, altered regulation of the HPA axis leads to anomalous response of this axis to stress in people with PTSD compared to normal individuals. Noradrenaline and 5-HT on the one hand and the HPA axis on the other influence each other. Thus, abnormalities in one could lead to altered regulation of the other, causing feed-forward abnormal response in the face of stress, either real or perceived. GCs, secreted by the adrenals, are also important substrates for the interaction between genes and environment. Repetitive stress or a single traumatic stress could, over a period of time, influence gene expression that modifies the connections among the neurons, their survival and growth. Finally, corticosteroids are also important for learning and memory. Chronic stress leads to the death of neurons in certain areas of brain, such as the hippocampus and the amygdala, that are important for learning and emotion. This could lead to disturbances in learning adaptive responses to stress.

PTSD has also been studied from the perspective of information-processing theories. These theories propose that the perception of stress, assigning meaning to it and response by behavioural outputs are organised in separate neural networks in a hierarchical manner. Exposure to traumatic stress sensitises these networks and makes them more prone to activation in response to either internal or external stimuli that match the traumatic stress. With greater sensitisation of the network, less closely matched cues can trigger the activation of the network. The network activation brings about intrusive memories and associated autonomic and behavioural responses, such as anxiety, hyperarousal, avoidance etc. Neuroanatomical regions and structures that are responsible for emotion and various behavioural outputs are described.

Acknowledgements

My thanks are due to Dr J. M. Santos MD CDM (Psiq), Professor A. P. Urdàniz MD PhD and Dr R. Greenwald for their useful comments on earlier drafts of this chapter.

References

Amaral, D. G. and Insausti, R. (1990) Hippocampal formation. In Paxinos, G. (ed.), The Human Nervous System. San Diego: Academic Press.

APA (1993) Diagnostic and Statistical Manual of Mental Disorders, 4th edn (DSM-IV). Washington, D. C.: American Psychiatric Association.

Bailey, C. H. and Kandel, E. R. (1996) Molecular and structural mechanisms underlying long-term memory. In Gazzaniga, M. S. (ed.), The Cognitive Neurosciences. Cambridge, MA: MIT Press.

Black, I. B. (1996) Molecular and cellular plasticity: Introduction. In Gazzaniga, M. S. (ed.), The Cognitive Neurosciences. Cambridge, MA: MIT Press.

Blanchard, E. B., Kolb, L. C., Prins A., Gates, S. and McCoy, G. C. (1991) Changes in plasma norepinephrine to combat-related stimuli among Vietnam veterans with PTSD. Journal of Nervous and Mental Disease 179, 371–373.

Boudarene, M. and Timsit-Berthier, M. (1997) Interest of events-related potential in assessments of post-traumatic stress disorder. Annals of the New York Academy of Sciences 821, 494–498.

Bremner, J. D. (1999) Does stress damage the brain? Biological Psychiatry 45, 797–805.

Bremner, J. D., Randall, P., Scott, T. M. et al. (1995) MRI-based measurement of hippocampal volume in patients with combat-related PTSD. American Journal of Psychiatry 152, 973–981.

Bremner, J. D., Licinio, J., Darnell, A. et al. (1997a) Elevated CSF corticotrophin releasing factor concentrations in post-traumatic stress disorder. American Journal of Psychiatry 154, 624–629.

Bremner, J. D., Randall, P. R., Vermetten E. et al. (1997b) Magnetic resonance imaging-based measurement of hippocampal volume in posttraumatic stress disorder related to childhood physical and sexual abuse: a preliminary report. Biological Psychiatry 41, 23–32.

Chemtob, C. M., Tomas, S., Law, W. and Cremniter, D. (1997) Postdisaster psychosocial intervention: a field study of the impact of debriefing on psychological distress. American Journal of Psychiatry 154, 415–417.

Chemtob, C., Roitblat, H. L., Hamada, R. S., Carlson, J. G. and Twentyman, C. T. (1988) A cognitive action theory of post-traumatic stress disorder. Journal of Anxiety Disorders 2, 253–275.

Coccaro, E. F., Siever, L. J., Klar, H. M. et al. (1989) Serotonergic studies in patients with affective and personality disorders. Archives of General Psychiatry 46, 587–598.

Davidson, J. R. T. (1995) Post-traumatic stress disorder and acute stress disorder. In Kaplan, H. I. and Sadock, B. J. (eds), Comprehensive Textbook of Psychiatry. Baltimore: Williams and Wilkins.

Davidson, J., Lipper, S., Kilts, C. D., Mahorney, S. and Hummett, E. (1985) Platelet MAO activity in post-traumatic stress disorder. American Journal of Psychiatry 142, 1341–1343.

De Bellis, M. D., Lefter, L., Trickett, P. K. and Putnam, F. W. (1994) Urinary catecholamine excretion in sexually abused girls. Journal of American Academy of Child and Adolescent Psychiatry 33, 320–327.

Foa, E. B., Steketee, G. and Rothbaum, B. O. (1989) Behavioral/cognitive conceptualization of post-traumatic stress disorder. Behavior Therapy 20, 155–176.

Goenjian, A. K., Yehuda, R., Pynoos, R. S. et al. (1996) Basal cortisol and dexamethasone suppression of cortisol among adolescents after the 1988 earthquake in Armenia. American Journal of Psychiatry 153, 929–934.

Goerner, S. J. (1995) Chaos and deep ecology. In Abraham, F. D. and Gilgen, A. R. (eds), Chaos Theory in Psychology. Westport, CT: Graeger.

Gray, J. A. (1994) Framework for a taxonomy of psychiatric disorder. In Van Goozen, S. H.M., Van de Poll, N. E. and Sergeant, J. A. (eds), Emotions: Essays on Emotion Theory, pp. 29–59. Hillsdale, NJ: Lawrence Erlbaum.

Gray, J. A., Fendon, J., Rawlins, J. N. P., Hemsley, D. R. and Smith, A. D. (1991) The neuropsychology of schizophrenia. Behavioral and Brain Sciences 14, 1–20.

Gross, R. (1996) Psychology: The Science of Mind and Behaviour, 3rd edn. London: Hodder and Stoughton.

Gurvits, T. G., Shenton, M. R., Hokama, H. et al. (1996) Magnetic resonance imaging study of hippocampal volume in chronic combat-related posttraumatic stress disorder. Biological Psychiatry 40, 1091–1099.

Hobbs, M., Mayou, R. A., Harrison, B. and Worlock, P. (1996) A randomised controlled trial of psychological debriefing for victims of road traffic accidents. British Medical Journal 313, 1438–1439.

Holsboer, F. (1995) Neuroendocrinology of mood disorders. In Bloom, F. E. and Kupfer, D. J. (eds), Psychopharmacology: The Fourth Generation of Progress. New York, Raven Press.

Ironson, G., Wynings, C., Schneiderman, N. et al. (1997) Posttraumatic stress symptoms, intrusive thoughts, loss, and immune function after Hurricane Andrew. Psychosomatic Medicine 59(2), 128–141.

Jaffe, J. A. (1995) Opioid dependence. In Kaplan, H. I. and Sadock, B. J. (eds), Comprehensive Textbook of Psychiatry. Baltimore: Williams and Wilkins.

Jensen, J. B., Pease, J. B., Bensel, R. and Garfinkel, B. D. (1991) Growth hormone response patterns in sexually or physically abused boys. Journal of American Academy of Child and Adolescent Psychiatry 30, 784–790.

Kellner, M., Baker, D. G. and Yehuda, R. (1997) Salivary cortisol in Operation Desert Storm returnees. Biological Psychiatry 42, 849–850.

Kosten, T. R., Mason, J. W., Giller, E. L., Ostroff, R. B. and Harkness, L. (1987) Sustained urinary norepinephrine and epinephrine levels in post-traumatic stress disorder. Psychoneuroendocrinology 12, 13–20.

Kosten, T. R., Wahby, V., Giller, E. L. and Mason, J. (1990) The dexamethasone suppression test and thyrotropin-releasing hormone stimulation test in post-traumatic stress disorder. Biological Psychiatry 28, 657–664.

Kounios, J., Litz, B., Kaloupek, D. et al. (1997) Electrophysiology of combat-related PTSD. Annals of the New York Academy of Sciences 821, 504–507.

Krystal, J. H., Kosten, T. R., Southwick, S. M. et al. (1989) Neurobiological aspects of PTSD: review of clinical and preclinical studies. Behaviour Therapy 20, 177–198.

Lang, P. J. (1993) From emotional imagery to the organisation of emotion in memory. In Birbaumer, N. and Öhman, A. (eds), The Structure of Emotion: Psychophysiological, Cognitive and Clinical Aspects. Seattle: Hogrefe and Huber.

Lang, P. J. (1994) The motivational organisation of emotion: affect–reflex connections. In Van Goozen, S. H. M., Van de Poll, N. E. and Sergeant, J. A. (eds), Emotions: Essays on Emotion Theory, pp. 61–96. Hillsdale, NJ: Lawrence Erlbaum.

Ledoux, J. E. (1996) In search of an emotional system in the brain: leaping from fear to emotion and consciousness. In Gazzaniga, M. S. (ed.), The Cognitive Neurosciences. Cambridge, MA: MIT Press.

Ledoux, J. E. (1998) The Emotional Brain. London: Phoenix.

Lerer, B., Epstein, R. P., Shestatsky, M. et al. (1987) Cyclic AMP signal transduction in post-traumatic stress disorder. American Journal of Psychiatry 144, 1324–1327.

Liberzon, I., Taylor, S. F., Amdur, R. et al. (1999) Brain activation in PTSD in response to trauma-related stimuli. Biological Psychiatry 45, 817–826.

Lisansky, J., Peake, G. T., Strassman, R. J. et al. (1989) Augmented pituitary corticotrophin response to a threshold dosage of human corticotrophin-releasing hormone in depressive pre-treated with metyrapone. Archives of General Psychiatry 46, 641–649.

Maes, M. and Meltzer, H. Y. (1995) The serotonin hypothesis of depression. In Bloom, F. E. and Kupfer, D. J. (eds), Psychopharmacology: The Fourth Generation of Progress. New York: Raven Press.

Mann, J. D. (1987) Psychobiologic predictors of suicide. Journal of Clinical Psychiatry 48 (Suppl 12), 39–43.

Marburg, M. M., McFall, M. E., Lewis, N. and Veith, R. C. (1995) Plasma norepinephrine kinetics in patients with post-traumatic stress disorder. Biological Psychiatry 38(12), 819–825.

Mason, J. W., Southwick, S. W., Yehuda, R. et al. (1994) Elevation of serum free T3, total T3, TBG and total T4 levels in combat-related post-traumatic stress disorder. Archives of General Psychiatry 51, 629–641.

Mason, J. W., Giller, E. L., Kosten, T. R., Ostroff, R. B. and Podd, L. (1986) Urinary free cortisol levels in post-traumatic stress disorder. Journal of Nervous and Mental Disease 176, 498.

Mayou, R. A., Ehlers, A. and Hobbs, M. (Submitted) A three year follow-up of a randomised controlled trial of psychological debriefing for road traffic accident victims.

McEwen, B. S. (1987) Glucocorticoid–biogenic amine interaction in relation to mood and behavior. Biochemistry and Pharmacology 36, 1755–1763.

McEwen, B. S. (1996) Stressful experiences, brain and emotions: developmental, genetic and hormonal influences. In Gazzaniga, M. S. (ed.), The Cognitive Neurosciences, Cambridge, MA: MIT Press.

McEwen, B. S., Angulo, J., Cameron, H. et al. (1992) Paradoxical effects of adrenal steroids on the brain: protection versus degeneration. Biological Psychiatry 31, 177–199.

McFall, M. E., Marburg, M. M., Ko, G. N. and Veith, R. C. (1990) Autonomic response to stress in Vietnam combat veterans with post-traumatic stress disorder. Biological Psychiatry 27, 1165–1175.

McFarlane, A. C., Weber, D. L. and Clark, C. R. (1993) Abnormal stimulus processing in PTSD. Biological Psychiatry 34, 311–320.

Mellman, T. A., Kumar, A., Kulik-Bell, R., Kumar, M. and Nolan, B. (1995) Nocturnal/daytime urine noradrenergic measures and sleep in combat-related PTSD. Biological Psychiatry 38, 174–179.

Metzger, L. J., Orr, S. P., Lasko, N. B., Berry, N. J. and Pitman, R. K. (1997) Evidence for diminished P3 in PTSD. Annals of the New York Academy of Sciences 821, 499–503.

Nemeroff, C. B., Widerlov, E., Bissette, G. et al. (1984) Elevated concentrations of CSF corticotrophin-releasing factor-like immunoreactivity in depressed patients. Science 226, 1342–1344.

Paige, S., Reid, G., Allen, M. and Newton, J. (1990) Psychophysiological correlates of PTSD. Biological Psychiatry 58, 329–335.

Perry, B. D. (1994) Neurobiological sequelae of childhood trauma: PTSD in children. In Marburg, M. M. (ed.), Catecholamine Function in Posttraumatic Stress Disorder: Emerging Concepts. Washington, D. C.: American Psychiatric Press.

Perry, B. D. and Pollard, R. (1998) Homoeostasis, stress, trauma and adaptation: a neurodevelopmental view of childhood trauma. Child and Adolescent Psychiatric Clinics of North America 7, 33–51.

Perry, B. D., Giller, E. L. and Southwick, S. M. (1987) Altered platelet alpha$_2$ adrenergic binding sites in post-traumatic stress disorder. American Journal of Psychiatry 144, 1511–1512.

Perry, B. D., Southwick, S. M. and Yehuda, R. (1990) Adrenergic receptor regualtion in post-traumatic stress disorder. In Biological Assessment and Treatment of Posttraumatic Stress Disorder, pp. 87–114. Washington D. C.: American Psychiatric Press.

Pitman, R. K. and Orr, S. (1990) Twenty-four hour urinary cortisol and catecholamine excretion in combat-related post-traumatic stress disorder. Biological Psychiatry 27, 245–247.

Pitman, R. K., Van der Kolk, B. A., Orr, S. P. and Greenberg, M. S. (1990) Naloxone-reversible stress-induced analgesia in post-traumatic stress disorder. Archives of General Psychiatry 47, 541–547.

Prasad, K. M. R. (1996) Psychoneuroimmunology and psychooncology. In Chandra, P. S. and Chaturvedi, S. K. (eds), Lecture Notes in Psycho-Oncology, pp. 1–8. Bangalore: NIMHANS Publications.

Rauch, S., Van der Kolk, B. A., Fisler, R. et al. (1996) A symptom provocation study using positron emission tomography and script driven imagery. Archives of General Psychiatry 53, 380–387.

Reiman, E. M., Lane, R. D., Ahern, G. L. et al. (1997) Neuroanatomical correlates of externally and internally generated human emotion. American Journal of Psychiatry 154, 918–925.

Resnick, H., Yehuda, R., Pitman, R. K. and Foy, D. W. (1995) Effect of previous trauma on acute plasma cortisol level following rape. American Journal of Psychiatry 152, 1675–1677.

Sapolsky, R. M. (1996) Why stress is bad for your brain? Science 273, 749–750.

Sartory, G. (1993) The associative network of fear: how does it come about? In Birbaumer, N. and Öhman, A. (eds), The Structure of Emotion: Psychophysiological, Cognitive and Clinical Aspects. Seattle: Hogrefe and Huber.

Shalev, A. Y. (1996) Severe stress versus traumatic stress: from acute homeostatic reactions to chronic psychopathology. In van der Kolk, B. A., McFarlane, A. C. and Weisaeth, L. (eds), Traumatic Stress: The Effects of Overwhelming Experience on Mind, Body, and Society. New York: Guilford Press.

Shin, L. M., Kosslyn, S. M., McNally, R. J et al. (1997) Visual imagery and perception in post-traumatic stress disorder. Archives of General Psychiatry 54, 233–241.

Smith, M. A., Davidson, J., Ritchie, J. C. et al. (1989) The corticotrophin-releasing hormone test in patients with post-traumatic stress disorder. Biological Psychiatry 26, 349–355.

Soubrie, P. (1986) Reconciling the role of central serotonin neurons in human and animal behavior. Behavioral and Brain Sciences 9, 319–364.

Southwick, S. M., Krystal, J. H., Bremmer, D. et al. (1997) Noradrenergic and serotonergic function in post-traumatic stress disorder. Archives of General Psychiatry 54, 749–758.

Starkman, M. N., Gebarski, S. S., Berent, S. and Schteingart, D. E. (1992) Hippocampal formation volume, memory dysfunction and cortisol levels in patients with Cushing's syndrome. Biological Psychiatry 32, 756–765.

Swerdlow, N. R. and Koob, G. F. (1987) Dopamine, schizophrenia, mania and depression: toward a unified hypothesis of cortico-striato-pallido-thalamic function. Behavioral and Brain Sciences 10, 215–217.

Taylor, S. F., Liberzon, I., Decker, L. R., Koeppe, R. A. and Minoshima, S. (1998) Viewing emotional stimuli increases skin conductance and blood flow in limbic brain. Biological Psychiatry 43, 12S.

Terr, L. C. (1996) Acute responses to external events and post-traumatic stress disorder. In Lewis, M. (ed.), Child and Adolescent Psychiatry: A Comprehensive Textbook, 2nd edn, pp. 757–758. Baltimore: Williams and Wilkins.

Valentino, R. J., Foote, S. L. and Aston-Jones, G. (1983) Corticotropin-releasing factor activates noradrenergic neurons in the locus coeruleus. Brain Research 270, 363–367.

Van der Kolk, B. A. and McFarlane, A. C. (1996) The black hole of trauma. In van der Kolk, B. A., McFarlane, A. C. and Weisaeth, L. (eds), Traumatic Stress: The Effects of Overwhelming Experience on Mind, Body, and Society. New York: Guilford Press.

Van der Kolk, B. A. (1997) The psychobiology of post-traumatic stress disorder. Journal of Clinical Psychiatry 58 (Suppl 9), 16–24.

Van der Kolk, B. A., Greenberg, M. S., Boyd, H. and Krystal, J. (1985) Inescapable shock, neurotransmitters and addiction to trauma: towards a psychobiology of post-traumatic stress disorder. Biological Psychiatry 20, 314–325.

Weinberger, N. M. (1996) Retuning the brain by fear conditioning. In Gazzaniga, M. S. (ed.), The Cognitive Neurosciences. Cambridge, MA: MIT Press.

Wolkowitz, O. M., Reus, V. I., Weingartner, H. et al. (1990) Cognitive effects of corticosteroids. American Journal of Psychiatry 147, 1297–1303.

Yehuda, R. (1998) Psychoneuroendocrinology of post-traumatic stress disorder. Psychiatric Clinics of North America 21, 359–379.

Yehuda, R., Southwick, S. M., Nussbaum, G. et al. (1990) Low urinary cortisol excretion in PTSD. Journal of Nervous and Mental Disease 178, 366–369.

Yehuda, R., Lowy, M. T., Southwick, S. M., Shaffer, D. and Giller, E. L. (1991) Increased lymphocyte glucocorticoid receptor number in post-traumatic stress disorder. American Journal of Psychiatry 148, 499–504.

Yehuda, R., Southwick, S. M., Ma, X. and Mason, G. W. (1992) Urinary catecholamine excretion and severity of symptoms in PTSD. Journal of Nervous and Mental Disease 180, 321–325.

Yehuda, R., Boisoneau, D., Mason, J. W. and Giller, E. L. (1993) Glucocorticoid receptor number and cortisol excretion in mood, anxiety and psychotic disorder. Biological Psychiatry 34, 18–25.

Yehuda, R., Boisoneau, D., Lowy, M. T. and Giller, E. L. (1995a) Dose–response changes in plasma cortisol and lymphocyte glucocorticoid receptors following dexamethasone administration in combat veterans with and without post-traumatic stress disorder. Archives of General Psychiatry 52, 583–593.

Yehuda, R., Kahana, B., Binder-Brynes, K., Southwick, S. M., Mason, J. W. and Giller, E. L. (1995b) Low urinary cortisol excretion in holocaust survivors with post-traumatic stress disorders. American Journal of Psychiatry 152, 982–986.

Yehuda, R., Levengood, R., Schmeidler, J. et al. (1996a) Increased pituitary activation following metyrapone administration in post-traumatic stress disorder. Psychoneuroendocrinology 21, 1–16.

Yehuda, R., Teicher, M. H., Trestman, R. L. et al. (1996b) Cortisol regulation in post-traumatic stress disorder and major depression: a chronobiological analysis. Biological Psychiatry 40, 79–88.

Yehuda, R., Siever, L., Teicher, M. H. et al. (1998) Plasma norepinephrine and MHPG concentrations and severity of depression in combat PTSD and major depressive disorder. Biological Psychiatry 44, 56–63.

Chapter 4
Post-traumatic stress and the space between: an interpersonal perspective

ANDREW WEST

This chapter shifts emphasis from an index traumatised person towards an index trauma and then offers a way of looking at trauma that takes in all the relationships surrounding it. The process of applying this in the clinical arena is left to readers to take at their own pace and in their own way, although an attempt is made to facilitate the process by listing some of the implications of the argument, and drawing up some tentative checklists.

Any view of post-traumatic stress disorder (PTSD) as a unitary condition affecting an individual needs to be challenged. The literature does not support that view, and yet clinicians and the public alike are repeatedly tempted towards it. This chapter alerts the reader to the interpersonal in relation to PTSD and provides some signposts to prevent us, in the clinical arena, from neglecting it.

Three vignettes will set the scene. They will be followed by a brief consideration of what constitutes 'trauma'. The section 'Whose trauma; whose disorder?' is an argument for broadening the relationship between the protagonist of the precipitating event and the person expressing the 'disorder'. They do not need to be the same person. There follows a discussion of the recursive cycles which can contribute to the maintenance of post-traumatic symptoms, and reference is made to literature supporting the use of systemic therapies in the management of PTSD and other psychological sequelae of trauma. The second part of the chapter addresses the implications that maintaining a systemic perspective might have on practice. An awareness of relationship links might enable a broader prediction of who (other than the directly traumatised) might reasonably be expected to be adversely affected by a traumatic event and thus who might fall within the treatment remit. Certain dynamics that are frequently found in groups of people functioning in the shadow of trauma are listed. Finally, some systemic methods drawn from the literature are described in order to illustrate how a systemic perspective might materialise in therapy.

Much of the literature cited here refers to adults. Child psychiatry and related disciplines have always had to borrow or extrapolate from adult literature and experience. The child's internal and external worlds are populated largely with adults, so the experiences of adults can hardly be considered irrelevant. Furthermore, this chapter is about finding links that lead one beyond the confines of a narrow focus; direct child work may not necessarily be the best way of helping the child protagonist.

An area of substantial relevance which this chapter deliberately neglects is that of intrafamilial violence, sexual abuse and rape. This area is a subject in its own right, and one in which it is all too easy to see how trauma and relationships become intertwined. This area is addressed in the chapter by Claire Frederick and Constance Sheltren where they discuss family therapy and intrafamilial trauma. Similarly, group therapy might be considered a form of systemic, or interpersonal response, but the topic is covered in the chapter by Deborah Glass and Susie Thompson and so will not be mentioned here other than in passing.

Vignettes

- A husband and father serves in Vietnam; he is subjected to, and commits, atrocities. Following his return to civilian life he appears moody, drinks heavily, often withdraws into himself without obvious warning, or snaps at his wife and children, sometimes assaulting them physically. His wife, who had witnessed domestic violence as a child but who thought she had left that behind, becomes anxious and depressed. Their children develop a range of emotional, behavioural and psychosomatic complaints. He has PTSD but, in the aftermath, it seems that his immediate family suffers at least as much as he does.

- A 13 year old girl is killed with a number of her peers in a tragic school bus accident. Her mother, who was not present at the accident, develops sleep disturbance, experiences intrusive images of tangled metal, broken glass, blood, and sounds of screaming, and is unable to travel by bus or coach. She has developed symptoms of PTSD as though she had been there with her daughter at the time of her death.

- A passenger ferry sinks, with the loss of many lives. A crew member, off duty on the day of the accident, develops PTSD, including the symptom of survivor guilt. It appears that the bond between him and the direct victims of the disaster, arising out of their shared work, was the mediating link between their own trauma and his disorder.

In these vignettes there is a considerable loss of clarity as to who was traumatised, who suffered what symptoms as a consequence, and to what extent a diagnosis of PTSD is appropriate. The linear path from trauma to PTSD is exposed as a fiction.

How trauma is defined by a relationship

Both the ICD-10 (WHO 1992) and the DSM-IV (APA 1994), as well as listing the symptoms characteristic of PTSD, state that they follow on from an experience 'outside the range of usual human experience'. Subjectivity and causal assumptions are generally avoided by classificatory systems, so it is interesting that they adopt this criterion. March (1993) illustrates nicely the problematic cohabitation of subjective criteria and rigid classification. It is questionable, for example, as to whether painful childbirth can be considered to be outside the range of normal human experience, yet it is now acknowledged as a precipitant of PTSD (Ballard et al. 1995, Fones 1996). If the trauma considered causative is judged to be within the range of normal human experience then a diagnosis such as Adjustment Disorder is used and individual vulnerability is invoked as responsible for the emergence of disorder (WHO 1992). The further outside 'normal human experience' the event falls, the less is the role deemed to be played by the individual's own constitution. This is an artefact of the classificatory system and a wish to explain disorder in such a way as to remain invulnerable to it.

Two things seem clear:

- There is a spectrum of both trauma and response and, for this reason, the acknowledgement of partial syndromes (Stein et al. 1997) and the use of a broader term such as 'traumatic stress' seem appropriate.
- There is a reciprocal relationship between the victim and the trauma and the victim defines to a large extent what constitutes trauma.

Whose trauma; whose disorder?

In the second and third vignettes, the disorder develops as though the person had been present at the traumatic event. They challenge an assumption made by many and reflected in the ICD-10, namely that the person experiencing the trauma and the person diagnosed with PTSD are the same. A number of reports and small studies in the literature support the contrary view – that a variety of relationships can mediate the development of post-traumatic symptoms in people other than those directly traumatised, and this has been increasingly recognised in the last two revisions of the DSM (APA 1987, 1994). In DSM-IV the precipitant might be 'learning about [trauma] experienced by a family friend or close associate'. Here are some examples from the literature:

- After the capsize of the *Herald of Free Enterprise* in 1987 a number of cross-channel ferry workers developed PTSD (Dixon et al. 1993). They were not present at the disaster, and were not bereaved relatives. Most had at least lost 'acquaintances' in the disaster. The authors suggest extending the definition of trauma to include vicarious experience. They speak of 'as if' victims of a disaster and suggest that a process of identification with victim crew members led to the subjects' assumptions of safety and stability in their own lives being shattered.
- The female partners of Vietnam veterans have, not infrequently, developed PTSD or post-traumatic symptoms (PTSs). Figley (1985) has described four routes by which family members might develop PTSs:
  - **simultaneous**, in which family members directly experienced the same trauma
  - **vicarious**, in which the family learns that a member has been directly traumatised (including fatally)
  - **intrafamilial**, where trauma has been caused within the family and has been directly experienced by more than one family member. This includes abuse and domestic violence
  - **secondary** (or **chiasmal**) which has been likened to an infectious route and affects people who come into close contact with the directly traumatised. This can include health and other professionals as well as family members.

  Distinct from all of these is the situation where the veteran, himself suffering from PTSD, is violent towards his partner who, as a consequence, develops PTSD in her own right.
- Siblings of child victims of disaster or violence can develop PTSD as one of many possible conditions and the effects on siblings is the topic of a recent review (Newman et al. 1997). An American study (Applebaum and Burnes 1991) demonstrates that PTSD is a common occurrence in the siblings and parents of children dead through accident or homicide, even if they did not themselves witness the event.
- The experiences of parents witnessing their children's bone marrow transplants have been described using a PTSD model (Heiney et al. 1994), and the mothers of paediatric cancer survivors have been reported to be at increased risk of subsequent PTSD (Pelcovitz et al. 1996). Mothers have developed PTSs when their daughters have disclosed sexual abuse (Green et al. 1995, Timmons-Mitchell et al. 1996).

This appears to be especially likely, but not exclusively, if the mother had herself been abused in the past.

This last example introduces the first of two considerations which are important to the development of vicarious traumatisation:

- The meaning, or contextual significance, of the event to the recipient of the news will, to some extent, determine the consequences for them.
- The way that news of an event is delivered might itself constitute trauma, or might modulate the traumatic effect of the news. PTSD has been reported in a child subsequent to her hearing a verbal description of her uncle's war-related death (Saigh 1992). The author cites an earlier paper of his in which he identified 13 of 230 childhood cases of PTSD as being mediated by 'information transmission' and points out the introduction, by DSM-III, of verbal mediation as one of three forms of traumatic stress, the other two being direct exposure, and observation. In a recent account (Winje and Ulvik 1998) of symptoms of intrusion, avoidance and distress in the parent and child survivors of a bus accident, not only is the receipt of the news sufficient to induce symptoms in non-passenger relatives, but there is some indication that they might be at greater risk than the passengers themselves. This is well discussed by the authors, who put it down to the fact that the passengers were not in a position to have much understanding of the circumstances at the time of the accident, which took place in the darkness of a long tunnel. Non-passenger relatives received the news through the mass media and were left in a state of partial knowledge for hours.

At this point it is necessary to take a step back. Clearly there is ample support in the literature for what has been called the 'ripple effect': following a traumatic event, the effects of traumatisation spread out like ripples in a pond, affecting many people in a variety of ways and mediated by a variety of means. An excellent article (Brende and Goldsmith 1991) simply begins, 'When one or more members of a family are traumatised, the entire family can suffer from post-traumatic symptoms'. To illustrate their model they provide four vignettes in which trauma in one generation is linked to PTSD in another. The *Herald of Free Enterprise* study indicates that this transmission of traumatic effect is not limited to intrafamilial relations and opens the way for us to look out for vicarious traumatisation through a range of possible relationships, especially where there is a degree of identification with those directly traumatised. This range includes that between therapist and client (Figley 1995).

Maintaining cycles

Any disorder that is not maintained will, by necessity, cease the moment it started. A common maintaining process is the recursive cycle, a sequence of influences which loops around on itself and thus keeps itself going. The condition brings about a circumstance which in turn maintains the condition. When it comes to the maintenance of PTSD the interpersonal continues to play a major role. Social isolation (Keane et al. 1985), alcoholism and depression (Breslau et al. 1997), violence, spousal stress (Barnes 1995, Rabin 1995), selectivity of memory (Southwick et al. 1997), and a number of other interpersonal factors (Craine et al. 1992) have been implicated in the maintenance of post-traumatic symptoms.

In the Applebaum and Burnes study (1991), cited above, parents were often not aware of the extent of the symptomatology in their surviving children, possibly because of their own distress. It has also been reported that, following simultaneous exposure, if parents develop PTSD or are otherwise unable to provide emotional support, their children are at greater risk of PTSD (Udwin 1993, Foy et al. 1996). This is discussed by Winje and Ulvik (1998) in which, despite high levels of intrusion and avoidance in both mothers and fathers, a correlation was found between the symptoms of mothers, but not fathers, and their children. With a nicely broad-minded twist they point out that this association has not been shown to be harmful and that it could even turn out to be helpful in the long term. Long-term follow-up studies would be needed to demonstrate a relationship between maternal symptoms and the prognosis of a child's PTSs.

When some of the interpersonal dynamics often to be found in PTSD-affected families are listed below it will be seen that many of those dynamics could have a significant maintaining effect on the disorder.

Systemic treatment methods in the literature

A large number of models and methods have been described in connection with traumatised families. These include behavioural family therapy (Glynn et al. 1995), interventions based on family adaptation theory (Craine et al. 1992) and crisis intervention models (Harris 1991), psychoeducational group work for improving marital relations (Rabin 1995), as well as papers that put forward interventions based on structural (Brooks 1991), strategic (Swanson et al. 1989) and narrative (Johnson et al. 1995, Bloom 1996) approaches. Family approaches are recommended in order to 'repair schemata' (Allen and Bloom 1994), so the child can help the adult to recover lost memories (Tilmans-Ostyn 1995), and on the grounds of the 'social nature of trauma' (Allen and

Bloom 1994). The chapter on family therapy in this volume (Chapter 10, by Frederick and Sheltren) gives an account of the history of family therapy in the context of trauma and the authors describe their own approach, with a clinical example.

Much less has been written, however, about family therapy in connection with PTSD as opposed to the more generic 'trauma'. One review, despite its appearance in *Family Therapy Collections* (Rosenthal et al. 1987), after a good preamble on PTSD and listing the effects of trauma on families, has surprisingly little about family therapy, which is raised on the penultimate page as an 'adjunct to group work', and only the effects on spouses and children of living with an individual with PTSD are offered as justification. The authors show their systemic colours, however, when they point out that 'maintenance of the secret may become more important in the family dance than the secret itself' and they warn therapists against replicating the family's power struggle over disclosure. These are two very important points which merit some emphasis. The issue of secrecy will be returned to below.

The review by Shalev et al. in *Psychosomatic Medicine* (1996), although placed well within the medical tradition, delivering an exhaustive review of individual therapies such as drug treatment and behaviour and cognitive-behavioural therapies, also offers a well-developed systemic perspective on the problem. Very little is said, though, about family therapy as such, giving as a reason the fact that most of the literature is in the form of 'anecdotal reports and theoretical formulation' and is therefore dismissed. This illustrates the loss to the broader medical sciences that flows on from too monogamous an espousal of the quantitative approach. In the family therapy literature, some of the most powerful writing is around case reports and vignettes.

Applying systemic methods in the management of PTSD

In the systemic approach it is the relationships between individuals and groups of individuals that are the focus of attention. It is as though the 'space between' people becomes the patient, rather than the people themselves and, instead of collecting features of the individuals and looking for changes in those features, appropriate shifts in the observed relationships are the goals of intervention.

Translating this perspective into action can be considered in three sections:

- To whom should we be offering help?
- What dynamics should we be looking out for?
- What therapeutic methods should we employ?

To whom should we be offering help?

Starting from the point of discovery that a traumatic event has occurred begs this chapter's opening question about the definition of trauma. An event usually comes to our attention through a symptomatic individual, and if there is an individual who appears to have developed PTSs as a consequence of an event, then the event is traumatic by definition. Occasionally an event is brought to our attention by another route, such as early news of a mass disaster. In these situations the event is usually well outside the 'range of usual human experience' and we can safely assume that people in contact, direct or otherwise, are at risk of developing significant symptoms.

Given the event, we need to consider people as being at risk if they fall into certain groups, defined by their relationship with the event. This will either be a direct relationship, where the person is a witness or a survivor, or an indirect one. In the latter case the person is connected to the event by virtue of some relationship with a direct witness, survivor or victim. The relationship of importance is described as a 'strong emotional connection' and has been compared to couvade, where the male partner of a pregnant woman can develop some of the symptoms of pregnancy, as well as *folie à deux* and mass hysteria (Nelson and Wright 1996). Such relationships can be divided into familial, quasi-familial, peer, professional/supportive, and other. Some of these require further elaboration:

- **Quasi-familial relationships** are those that have taken on a significance similar to that of familial relationships. For children this might include teachers, activity leaders and guardians. If one considers the relationship deriving significance from a process related to transference, it becomes easy to see how damage to one person could disrupt the internal world of another.
- In the **peer relationship** the mechanism that springs to mind is along the lines of 'If it happened to him then it could happen to me'. We can all find something in common with one another, yet we do not appear to be equally at risk. It is therefore probable that the intensity or extent of shared life is crucial. In the *Herald of Free Enterprise* the relationship was a working one. Possibly being in the same class at school is sufficient. It may be that children are more susceptible to the peer link than adults, or that school holds children together in greater proximity and stress than we would like to imagine. Following a school shooting incident, physical proximity was not the most important predictive factor in the development of PTSD (Schwartz and Kowalski 1991) and perceived degree of friendship with the victim appeared to be a predictor of PTSs in school-children following a school-based death (Parker et al. 1995).

- The **professional/supportive** category refers to the observed fact that anyone working with or supporting the directly or indirectly traumatised is themselves at risk of indirect traumatisation. This has been termed compassion fatigue or compassion stress (Figley 1995).
- A residual category of '**other**' reminds the reader to look beyond the familiar and to maintain a broad view of who might be in need of support or therapeutic intervention.

Attention should be paid, not only to the symptomatic, but also to those who have a role in perpetuating the disorder. With a child protagonist, such people are likely to be in the family, family substitute, or school, but not exclusively so, and the taking of a careful interpersonal history would be necessary in order to reveal significant others in the child's life (Box 4.1).

Box 4.1 People to consider in therapy or intervention

At risk
Direct
   Witness
   Survivor

Indirect
   Familial
   Quasi-familial
   Peer
   Professional/supportive
   Other

Those potentially perpetuating the disorder

What dynamics should we be looking for?

The list in Box 4.2 is not exhaustive, but aims to include the most important interpersonal dynamics encountered. It should also be pointed out that such dynamics are unlikely to be encountered in isolation, but rather intermingled and overlapping, woven into a sort of seamless web.

Secrecy

As Rosenthal et al. (1987) point out, a secret can take on great significance and its maintenance can become an end in itself. One has to speculate as to how the secret is maintained; who is most involved in its maintenance; who most threatens to reveal it; who is 'in the know' and who is not; what the secret achieves, and what the believed consequences of revelation might be. The importance of secrecy in enabling sexual and other abuse is well known; a family secret may be a more innocent, but nevertheless powerful key to the maintenance of a problem and therefore also its resolution. A systemic or family therapist will tend to be instinctively curious about any secrets they might encounter.

Box 4.2 What dynamics should we be looking for?

Secrecy
Minimisation and overemphasis
Disenfranchisement and disempowerment
Traumatic re-enactment
Caretaking
Overidentification
Triangulation
Neglected needs
Role rigidity
Confusion and chaos
Communication breakdown
Alienation
Positive feedback loops

Minimisation and overemphasis

The trauma, or the consequent symptoms, may be minimised by some members of the system. As with the secret, this will have functions and effects, real and imagined. It could result in the protagonist not receiving necessary support or therapy, or it could result in a prolongation and amplification of symptoms in a face-saving tug-of-war. Alternatively, though possibly simultaneously, the trauma and its sequelae may be given too much emphasis and power, as though they are an immovable obstacle to achieving healthy functioning. Denial can be seen as an extreme form of minimisation (or minimisation a form of denial) and we must watch for not only denial of the trauma or its impact and denial of the protagonist's resources, but also denial of current ongoing traumatisation, including abuse. Both minimisation and overemphasis can disempower and disenfranchise the protagonist.

Disenfranchisement and disempowerment

Disenfranchisement and disempowerment can occur without minimisation and overemphasis, and can affect people other than the directly traumatised protagonist. The protagonist's disenfranchisement and disempowerment may prove to be something that other family members have come to cling on to and value, whereas the protagonist might be resenting the extent to which their past experience has been encouraged to control him. Sometimes the protagonist may collude in the process: losing their voice may simply be the price they have to pay for handing responsibility over to the past, and to their caretaker. Alternatively, the protagonist and caretaker may collaborate, using the trauma as a means to disenfranchise a third party. These descriptions may make the process appear machiavellian until one remembers that they are usually entered into unconsciously. Often, when the full range of consequences is made explicit within the system, the process ceases or shifts.

Traumatic re-enactment

The Freudian concept of transference neurosis (e.g. Sandler et al. 1970) and Malan's (1979) description of the 'triangle of people' help to explain how a past conflict can be re-experienced in a current situation, often bringing the patient to therapy, and in the transference in therapy itself. Johnson et al. (1995), in a paper well worth obtaining and reading and returned to below, describe what they call the 'critical interaction'. They are writing in the context of couples work with Vietnam veterans and their partners, and describe a 'repetitive conflict between the couple that is covertly associated with a traumatic memory'... 'an attempt both to symbolise the traumatic experience within the couple's interaction and to avoid awareness of the trauma'. It is easy to see how this dynamic could have a perpetuating role in the disorder. Johnson's critical interaction therapy will be considered in more detail in the next section, but is introduced here in order to encourage a sensitivity to this kind of recapitulation, which can be expressed in a very subtle form, or may take the form of intrafamilial or other abuse.

Caretaking

Caretaking becomes a problem when it is no longer clear whose needs are being met. Care may be given compulsively when one person gives to another, usually a visibly worthy recipient, care which he would like to receive himself (Malan 1979). The partnership calls to mind the dysfunctional victim–rescuer–persecutor triangle (Karpman 1968). Where there is a victim, there is usually an overenthusiastic or overburdened caretaker. In this context the most obvious persecutor is the traumatic event itself, unless there is a clearly identified perpetrator who can take on that role. The crucial aspect of the dysfunctional triangle here is that the caretaker does too much, and the victim's internal resources are denied, ignored or dismissed, itself a form of disempowerment. I do not mean to suggest that taking care of someone is wrong;

appropriate support and care of the traumatised is desirable. There has to be an appropriate boundary, however, between the needs of one individual and those of another.

Overidentification

Overidentification is one possible product of a strong emotional connection. Again I would suggest that it becomes a problem when the boundaries between individuals' feelings, thoughts and needs become blurred or invisible. A process akin to projective identification may have a role to play here. Arguably, most of us have experienced at least one event in our past, distant or otherwise, which, because of its unpalatability, we were unable to fully metabolise. When we come into contact with someone who is visibly struggling with a trauma, there is a temptation for us to borrow, as it were, from their efforts. In projective identification an unacceptable or threatening part of the self is projected into another who will experience it, and process it to a degree. It is then taken back, in its modified form, and re-internalised (Ogden 1979). Put more simply, it is a bit like saying 'If you're putting on a wash, maybe you could pop my socks in at the same time', except that permission is not asked. In the context of systemic or family therapy it may be useful at some point to say, 'Let's get this straight, are you asking me to wash your socks for you?'. Perhaps overidentification, or intense identification, is one way in which vicarious or secondary traumatisation can occur. At the risk of taking the analogy too far, the recipient and the donor of care share the risks of, for example, non-colour-fastness!

Triangulation

The Karpman triangle has been mentioned above but it is only one example of the dynamic triangles that can form. Johnson et al. (1995) describe how the spouse of the Vietnam veteran takes on the role of intermediary, between the veteran on the one hand and, on the other, their entire social circle. In their depiction of the critical interaction, they capture the intensity of the almost living presence of the traumatic history with the phrase, 'The veteran and spouse are triangulated with a shadow'. And, later, 'The demands of the spouse upset the veteran, whilst the past appears to embrace and tolerate [him]'. It is easy to see the potential of this as a perpetuating influence.

Neglected needs

The focusing of attention on the visible needs of the protagonist can result in the neglect of others in the system. The denial of needs in the caretaker is an example, but we need to be on the lookout for siblings, peers, and other members of the system. Paradoxically, strenuous attempts to meet the apparent or assumed needs of the protagonist may even result in the protagonist's actual needs being overlooked.

Role rigidity

Rigidity within a system suggests fear of movement, or the real or imagined absence of crucial resources. An important aim of therapy should be to increase the functional flexibility within the system.

Confusion and chaos

The shadow of the trauma may be like a physical presence for some and yet invisible to others, so that the outburst or withdrawal of the traumatised person can appear unpredictable. The patterns of interaction and behaviour that used to assure family members a calm passage no longer do so, and the result can be confusing, to say the least. The confusion can lead to fear.

Communication breakdown

There is a discontinuity of experience between the protagonist and those around them, and between the traumatised family and its social environment. There may be a fear of 'saying the wrong thing'. There may be secrets to be maintained. Each of these makes for problematic communication. The common ground that bound people together is common no longer, and they can find that they are drifting apart.

Alienation

The discontinuity of experience, compounded by the breakdown in communication, can lead to alienation, either of the individual or of the family or group as a whole. Races have been alienated following trauma.

Positive feedback loops

The unfolding of events within the system, including traumatic re-enactment, outbursts, and withdrawal, tend to consolidate further the separate narratives held by the individuals. There is a tendency not to say and not to do the things that would challenge the dysfunctional assumptions that people are making.

Therapeutic application

Advocated here, rather than specific techniques, is a change in the culture of the therapy, enabled by the adoption of two specific standpoints:

- Firstly, a shift in orientation from identifying a person as the 'index patient' towards identifying an event as the 'index trauma' would enable a more broad-minded assessment of whom to include in an offer of intervention. The reader's own version of Box 4.1 could be used to identify additional secondarily affected people, as well as those with possible perpetuating roles. The immediate family or household should certainly be included and, in the case of children, one should also consider peer groups and schools.

- Secondly, emphasis is placed on relationships, the changes in relationships, and on meaning. 'Meaning' refers to the significance that objects, events and communications have to an individual or to a system. It is important for the therapist to attempt an understanding of the meanings (there will be more than one) of, for example, the trauma, the relationships, survival and loss.

Nelson and Wright (1996) divide the work into four categories – psychoeducation, concurrent individual therapy, couples and family therapy, and work addressing the needs of the involved professionals. This structure will be used here in listing the aims and methods one might consider for one's intervention. Following this, two other papers will be referred to; each describes a specific technique in some detail. These techniques, which are included for illustrative purposes and because they describe in explicit terms a therapeutic technique, originate in adult work and would require adaptation if they were to be applied in direct work with children.

Some particular notes of caution must be sounded. One is that any revelation must take place at a pace which suits the protagonist and the people around them. The description of a trauma can be traumatic in itself, both to the describer and their audience. A delicate balance must be found between colluding with the silence, on the one hand and, on the other, encouraging a traumatic re-enactment. One way of enabling this balance is to run individual work alongside the family work so that the individual can experiment with disclosure. Individual work need not be limited to the protagonist. This caution is part of a more general one of safety. Particularly when there has been intrafamilial and abusive trauma there is a need to establish safety, both physical and psychological. Individual work can promote this. What this paragraph should be making clear is that working systemically should in no way be taken to mean that everyone must be in the room at the same time. The contrary is the case: sensitive systemic work might dictate that certain individuals need to be seen alone.

Box 4.3 Aims and methods of systemic work

Psychoeducation
Teach the effects of trauma and demystify
Teach coping strategies
Teach communication skills
Improve communication between family/system members
Teach problem solving skills
Identify support networks
Improve access to available and appropriate support

Concurrent individual work
Help the protagonist to differentiate the past from the present
Make peace with the past
Help the protagonist to pace disclosure

Family work and direct work with the system
Clarify the chaos
Promote safety
Overcome the conspiracy of silence
Pace the revelation
Address secrets, shame, alliances, expectations, needs
Decrease blaming, scapegoating, and the tendency for affect, pain and pathology to be located in one individual
Locate the problem outside the individual (Bentovim 1995 states the value of circular, future, and hypothetical questioning – all well within the systemic repertoire, as well as play therapy and the use of dolls and toys, in externalising the problem)
Engage any disempowered person more in a caretaker role
Decrease co-dependency
Make interactions and narratives explicit
Elicit family-of-origin patterns
Engage others as witnesses to the protagonists mourning, pain, fear, etc.
Achieve a mutually held perspective
Achieve a solution focus
Co-construct alternative stories
Increase the functional flexibility within the system

Support for professionals
Guard against compassion fatigue and secondary trauma by:

• maintaining clear boundaries
• supervision
• professional support

Critical interaction therapy

Johnson and colleagues (1995) describe how, in the context of Vietnam veterans and their spouses, there is often traumatic re-enactment in the form of a conflict arising in free discussion between the pair. Left unchecked, this serves to increase alienation between them and confirm their conflicted narratives. However, if it is dealt with in an appropriate way the outcome is therapeutic. In the process that they describe, the first crucial role of the therapist is to notice when the veteran withdraws, usually with broken eye contact, shift of posture, or a pause. This signals that his attention has shifted to the traumatic memory. He is sensitively asked if he is thinking about something else. As he describes the memory his spouse is encouraged to give him physical comforting while eye contact is maintained. Emphasis is placed on physical comforting. The therapist makes explicit the link between the memory and the current conflict and then asks the veteran to find out how the spouse is and to offer her support if appropriate. This is also a crucial step because it is challenging the co-dependent, rescuer–victim dyad discussed above. In this way some of the spouse's needs may be met and the veteran is empowered. This process is reinforced with summary, rehearsal and homework.

The authors express their reservations about the generalisability of their approach, and this is something that we should clearly pay attention to. They think that it may not be appropriate:

- where the trauma did not involve some close attachment;
- where secrecy is in no way an issue;
- where the trauma consisted of intrafamilial abuse.

They leave open the possibility that modifications of the approach might nevertheless be applicable in these situations.

Writing assignments

Lange (1996) describes the use of writing assignments in the context of working with Jewish families traumatised as a result of the Holocaust. The letters may be written to the living or to the dead, and they may be given to the addressee or not. What happens is partly behavioural, in that the protagonist is required to confront painful stimuli in a controlled way; partly cognitive, in that a degree of reappraisal is possible; and partly strategic, in that the agenda is often changed by the prescription of an action.

What Lange's and Johnson et al'.s approaches have in common is that they address the relationships between people and they prescribe methods of communication that are, to a degree, ritualised, thereby reducing the potential for emotional abuse or re-traumatisation. A caveat that must apply in drawing from work done with veterans of the Vietnam war and Holocaust survivors is that these represent a particular kind of institutionalised trauma, in which there is also an element of camaraderie. The traumas that we are helping child protagonists and their families deal with are usually different in this respect and this should be born in mind when generalising from one context to another.

Needless to say, the methods just described come from within the context of work primarily with adults. If direct work is to be done with children then media and approaches such as those described in the chapter by Claire Frederick and Constance Sheltren should be employed.

The reader should not leave this chapter without being recommended to read the work of Charles Figley. As mentioned above, Figley is responsible for a significant proportion of the literature on the treatment of traumatic stress. His book, *Helping Traumatized Families* (1989) is an account of his treatment method, clearly systemically grounded, and includes a chapter specific to the needs of children. The interested reader of this chapter is advised to find a copy of that work if it is not already familiar to them.

In conclusion

Hopefully the previously unconvinced are convinced, and those who were in need of a reminder are reminded, of the importance of an interpersonal perspective on the process of traumatisation, its aftermath, and its clinical management.

This chapter has taken the reader on what may have felt like a journey into territory far from the starting point, across generations and into war-torn parts. This is appropriate. Work with traumatised children is not an hermetically sealed endeavour and connections that cross boundaries are ignored at the child's peril.

References

Allen, S. N. and Bloom, S. L. (1994) Group and family treatment of post-traumatic stress disorder. Psychiatric Clinics of North America 17(2), 425–437.

APA (1987) Diagnostic and Statistical Manual of Mental Disorders, 3rd edn, revised (DSM-IIIR). Washington, D. C.: American Psychiatric Association.

APA (1994) Diagnostic and Statistical Manual of Mental Disorders, 4th edn (DSM-IV). Washington, D. C.: American Psychiatric Association

Applebaum, D. R. and Burns, G. L. (1991) Unexpected childhood death: posttraumatic stress disorder in surviving siblings and parents. Journal of Clinical Child Psychology 20(2), 114–120.

Ballard, C. G., Stanley, A. K. and Brockington, I. F. (1995) Post-traumatic stress disorder after childbirth. British Journal of Psychiatry 166, 525–528.

Barnes, M. F. (1995) Sex therapy in the couples context: therapy issues of victims of sexual trauma. American Journal of Family Therapy 23(4), 351–360.

Bentovim, A. (1995) Trauma-Organized Systems, p. 53. London: Karnac Books.

Bloom, S. L. (1996) Postscript. British Journal of Psychotherapy 12(3), 362–366.

Brende, J. O. and Goldsmith, R. (1991) Post-traumatic stress disorder in families. Journal of Contemporary Psychotherapy 21(2), 115–124.

Breslau, N., Davis, G. C., Peterson, E. L. and Schultz, L. (1997) Psychiatric sequelae of posttraumatic stress disorder in women. Archives of General Psychiatry 54(1), 81–87.

Brooks, G. R. (1991) Therapy pitfalls with Vietnam veteran families: linearity, contextual naïvetè, and gender role blindness. Journal of Family Psychology 4(4), 446–461.

Craine, M. H., Hanks, R. and Stevens, H. (1992) Mapping family stress: the application of family adaptation theory to post-traumatic stress disorder. American Journal of Family Therapy 20(3), 195–203.

Dixon, P., Rehling, G. and Shiwach, R. (1993) Peripheral victims of the Herald of Free Enterprise disaster. British Journal of Medical Psychology 66(2), 193–202.

Figley, C. R. (1985) From victim to survivor: social responsibility in the wake of catastrophe. In Figley, C. R. (ed.) Trauma and its Wake: The Study and Treatment of Post-traumatic Stress Disorder. pp. 409–411. New York: Brunner/Mazel.

Figley, C. R. (1989) Helping Traumatized Families. San Francisco: Jossey-Bass.

Figley, C. R. (ed.) (1995) Compassion Fatigue: Coping with Secondary Traumatic Stress in Those who Treat the Traumatized. New York. Brunner/Mazel.

Fones, C. (1996) Posttraumatic stress disorder occurring after painful childbirth. Journal of Nervous and Mental Disease 184(3), 195–196.

Foy, D. W., Madvig, B. T., Pynoos, R. S. and Camilleri, A. J. (1996) Etiologic factors in the development of posttraumatic stress disorder in children and adolescents. Journal of School Psychology 34(2), 133–145.

Glynn, S. M., Eth, S., Randolph, E. and Foy, D. W. (1995) Behavioural family therapy for Vietnam combat veterans with posttraumatic stress disorder. Journal of Psychotherapy Practice and Research 4(3), 214–223.

Green, A. H., Coupe, P., Fernandez, R. and Stevens, B. (1995) Incest revisited: delayed post-traumatic stress disorder in mothers following the sexual abuse of their children. Child Abuse and Neglect 19(10), 1275–1282.

Harris, C. J. (1991) A family crisis-intervention model for the treatment of post-traumatic stress reaction. Fourth annual meeting of the Society for Traumatic Stress. Journal of Traumatic Stress 4(2), 195–207.

Heiney, S. P., Neuberg, R. W., Myers, D. and Bergman, L. H. (1994) The aftermath of bone marrow transplant for parents of pediatric patients: a post-traumatic stress disorder. Oncology Nurses Forum 21(5), 843–847.

Johnson, D. R., Feldman, S. and Lubin, H. (1995) Critical interaction therapy: couples therapy in combat-related posttraumatic stress disorder. Family Process 34, 401–412.

Karpman, S. (1968) Fairy tales and script drama analysis. Transactional Analysis Bulletin 7(26), 39–44.

Keane, T. M., Scott, W. O., Chavoya, G. A., Lamparski, D. M. and Fairbank, J. A. (1985) Social support in Vietnam veterans with posttraumatic stress disorder: a comparitive analysis. Journal of Consulting and Clinical Psychology 53(1), 95–102.

Lange, A. (1996) Using writing assignments with families managing legacies of extreme trauma. Journal of Family Therapy 18, 375–388.

Malan, D. H. (1979) Individual Psychotherapy and the Science of Psychodynamics. London: Butterworths.

March, J. S. (1993) What constitutes a stressor? The 'Criterion A' issue. In Davidson, J.

R. T. and Foa, E. B. (eds), Posttraumatic Stress Disorder: DSM-IV and Beyond. Washington, D. C.: American Psychiatric Press.

Nelson, B. S. and Wright, D. W. (1996) Understanding and treating post-traumatic stress symptoms in female partners of veterans with PTSD. Journal of Marital and Family Therapy 22(4), 455–467.

Newman, M., Black, D. and Harris-Hendriks, J. (1997) Victims of disaster, war, violence, or homicide: psychological effects on siblings. Child Psychology and Psychiatry Review 2(4), 140–149.

Ogden, T. H. (1979) On projective identification. International Journal of Psycho-Analysis, 60, 357–373.

Parker, J., Watts, H. and Allsopp, M. R. (1995) Post-traumatic stress symptoms in children and parents following a school-based fatality. Child: Care, Health and Development 21(3), 183–189.

Pelcovitz, D., Goldenberg, B., Kaplan, S. et al. (1996) Posttraumatic stress disorder in mothers of pediatric cancer survivors. Psychosomatics 37(2), 116–126.

Rabin, C. (1995) The use of psychoeducational groups to improve marital functioning in high risk Israeli couples. A stage model. Contemporary Family Therapy 17(4), 503–515.

Rosenthal, D., Sadler, A. and Edwards, W. (1987) Families and post-traumatic stress disorder. Family Therapy Collections 22, 81–95.

Saigh, P. A. (1992) Verbally mediated childhood post-traumatic stress disorder. British Journal of Psychiatry 161, 704–706.

Sandler, J., Dare, C. and Holder, A. (1970) Basic psychoanalytical concepts: III Transference. British Journal of Psychiatry 116, 667–672.

Schwarz, E. D. and Kowalski, J. M. (1991) Malignant memories: PTSD in children and adults after a school shooting. Journal of the American Academy of Child Psychiatry 30(6), 936–944.

Shalev, A. Y., Bonne, O. and Eth S. (1996) Treatment of posttraumatic stress disorder: a review. Psychosomatic Medicine 58, 165–182.

Southwick, S. M., Morgan, C. A., Nicolaou, A. L. and Charney, D. S. (1997) Consistency of memory for combat-related traumatic events in veterans of Operation Desert Storm. American Journal of Psychiatry 154(2), 173–177.

Stein, M. B., Walker, J. R., Hazen, A. L. and Forde, D. R. (1997) Full and partial post-traumatic stress disorder: findings from a community survey. American Journal of Psychiatry 154 (8), 1114–1119.

Swanson, G., Frey, J. and Hyer, L. (1989) The strategic approach to unfreeze symptoms of PTSD. Clinical Gerontologist 8(3), 83–86.

Tilmans-Ostyn, E. (1995) La therapie familiale face a la transmission intergenerationelle de traumatismes. Therapie Familiale 16(2), 163–183.

Timmons-Mitchell, J., Chandler-Holtz, D. and Semple, W. E. (1996) Post-traumatic stress symptoms in mothers following children's reports of sexual abuse: an exploratory study. American Journal of Orthopsychiatry 66(3), 463–467.

Udwin, O. (1993) Annotation: Children's reactions to traumatic events. Journal of Child Psychology and Psychiatry 34(2), 115–127.

WHO (1992) The ICD-10 Classification of Mental Disorders. Geneva: World Health Organisation.

Winje, D. and Ulvik, A. (1998) Long-term outcome of trauma in children: the psychological consequences of a bus accident. Journal of Child Psychology and Psychiatry 39(5), 635–642.

Chapter 5
Clinical aspects of post-traumatic stress disorder in children and adolescents

NILESH SHAH AND SANTOSHKUMAR MUDHOLKAR

An innocent victim

Ruksana, a very active and social girl, had just turned 12 a week before she was abducted, abused, tortured and gang-raped by three men in Dharavi, one of the notorious slums of Asia. Three days later she was found in a semiconscious state lying half-naked on the road. Her face was swollen, and she had bruises and burn marks all over her body. Frightened of the perpetrators, her mother never took her to hospital. The incident was not reported by any newspaper or recorded at any police station. Later her mother brought her to the psychiatric out-patients department.

Over a period of 2–3 weeks her physical condition improved but her mental condition worsened. She would suddenly wake up from sleep with terrifying dreams about the event. She would remain withdrawn and aloof, preoccupied with the distressing thoughts. She would remain sad, uninterested, be tearful or get irritated and angry at the slightest recollection of the incident. She stopped going out of the house and also refrained from any kind of interaction with visitors. She did not find life worth living and made three attempts to end her life.

As is typical for many children and adolescents, Ruksana re-experienced the event in the form of terrifying dreams. The symptoms had persisted beyond 3 months. She was diagnosed to have post-traumatic stress disorder (PTSD).

It is natural and logical to expect some physiological or pathological reaction in children and adolescents after exposure to a stressful traumatic event, especially when there is an exposure to an event which is outside the range of usual human experience. As the name suggests, the concept of PTSD involves exposure to a stressful traumatic event and

97

the subsequent development of a disorder. The cardinal features of this disorder consist of:

- the re-experiencing of the trauma
- persistent avoidance of reminders of the trauma
- persistent hyperarousal.

The symptoms may either develop immediately after the exposure to the traumatic event or at a later date after a relatively symptom-free intervening period, and persist for at least a month.

The study of clinical aspects of PTSD in children and adolescents requires special consideration, for a variety of reasons:

- It is likely that apparently catastrophic events which may induce severe psychological reaction in adults may not be of any consequence to children and vice versa, as children's ability to appraise the gravity of a situation and foresee the ramifications may be limited.
- Because of temperamental traits, underlying psychiatric disorders, family psychopathology and socio-cultural background, some children and adolescents may be at a particularly high risk of exposure to stressful traumatic events and may be susceptible to developing PTSD.
- The clinical manifestations, course and outcome of PTSD in children and adolescents may be somewhat different from what they are in adults. PTSD may have significant effects on a number of other areas like their emotional development, cognition and memory, scholastic performance, etc.

Clinical aspects of PTSD in children and adolescents encompass the study of the following areas:

- the type of stressful traumatic event to which the person is exposed
- various contributory factors in the development of PTSD
- the essential and associated features
- psychiatric co-morbidity associated with PTSD
- diagnosis and differential diagnosis
- course and outcome.

Type of stressful traumatic event

Symptoms of PTSD in children and adolescents have been reported after exposure to a variety of traumatic events. These events are experienced as emotionally stressful by almost everyone exposed to them. The traumatic event involves actual or threatened death or serious physical injury to self and others, or loss of self-esteem. The person may have either experienced the traumatic event or simply witnessed it and felt intense fear, helplessness or horror. The risk of PTSD seems to vary with the nature of the trauma and the number of traumas experienced (Deykin and Buka 1997). It is also interesting to note that the clinical profile of symptoms, its severity and contents in an individual child depend on the type of traumatic event to which they are exposed. For example, the content of a dream or a play theme may be related to rescue operations in cases of children exposed to natural disasters. Similarly, in cases of children exposed to war situations and civilian violence, the contents of dreams may be very frightening and horrifying, depicting assault, murder and violence.

Children and adolescents who are not actually victims but have only witnessed the traumatic event also frequently develop symptoms of PTSD. In such children the development of symptoms of PTSD depends on their proximity to the traumatic event and emotional closeness to the actual victims. Parker et al. (1995) have reported that after a roof blew off a primary school killing one child, those children who were close friends of the dead child developed more symptoms than other children. This suggests that it is the experience of personal loss that contributes to symptoms formation as well as experience of personal danger.

Traumatic events may be broadly grouped into five categories:

- combat (war)
- natural disaster
- exposure to civilian violence, assaults and murders
- accidents
- rape and incest.

Combat (war)

The concept of PTSD as it is known today has developed mainly from the study of psychiatric morbidity in war veterans. The description of shell shock in the veterans of World War I, combat neurosis or operational fatigue in survivors of the Nazi concentration camps and the survivors of the atomic bombing in Japan are similar to the clinical picture of what today we know as PTSD. The psychiatric morbidity in Vietnam war veterans finally crystallised the concept of PTSD.

Subsequently, a number of studies have tried to examine the immediate and long-term effect of exposure to war violence in children and adolescents. Exposure to war violence has been found to be a strong and consistent predictor of the development of PTSD. It also has a negative effect on the cognitive and emotional development of children (Diehl et al. 1994). It is worth noting that as war stress increases, the reported symptoms of psychopathology in children increase too and the children in the vicinity of the war zone have highest rates of psychopathological symptoms (Elbedour et al. 1993). For children and adolescents trapped in a war zone, witnessing death or injury and the viewing of explicit graphic images of mutilation on television influence the severity of PTSD (Nader et al. 1993).

Natural disasters

An earthquake measuring 6.5 on the Richter scale struck the Marathawada region in rural India on 30 September 1993, leaving approximately 10 000 dead and many more seriously injured. As a result of massive destruction of property, 70 villages were reduced to a rubble of stone and mud. The authors of this chapter had an opportunity to visit earthquake-affected areas of the Latur and Osmanabad district of Maharashtra state. A head teacher at one of the schools in this area reported the symptoms listed in Table 5.1 in a group of 79 students (46 boys and 33 girls), aged 5–15 years.

Table 5.1 Symptoms found in schoolchildren after an earthquake (see text for details)

Symptoms	n = 79
Startle response and distractibility with poor attention and concentration	30
Night terrors	15
Secondary nocturnal enuresis	13
Conversion symptoms	09
Somatic symptoms including headache and abdominal pain	03
Elective mutism	01
Conduct problems	01

On interview, most of the children reported difficulty in falling asleep and frequent awakening with startle after even the slightest noise due to blowing of wind or the clanging of the temporary metal roofs of their houses. This was understandable, as the first wave of earthquake shocks had struck these villages in the middle of the night when most of them were fast asleep, leading to massive destruction and casualties. Some of the children also reported frightening dreams of dacoits attacking these villages after a rumour of such incidents in other villages.

Mohammad, an 11 year old schoolboy, was one of the survivors of an earthquake. He was trapped in the rubble while he struggled to run out of his house and fractured his hip in the process. Unfortunately other members of his family did not survive. Six months after the tragedy, while recovering from his hip injury in an orthopaedic ward, he was still haunted by the memories of the earthquake. He experienced vivid nightmares about the hue and cry at the time of impact. He slept very poorly. When awake, he was often tearful during the day and panic stricken at the slightest noise. He appeared numb and lost in his own thoughts. He had lost hope in his life.

In a similar study in children of an earthquake-affected area it was found that there was a strong positive correlation between proximity to the epicentre and overall severity of PTSD (Pynoos et al. 1993).

Exposure to civilian violence, assaults and murders

Exposure to civilian violence forms a very special form of traumatic experience as in most of the cases the harm is inflicted by the perpetrators on the victims with a clear intention to do so. Thus, it is associated with insult and loss of self-esteem for the victims, making them more prone to development of symptoms of PTSD, anxiety and depression. It is often associated with an element of aggression towards the culprit and a strong desire to take revenge. This is usually not the case when a child or an adolescent is exposed to a natural disaster or an accident where element of intention is absent and they are just one of the many victims. It is pointed out that inner-city children who frequently become victims or witnesses of civilian violence in their environment develop symptoms of PTSD (Duncan 1996).

Accidents

As opposed to traumatic events like war, natural disasters, and civilian violence such as riots, which are episodic, accidents – especially road traffic accidents – are of daily occurrence in children and adolescents. It is interesting to note that, as reported by Jones and Peterson (1993), PTSD can develop in a child as young as 3 years old following an automobile accident.

As many schoolchildren travel daily to school by their school bus, they are at a high risk of exposure to school bus accidents. They are particularly at a higher risk of developing symptoms of PTSD as most of the time they are alone and not with their parents or any adults except the bus driver and the conductor. In a study of PTSD in children 2 years after a non-fatal school coach accident, significantly less morbidity was found in boys than in girls (Curle and Williams 1996).

Another variable that needs to be considered in the case of vehicle accidents is associated head injury. Adolescents on motor bikes frequently suffer head injuries, and it may often be difficult to differentiate symptoms of PTSD from those of postconcussion syndrome. It has been reported that PTSD in children and adolescents can develop after

closed head injury, although it is likely to be rare. The loss of consciousness and post-traumatic amnesia after accident and closed head injury
need not prevent PTSD (McMillan 1996).

Rape and incest

The traumatic events most frequently experienced in a community
setting by adolescent girls leading to PTSD are rape and incest. A very
high level of PTSD symptomatology has been reported in young victims
(10–16 years) of sexual assaults (Boney-McCoy and Finkelhor 1995).

As it happens in cases of civilian violence, assaults and murders, even
in cases of rape and incest, the attack is intentional. But, unlike civilian
violence like ethnic riots and bomb blasts, in many of the cases of rape
and incest, the perpetrator is known to the victim. In addition to that,
the victim may have a close emotional bond with the perpetrators who
may be a father or a stepfather, a cousin or a boyfriend. In such cases the
symptoms of PTSD are ringed with a strong feeling of shame, guilt and
helplessness. Suicidal ideation and attempts are not uncommon in such
cases.

In a study by McLeer et al. (1992) it was observed that a greater
number of children and adolescents developed PTSD when they were
sexually abused by their fathers and trusted adults than when they were
sexually abused by a stranger or older child.

Contributory factors in the development of PTSD

Alhough most people are exposed to stressful traumatic experiences in
their lifetime, only a small proportion of them develop PTSD. Although
PTSD is most prevalent in young adults, children and adolescents are in
no way immune to this disorder.

High risk groups

As a result of their own temperament or family and social environment,
some children and adolescents seem to be particularly at risk of
exposure to such traumatic events and more susceptible to develop
PTSD. Burton et al. (1994) studied PTSD in delinquent adolescents.
Their findings suggest that juvenile offenders may constitute a high-risk
group for exposure to multiple types of trauma and the development of
PTSD. Children and adolescents dependent on substances such as
alcohol, heroine or cocaine seem to be at a higher risk of exposure to
traumatic events and subsequent development of PTSD. Deyking and
Buka (1997) have reported a very high lifetime prevalence rate of PTSD
(29.6%) (five times higher than that reported for a community sample)
in chemically dependent adolescents. Berton and Stabb (1996) have

observed in their study of PTSD in high school juniors that black adolescents are exposed to more violent crimes in their neighbourhoods and schools than white adolescents. It was also observed that in the schools with the highest rates of murder, assault and individual robbery, boys achieved low to mid-range PTSD scores while the scores for girls were the highest of all the subjects tested.

Perception and evaluation of the traumatic event

It seems that the extent of conceptual processing of the trauma discriminates between people who exhibit a PTSD response initially but quickly resolve the distress, and people who remain symptomatic (Sewell 1996). Children exposed to community violence are most likely to cope if they have an internal locus of control, a strong sense of self-efficacy and an optimistic and constructive attitude towards the future (Duncan 1996).

Availability of support

In general, children seem to be quite resilient to the effects of the traumatic events and less likely to develop PTSD as long as they are with their parents. But, as it happens in a number of situations, when they are away from their parents or when they are separated from them the risk of developing PTSD sharply increases. Once they are exposed to the stressful traumatic event the availability of parental support and open communication within the family is particularly important in helping children to cope with stress (Duncan 1996).

Life events in the subsequent period

In an individual exposed to a traumatic event the life events in the subsequent period should be examined for two reasons:

- the subsequent events may explain the persistence or mitigation of the symptoms of PTSD
- it may explain the delayed onset of PTSD.

It is often noted that the recent stressful event may revive the past traumatic experience and an individual may experience the symptoms of PTSD. It is important to recognise that common stressful events occurring after disasters may be more strongly associated with PTSD than magnitude of contact with the actual disaster (Garrison et al. 1995).

Joseph et al. (1994) have reported that in survivors of ferryboat disasters crisis support and subsequent life events were the two best predictors of variance on the General Health Questionnaire, whereas the perception of helplessness and bereavement were the two best predictors of intrusive symptomatology. In contrast to the popular belief, in a study on relocation from the disaster zone and the subsequent development of PTSD in children exposed to earthquake in Armenia, it was observed that children who were relocated after a natural disaster did no worse than children who remained in the disaster zone as far as PTSD, depression and behavioural problems were concerned (Najarian et al. 1996).

Essential and associated features (symptom profile)

Onset

Many individuals develop clinical features of PTSD immediately after or within a short period after exposure to a traumatic event, whereas others may develop symptoms of PTSD only after a couple of months, a couple of years or even a couple of decades have elapsed since the exposure to the traumatic event. Long-term follow-up studies of children exposed to traumatic events have emphasised the need for regular periodic follow-up of disaster victims for identification of delayed onset PTSD (Webb 1994). A stressful event or stimulus that reminds the person of the past traumatic event usually precipitates the delayed onset of PTSD.

Essential features

One of the most important and central features of PTSD is the persistent re-experiencing of the traumatic event.

Dreams

In children this phenomenon of re-experiencing the traumatic event is seen in the form of distressing dreams related to the event. Occasionally there may be frightening dreams without recognisable content. After several weeks, the actual content of the dream may change into generalised nightmares, dreams related to harm to self and others or dreams depicting rescue operations. As a result they may refuse to sleep alone or at any new place. They may insist on sleeping with their parents. The sleep may be restless and the child may weep and cry in their sleep.

Play

Another area in which the re-experiencing of the event is indirectly noticed in children is when they are playing. Most of the time children may not be aware that they are reliving the traumatic experience. The reliving of trauma may occur through repetitive play. For example, the boy involved in a serious automobile accident may repeatedly enact car crashes with toy cars. Similarly, the girl who has witnessed an accident which killed many people may repeatedly engage in a game where she plays a role of a doctor or a nurse cleaning, dressing and bandaging the wounds of the injured playmates.

Recollection

Most schoolchildren and adolescents, when asked about the traumatic event, are able to describe it vividly. Some of them have recurrent images of some part of the event. For example, they may have a recurrent image of injured people lying bleeding at the site of the accident, or images of people shouting, screaming and trying to escape from a building or apartment on fire.

This recollection may occur in response to some clue that symbolises or resembles some aspect of the traumatic event: for example, watching some similar scene on television or reading of an incident resembling the traumatic event in a book, a newspaper or a magazine.

The re-experiencing of events in children and adolescents is frequently associated with feelings of helplessness and guilt, especially when they have witnessed an event in which they could not help the victims or when they have survived the tragedy which killed their friends and relatives.

Avoidance of stimuli associated with the trauma and numbing of general responsiveness

Avoidance behaviour is quite frequently encountered in children. The child may avoid any sort of conversation about the traumatic event and their thoughts and feelings associated with it. Children who have been involved in a school bus accident or who were exposed to some traumatic event in school may refuse to go to school.

Many children and adolescents may fail to recollect some important aspect of a trauma. This is especially true in cases of sexual abuse where adolescent girls may not be able to provide any details of the event and may claim inability to recall the event.

It may be difficult for children to report numbing of responses, diminished interest in significant activities and constriction of affect. Presence or absence of these symptoms should therefore be carefully evaluated with reports from parents, teachers and other significant people.

In children, the sense of a foreshortened future may be evident from the belief that life will be too short and may end before they can grow to adulthood. There may also be 'omen formation': that is, belief in the ability to foresee the untoward future events.

These symptoms are likely to have an impact on other aspects of their life and may result in loss of interest in studies and diminished participation in play or other group activities. Such children may not be able to continue their friendships or make new friends.

Persistent symptoms of increased arousal

Symptoms of increased arousal are frequently seen in children and adolescents immediately after the exposure to the traumatic event. Generally the severity of these symptoms diminishes over a period of a couple of months, but in some cases it may persist for a very long time and there may be intermittent reactivation after exposure to cues that remind them of some aspect of the event.

Increased arousal may manifest clinically as difficulty in falling or staying asleep, inability to concentrate, hypervigilance and exaggerated startle response.

Associated features

Apart from the cardinal symptoms of PTSD, children and adolescents may show a variety of associated symptoms.

Young children after exposure to a traumatic event may refuse to separate from their mother or may show regressive infantile behaviour. They may develop enuresis or encopresis. Older children may become irritable and may show angry outbursts and destructive behaviour (Yule and Canterbury 1994). There may be negative effects on their cognitive and emotional development and their scholastic performance may deteriorate (Diehl et al. 1994).

Children may also exhibit various physical symptoms such as headache, vertigo, stomach ache or breathlessness. It is also hypothesised that if re-experiencing of the traumatic event is suppressed, then generalised arousal increases leading to problems with impulse control and somatic complaints (Nader and Fairbanks 1994).

Anxiety symptoms such as restlessness, nervousness, tremulousness and autonomic lability may also be associated with symptoms of PTSD in schoolchildren. Alcohol and drug abuse may be associated with symptoms of PTSD in adolescents.

Co-morbidity

Although PTSD is the most common disorder that develops after the exposure to a traumatic event, a variety of psychiatric co-morbidity is usually found to be associated with this disorder in children and adolescents. From the therapeutic point of view it is very important to identify such psychiatric co-morbidity in the affected population.

Children and adolescents may have some psychiatric morbidity such as attention deficit hyperactivity disorder (ADHD), conduct disorder, and substance abuse disorder, which make them more prone to exposure to traumatic events and susceptible to development of PTSD. In such cases the co-morbid condition exists before the onset of PTSD and may persist even after the recovery from PTSD. In other cases, children and adolescents may develop one or more psychiatric co-morbidity after the exposure to the traumatic event.

Mood disorders, anxiety disorders and PTSD

High rates of mood disorders and anxiety disorders may be observed along with PTSD. Immediately after the exposure to a traumatic event, quite a few children may develop symptoms of anxiety and attacks of panic. During the course, development of depressive symptoms is the rule.

In a longitudinal analysis of victims of Hurricane Andrew, a number of adolescents were found to have depressive symptoms and suicidal ideation (Warheit et al. 1996). Similarly, in a study of psychiatric co-morbidity in children after the earthquake in Armenia it was observed that after a catastrophic natural disaster, children are at risk for co-morbid PTSD and secondary depression (Goenjian et al. 1995).

ADHD and PTSD

Cuff et al. (1994) have reported four co-morbid cases of ADHD and PTSD. They have put forward two hypotheses to explain this co-morbid relationship:

- Children with ADHD are at a higher risk of trauma due to their impulsivity and dangerous behaviours.
- Hyperarousal induced by severe trauma is manifested by hypervigilance, and poor concentration may impair attention to create an ADHD-like syndrome.

Dissociative disorders, conversion disorder and PTSD

After the exposure to the traumatic event, along with symptoms of PTSD, symptoms of dissociative disorders and conversion disorder may be seen particularly in children and adolescents with borderline intellectual capacity. Children may complain of complete or partial amnesia for the event (**dissociative amnesia**) or may develop one or more neurological symptoms like weakness in limbs, blindness or aphonia that cannot be explained by a known medical disorder (**conversion disorder**).

Diagnosis and differential diagnosis

Diagnosis

The term 'post-traumatic stress disorder' (acute 308.30 and chronic or delayed 309.81) as a diagnostic category first appeared in the third edition of the *Diagnostic and Statistical Manual of Mental Disorder* (DSM-III) (APA 1980) under the category of 'Anxiety disorders'. In DSM-IV (APA 1994; 309.81 PTSD) re-experiencing, avoidance and hyperarousal were identified as the most specific symptoms of PTSD. It further specifies it as 'acute' if the duration is less than 3 months and 'chronic' when it is more than 3 months. When the onset of the symptoms is after 6 months of exposure to the stressor then it is specified as 'with delayed onset'. In ICD-10 (WHO 1992), PTSD (F43.1) appears under a separate heading of 'Reaction to severe stress and adjustment disorders'.

Special notes have been added in the DSM-IV diagnostic criteria for PTSD describing the differences in clinical manifestations in children. The response to a traumatic event in children may be expressed by disorganised and agitated behaviour rather than fear, helplessness or horror. In children, the traumatic event may be re-experienced by repetitive play of some aspect of trauma, frightening dreams without recognisable contents and trauma-specific re-enactment.

When making the diagnosis of PTSD, it is important to note that children with acute forms of PTSD exhibit a relative increase in spontaneous acting out (as though the trauma has recurred), difficulty in falling asleep, hypervigilance, nightmares, exaggerated startle response and generalised anxiety and agitation. Those presenting with the chronic form, on the other hand, will have a relative increase in symptoms of detachment, restricted range of affect, dissociative episodes, sadness and a belief that life will be too hard (Famularo et al. 1990).

Differential diagnosis

Acute stress reaction

DSM-IV (APA 1994) introduced a new diagnostic category for patients in whom symptoms similar to those found in PTSD develop within 4 weeks of exposure to the traumatic event and persist for less than 4 weeks. This is termed 'acute stress reaction'. When the symptoms persist beyond 4 weeks the diagnosis is changed from acute stress reaction to PTSD.

Adjustment disorder

In PTSD the symptoms develop after a psychologically traumatising event which is outside the range of normal human experience. In contrast, adjustment disorder is a short-term maladaptive reaction to the day to day stressful event (psychosocial stressors) which are within the range of normal human experience. When the severity of emotional and behavioural symptoms in response to an identifiable psychosocial stressor exceeds what is expected from the exposure to the stressor and leads to significant impairment in psychological, social and occupational functioning, a diagnosis of adjustment disorder is considered. For example, a child who develops emotional and behaviour problems (such as temper tantrums or fighting with other children at school) after a moderate to severe stress, such as quarrels in the house or problems in school, may be diagnosed as having adjustment disorder.

Brief psychotic disorder (brief reactive psychosis)

As in PTSD, even in brief reactive psychosis (brief psychotic disorder with marked stressors) the symptoms occur shortly after and apparently in response to the events, which are markedly stressful to almost anyone in similar circumstances. But, in contrast to PTSD, the clinical picture of brief reactive psychosis is dominated by delusions, hallucinations and disorganised speech and behaviour. The symptoms do not persist beyond a month, resulting in full recovery to premorbid level. Brief reactive psychosis may be seen in adolescents in response to stressors such as the death of a loved one, failure in a relationship or violence involving threats to life.

Postconcussion syndrome

Postconcussion syndrome has been described in the psychiatric literature, but is not listed as a diagnosis in DSM-IV. The clinical picture in patients who have developed PTSD following traumatic brain injury may be somewhat different from those following other traumatic events. It may be dominated by difficulty in remembering aspects of the event, difficulty in concentrating, startle responses and physiological reactivity. This may cause difficulties in differentiating between PTSD and postconcussion syndrome (Ohry et al. 1996).

In some cases when there is an overlap of symptoms of PTSD and postconcussion syndrome, both diagnoses may be given. However, in most cases of postconcussion syndrome the traumatic event is not relived or re-experienced and persistent avoidance behaviour and numbing of responsiveness is usually not present.

Course and outcome

It is very important for a clinician to realise that symptoms of PTSD in children and adolescents may persist for a very long time. It may become chronic or follow a remission–relapse cyclical pattern. It may also lead to long-term social, occupational and interpersonal dysfunction.

Terr (1983) followed up a group of schoolchildren after 4 years and studied the effect of kidnapping on them. She found that all remained influenced by the trauma in some debilitating way. Earlier developmental accomplishments were lost to some extent and they had become less autonomous. The children were preoccupied with self-preservation and had a heightened sense of vulnerability. Some of them had developed time distortions and perceptual changes. Similarly, a follow-up study of 334 children, survivors of the sinking of the cruise ship *Jupiter*, revealed that even a year after the accident nearly half of them had symptoms of PTSD (Yule 1992). The same trends were also observed in a 21 month follow-up study of school-age children exposed to Hurricane Andrew. Even after 21 months 70% of the children demonstrated moderate to severe PTSD symptoms. Boys demonstrated significant increases in internalising symptoms and in Withdrawn, Anxious/ Depressed, Social Problems and Attention Problem scales of the Teacher's Report Form, whereas girls showed a significant increase in the Anxious/Depressed scale (Shaw et al. 1996).

In another follow-up study by Goenjian et al. (1997) of adolescents exposed to earthquake, it was observed that severity of PTSD symptoms significantly decreased among subjects who were given psychotherapy, but increased significantly among subjects not treated with psychotherapy.

Conclusion

We have come a long way in identifying and delineating the syndrome of PTSD. Recent clinical and research literature on PTSD in children and adolescents provides a fairly good idea of the different types of traumatic events and other contributory factors that influence the development of PTSD.

Various studies have also focused their attention on how clinical manifestations of PTSD differ in children and adolescents from those in adults. As far as the diagnosis of PTSD is concerned, it seems that it is more appropriately classified under a separate heading of 'Reaction to severe stress and adjustment disorder' along with acute stress reaction and adjustment disorder in ICD-10. However, in DSM-IV, it appears under 'anxiety disorder' along with acute stress reaction.

A number of studies have followed up children and adolescents exposed to traumatic events and have reaffirmed the need for such longitudinal studies, as there may be a delayed onset or chronic persistence of symptoms of PTSD.

References

APA (1980) Diagnostic and Statistical Manual of Mental Disorders, 3rd edn (DSM-III). Washington, D. C.: American Psychiatric Association.

APA (1994) Diagnostic and Statistical Manual of Mental Disorders, 4th edn (DSM-IV). Washington, D. C.: American Psychiatric Association.

Berton, M. W. and Stabb, S. D. (1996) Exposure to violence and post-traumatic stress disorder in urban adolescents. Adolescence 31(122), 489–498.

Boney-McCoy, S. and Finkelhor, D. (1995) Psychosocial sequelae of violent victimisation in a national youth sample. Journal of Consulting and Clinical Psychology 63(5), 726–736.

Burton, D., Foy, D. W., Bwanausi, C. et al. (1994) The relationship between traumatic exposure, family dysfunction, and post-traumatic stress symptoms in male juvenile offenders. Journal of Traumatic Stress 7(1), 83–93.

Cuff, S. P., McCullough, E. L. and Pumariega, A. J. (1994) Comorbidity of attention deficit hyperactivity disorder and post-traumatic stress disorder. Journal of Child and Family Studies 3(3), 327–336.

Curle, C. and Williams, C. (1996) Post-traumatic stress reaction in children: gender differences in the incidence of trauma reaction at two years and examination of factors influencing adjustment. British Journal of Clinical Psychology 154(6), 752–757.

Deykin, F. Y. and Buka, S. L. (1997) Prevalence and risk factors for post-traumatic stress disorder among chemically dependent adolescents. American Journal of Psychiatry 154(6), 752–757.

Diehl, V. A., Zea, M. C. and Espino, C. M. (1994) Exposure to war violence, separation from parents, post-traumatic stress and cognitive functioning in Hispanic children. Revista Interamericana de Psicologia 28(1), 25–41.

Duncan, D. F. (1996) Growing up under the gun: Children and adolescents coping with violent neighbourhood. Journal of Primary Prevention 16(4), 343–356.

Elbedour, S., Ten-Bensel, R. and Maruyama, G. M. (1993) Children at risk: psychological coping with war and conflict in the Middle East. International Journal of Mental Health 22(3), 33–52.

Famularo, R., Kinscherff, R. and Fenton, T. (1990) Symptom differences in acute and chronic presentation of childhood post-traumatic stress disorder. Child Abuse and Neglect 14(3), 439–444.

Garrison, C. Z., Bryant, E. S., Addy, C. L., Spurrier, P. G., Freedy, J. R. and Kilpatrick, D. G. (1995) Posttraumatic stress disorder in adolescents after Hurricane Andrew. Journal of the American Academy of Child and Adolescent Psychiatry 34(9), 1193–1201.

Goenjian, A. K., Karayan, I., Pynoos, R. S. et al. (1997) Outcome of psychotherapy among early adolescents after trauma. American Journal of Psychiatry 154, 542–563.

Goenjian, A. K., Pynoos, R. S., Steinberg, A. M. et al. (1995) Psychiatric comorbidity in children after the 1988 earthquake in Armenia. Journal of American Academy of Child and Adolescent Psychiatry 34(9), 1174–1184.

Jones, R. W. and Peterson, L. W. (1993) Post-traumatic stress disorder in a child following an automobile accident. Journal of Family Practice 36(2), 223–225.

Joseph, S., Yule, W., Williams, R. and Hodgkinson, P. (1994) Correlates of post-traumatic stress at 30 months: the Herald of Free Enterprise disaster. Behaviour Research and Therapy 32(5), 521–524.

McLeer, S. V., Deblinger, E. B., Henry, D. and Orvaschel, H. (1992) Sexually abused children at high risk for post-traumatic stress disorder. Journal of American Academy of Child and Adolescent Psychiatry 31(5), 875–879.

McMillan, T. M. (1996) Post-traumatic stress disorder following minor and severe closed head injury: 10 single cases. Brain Injury 10(10), 749–758.

Nader, K. O., Fairbanks, L. A. (1994) The suppression of reexperiencing: impulse control and somatic symptoms in children following traumatic exposure. Special Issue: War and stress in the Middle East. Anxiety, Stress and Coping 7(3), 229–239.

Nader, K. O., Pynoos, R. S., Fairbanks, L. A., Al-Ajeel, M. and Angeles, U. S. (1993) A preliminary study of PTSD and grief among the children of Kuwait following the Gulf crisis. British Journal of Clinical Psychology 32(4), 407–416.

Najarian, L. M., Goenjian, A. K., Pelcovitz, D., Mandel, F. and Najarian, B. (1996) Relocation after a disaster: posttraumatic stress disorder in Armenia after the earthquake. Journal of the American Academy of Child and Adolescent Psychiatry 35(3), 374–383.

Ohry, A., Rattok, J. and Solomon, Z. (1996) Post-traumatic stress disorder in brain injury patients. Brain Injury 10(9), 687–695.

Parker, J., Watt, H. and Allsopp, M. R. (1995) Post-traumatic stress symptoms in children and parents following a school-based fatality. Child Care, Health and Development 21(3), 183–189.

Pynoos, R. S., Goenjian, A., and Tashjian, M. (1993) Post-traumatic stress reaction in children after the 1998 Armenian earthquake. British Journal of Psychiatry 163, 239–247.

Sewell, K. W. (1996) Constructional risk factors for a post-traumatic stress response after a mass murder. Journal of Constructivist Psychology 9(2), 97–107.

Shaw, J. A., Applegate, B. and Schorr, C. (1996) Twenty one month follow up study of school age children exposed to Hurricane Andrew. Journal of the American Academy of Child and Adolescent Psychiatry 35(3), 359–364.

Terr, L. (1983) Chowchilla revisited: the effects of psychic trauma four years after a school bus kidnapping. American Journal of Psychiatry 140, 1543–1550.

Warheit, G. J., Zimmerman, R. S., Khoury, E. L., Vega, W. A. and Gil, A. G. (1996) Disaster related stresses, depressive signs and symptoms, and suicidal ideation among a multi-racial/ethnic sample of adolescents: a longitudinal analysis. Journal of Child Psychology and Psychiatry and Allied Disciplines 37(4), 435–444.

Webb, N. B. (1994) School based assessment and crisis intervention with kindergarten children following the New York World Trade Center bombing. Crisis Intervention and Time Limited Treatment 1(1), 47–59.

WHO (1992) The ICD-10 Classification of Mental and Behavioural Disorders: Clinical Descriptions and Diagnostic Guidelines. Geneva: World Health Organisation.

Yule, W. (1992) Post-traumatic stress disorder in child survivors of shipping disasters: the sinking of the 'Jupiter'. Psychotherapy and Psychosomatics 57(4), 200–205.

Yule, W. and Canterbury, R. (1994) The treatment of post-traumatic stress disorder in children and adolescents. International Review of Psychiatry 6(2–3), 141–151.

Chapter 6
The assessment of post-traumatic stress reactions in children and adolescents

Leonard Thornton

It is now well established that children and adolescents can exhibit post-traumatic stress reactions following their exposure to extreme adverse events. A wide range of acute stressors has been identified. These include traumatic events which are clearly outside the range of normal experience such as those occurring in war zones and during both natural and technological disasters. However, relatively more prevalent adverse single events such as being involved in a motor vehicle accident or witnessing similar traumas may also result in the development of post-traumatic stress symptoms. In addition to these acute events, some traumatic stressors such as experiencing child sexual abuse and witnessing marital violence may occur as multiple episodes over a lengthy period of time and lead similarly to post-traumatic psychological problems.

The child's clinical presentation in response to acute or chronic stressors can include the full syndrome or partial features of post-traumatic stress disorder (PTSD) and a broad range of co-morbid psychological conditions. However, these trauma-specific and general psychopathological symptoms are developmentally linked and the overall presenting clinical picture varies with the age of the child. The post-traumatic reactions experienced by children and adolescents can be severe and long lasting, and may result in significant impairment of adaptive functioning and development.

The increased public awareness of post-traumatic disorders in children and adolescents has led to a rise in demand for early recognition and accurate assessment of affected individuals. The aim of this chapter is to describe the framework for a practical comprehensive assessment of the traumatised child. However, the exact format of an assessment will depend on the reasons for the child's referral, which

113

may include, for example, assessment for a treatment intervention or for the purposes of preparing a report in a compensation litigation case. In situations where the child has been subjected to certain stressors such as physical, sexual or emotional abuse, further more specialised multipro-fessional assessment procedures may be required in order to address issues such as child protection, parental custody/access and criminal prosecution. Details of these multiple assessment formats are beyond the scope of this chapter and the interested reader is referred to the relevant specialist texts for further information.

Assessment principles and format

The assessment should provide a detailed picture of the child's clinical presentation. This includes the primary and co-morbid psychiatric disor-ders present, the symptom severity, the degree of psychosocial impair-ment arising as a direct result of the traumatic event and the contributory role of any predisposing and maintaining factors. This diagnostic formulation should also provide a provisional indication of prognosis and where appropriate the possible outcome of treatment interventions.

The assessment process focuses on three main areas: the child's pre-event level of functioning, the traumatic event itself and the child's subsequent symptomatic response and adjustment. In order to make a comprehensive assessment, it is essential that information is obtained from several sources, in order to build up a range of perspectives regarding the child and their circumstances. These informant sources can include:

- separate clinical interviews with the child, parents and family
- school-based observations
- parent- and child-completed symptom rating scales
- school reports
- medical records or reports
- witness statements.

It is advisable that the various background documents are reviewed before the assessment is carried out in order that the clinician is familiar with the child's circumstances preceding, during and following the traumatic event.

Clinical interviews

The cornerstone of assessment is the detailed biographical clinical inter-view. However, it is well recognised that parents underestimate the level of post-traumatic distress experienced by their children (Handford et al. 1986, Earls et al. 1988, Sack et al. 1994). This finding reflects the generally low rates of agreement between parents and children regarding the presence of child psychopathology (Achenbach et al. 1987). In particular, children tend to report more internalising symptoms than their parents do about them, whereas parents are more likely to identify the child's externalising behaviour problems (Kashani et al. 1985). In addition, traumatised children may not report post-traumatic symptoms in order to avoid both reliving the unpleasant experience and causing the parents distress (Yule and Williams 1990). The parents may collude with this behaviour in order to protect themselves and the child. In view of these parent–child discrepancies in reporting, it is therefore important that separate interviews are carried out.

The parental interview provides information regarding family background, the child's developmental history and pre-event level of functioning, plus the parents' account of the traumatic event (where applicable) and the child's subsequent symptom response and adjustment from the parents' perspective.

The interviewing of older children and adolescents covers their account of pre-event adjustment and subsequent post-traumatic symptoms and impairments. In addition, the assessment should include a detailed mental state examination. Children and adolescents are the sole informants about their own feelings and perceptions. In particular, their subjective appraisal of the traumatic event is a central component of the assessment. In some instances they may also be the only informant regarding objective details of the event. This is particularly the case for 'private' traumatic events such as episodes of child sexual abuse.

In recent years, there has been a greater understanding of post-traumatic presentations in very young children. It has been shown that children under the age of 4 can exhibit some of the post-traumatic symptoms also found in older children and adolescents (Scheeringa et al. 1995). However, in order to take account of the very young child's relatively limited cognitive and language abilities, a more specialised assessment format is required. The parental interview becomes the main source of reported information regarding the young child. In addition to the detailed family and developmental history, attention should be paid to the emergence of new symptoms and behaviours plus any associated changes in the child's expected developmental trajectory. The presence of specific post-traumatic symptoms in very young children can be more reliably established by the use of alternative diagnostic criteria which are more developmentally sensitive and which provide objective descriptions of observable behaviours such as post-traumatic play (Scheeringa et al. 1995). The young child's mental state assessment is made via observations of their interactions with the examiner alone and with the parents during both free play and structured activities (AACAP 1997, Boris et al. 1997). In addition, an observational assessment of the young child's behaviours and relationships with other children and adults in the kindergarten or infant school setting may provide valuable details regarding their social and emotional adjustment which are not apparent in the clinic.

Assessment instruments

A wide variety of rating scales and interview schedules are available to assess the presence of PTSD in children and adolescents (see AACAP 1998 for a review). Parent- and child-completed symptom rating scales are valuable adjuncts to the clinical interviews. Although no current single measure can cover the full range of psychopathology experienced by the traumatised child, a small battery of such instruments can provide a rapid and 'user friendly' screening of a broad spectrum of specific PTSD and related features plus commonly occurring co-morbid symptoms such as anxiety, depression and disturbances of conduct. Self-report measures are of particular value in accessing the child's internal world and, when completed before the clinical interview, they orient the child to the areas which will be covered later in the assessment. In addition, these rating forms act as a guide for the clinician regarding the breadth of symptoms experienced by the child about which further enquiries can be made at subsequent interview.

Well-established and practical child report measures include the Child PTSD Reaction Index (Frederick and Pynoos 1988). The adult Impact of Event Scale (Horowitz et al. 1979) has also been used with children and an eight-item subscale has been validated for this age group (Dyregrov and Yule 1995).

However, PTSD instruments have their limitations. They often require a traumatic event to have been recognised beforehand, may only be applicable to certain types of trauma and may focus only on a narrow range of post-traumatic features. In an attempt to overcome some of these difficulties, more recently developed rating scales such as the Child Report of Post-traumatic Symptoms and its parent report version (Greenwald and Rubin 1999) aim to tap a broader spectrum of post-traumatic phenomena in children where a traumatic stressor may not necessarily have been identified. In the future such instruments may prove to be of practical value in clinical assessments.

As an adjunct to specific measures of post-traumatic stress in children, information may be obtained regarding the presence of more generic co-morbid symptoms via the use of self-rating instruments such as the Revised Children's Manifest Anxiety Scale (Reynolds and Richmond 1978), the Children's Depression Inventory (Kovacs 1985) and the parent-completed Child Behaviour Checklist (CBCL) (Achenbach and Edelbrock 1983). In addition, use of the Teacher's Report Form and the Youth Self Report versions of the CBCL (Achenbach and Edelbrock 1986, 1987) allow direct comparisons to be made between the three informants across a wide range of general problem behaviours (Achenbach 1991).

The limitations of PTSD measures and the relative insensitivity of generic instruments to elicit specific post-traumatic symptoms means that rating scales should not be employed alone to establish the child's clinical diagnosis. Their main practical value is in assessing the current severity of specific post-traumatic symptoms and general child psychopathology. These measures can then provide a baseline to monitor the progress of symptoms over time and in particular the child's response to treatment interventions.

With regard to more detailed semi-structured interview schedules, although they are widely employed in research studies of traumatised children, such instruments are usually too lengthy and unwieldy for use in routine clinical assessments and additionally may require specific training in their administration. In general, the well-conducted detailed clinical interview will elicit the full range of symptoms and impairments experienced by the child without need for a more structured interview schedule.

Assessment of pre-event functioning

Studies have shown that pre-existing adverse family environmental factors including discordant family interactions, disruption of the parent–child relationship and a family history of anxiety disorders may contribute to the risk of developing PTSD (Breslau et al. 1991, Green et al. 1991, Brent et al. 1995).

In the child's background, a history of special educational or emotional needs, pre-existing child psychiatric disorder including anxiety and depression, and a history of early trauma exposure have been associated with increased vulnerability to developing post-traumatic difficulties (Burke et al. 1982, Earls et al. 1988, Garrison et al. 1993).

It is therefore important that assessment of pre-event functioning identifies pre-existing family and personal vulnerabilities and establishes the child's level of adjustment immediately prior to the traumatic event. The following areas should be covered:

- **Family**: This includes details of family structure and functioning plus information on relevant parent and sibling medical/psychiatric history.
- **Early development and temperament**: This includes details of the child's birth; attainment of locomotor, language and toileting

milestones; sleep and appetite patterns; general level of motor activity and attention; response to new situations; affect regulation; development of play; attachment behaviours; and the presence of developing traits, e.g. obsessionality.

- **Education**: This includes a sequential list of the child's pre-school and school placements; attendance records with reasons for non-attendance, e.g. ill-health, separation difficulties, truancy; academic abilities with particular attention being paid to general or specific learning problems; classroom behaviour including any pre-existing attention difficulties; and the child's peer and teacher relationships. The parental report should be supplemented by a school report covering the period up to the time of the traumatic event.
- **Previous medical history**: This includes significant illnesses and injury (including head injury) plus the treatments required.
- **Previous exposure/response to adverse events**: This includes details of previous personal and family adverse life events, e.g. hospitalisation, bereavement, parental separation or divorce and the child's emotional response to them, plus any adverse reactions to normal stressors such as the birth of a sibling.
- **Psychological difficulties**: This includes details of previous emotional, behavioural or relationship difficulties which the child has exhibited; contact with child mental health services; response to any therapeutic interventions; and the child's level of symptom disturbance or impairment before the traumatic event.
- **Relationships and activities**: This includes details of the child's family, peer and other relationships plus information regarding their interests or hobbies and participation in social activities and organisations.

Assessment of the traumatic event

Several traumatic event-related factors contribute to the risk of children and adolescents developing post-traumatic stress reactions. These include direct exposure to the trauma, indirect components and the child's subjective appraisal of the event.

The child's proximity and degree of exposure to the traumatic event are associated with an increased risk of developing PTSD symptoms (Pynoos et al. 1987, Lonigan et al. 1991, Shannon et al. 1994, March et al. 1997). Indirect effects include children who have been informed of a friend's or family member's death or injury in a traumatic event or who have witnessed directly an accident or medical emergency (March et al. 1997, Cuffe et al. 1998). The child's subjective appraisal and immediate response are particularly significant factors when assessing the impact of the traumatic event. The increased realisation that a personal perspective is required was reflected in DSM-IV with the introduction of a subjective response component in category A of the diagnostic criteria for PTSD. This response can include 'fear, helplessness or horror' and in children 'disorganised or agitated behaviour'.

Assessment issues

Information should be obtained from the parents if they were involved in or witnessed the trauma. In addition to providing the parental perspective of what occurred, they may be able to relate a more accurate account of the sequence and timing of events than the child. If available, witness statements made to police and solicitors shortly after the episode may provide further factual information. Finally, hospital records detailing the child's physical injuries including loss of consciousness and any immediate medical treatment received should be consulted.

The aim of the child interview is to obtain their narrative account of the traumatic event and its immediate sequelae. This should include details of the objective aspects of the episode, the child's subjective appraisal of the event and their emotional responses during it. It must be borne in mind that the assessment interview may be the first occasion in which the child has recalled the traumatic event in any detail, even though it may have occurred several months or years previously. The clinician must therefore be alert to the risk of retraumatising the child and deal sensitively with any subsequent distress which the child may exhibit during the interview. In certain cases, where the child becomes particularly upset, it may be necessary to carry out several short interviews over a period of time to complete the assessment and minimise the child's distress.

In order to facilitate recall, particularly in young children, various assessment aids can be employed. These can include the use of toys and dolls to represent the sequence of events in a road traffic accident, for example. The child's drawings of the trauma are also of value in promoting discussion of the event (Pynoos and Eth 1986).

In more complex traumas involving older children and adolescents, detailed diagrams may be helpful. The author, when assessing survivors of the *Jupiter* disaster (see Yule et al. 1990), found that using a deck plan of the cruise ship helped improve the recall of the adolescents and graphically illustrated the difficulties and dangers involved in trying to escape the sinking ship. The child's own witness statements can also be used during the interview to prompt recollections of the trauma.

In order to facilitate the narrative flow and establish the child's associated emotional feelings at different times during the traumatic event, simple verbal prompts such as 'What happened next?', 'How did you feel then?' should be employed. The child should be guided sequentially through the circumstances leading up to the event, details of what actually happened during the event itself and finally the immediate sequelae such as being taken to hospital.

Information is required about objective details of the trauma. This includes how much forewarning the child had of the trauma, its speed of onset, whether the child was trapped and for how long, details of their escape or rescue and whether they suffered physical injuries. Other objective areas to enquire about include separation from significant others, and how long before they were reunited. Information should also be obtained as to whether the child witnessed other people, particularly family members, being injured or killed or if they saw the dead bodies subsequently.

The clinician should enquire specifically:

- whether the child thought either they or a family member was going to die during the event
- who they felt was responsible for the trauma
- whether they thought they could do anything to help themselves at the time or if they felt that events were essentially out of their control
- when they finally felt safe.

The child should also be asked to rate subjectively the most frightening aspects of the overall traumatic experience. It should be remembered that the indirect exposure aspects and immediate sequelae may be perceived by the child to have been more distressing than their exposure to the core trauma.

The need for this subjective appraisal is illustrated by two case examples assessed by the author. One 14 year old boy who was involved in a car accident, in which his mother had been the driver, reported that the most frightening aspect of the crash had been when he thought (incorrectly) that his mother had been killed. He rated this higher than his fears about his own serious chest injuries. Another child, a girl aged 10, reported that being prepared in hospital for emergency surgery on her leg was more upsetting than the preceding cycling accident which had caused her injuries.

The assessment of children who have experienced multiple traumatic stressors, such as physical or sexual abuse, poses more practical difficulties. Such events may stretch over several years and begin at an early age. In addition, the child may be reluctant to describe the traumas. Details should be obtained regarding the age of onset, duration, approximate frequency and range of the stressors. Two or three examples of the most severe episodes should then be examined using a format similar to that described above for single-event stressors. In addition, the child's perception of the potential risk of the events recurring should be assessed. More specific assessment procedures for sexually abused children have been developed such as the Step-Wise Interview technique (Yuille et al. 1993). This contains several interview components including rapport building, free narrative and the use of general and specific questions about the abuse.

Assessment of post-event adjustment

Physical injuries and impairments

Details should be obtained from the parents and relevant hospital or medical records, regarding the duration of any hospitalisation after the traumatic event, any subsequent physical immobility and the length of time before the child was able to return to school and participate in their usual interests and social activities.

It is important to establish from the background medical reports whether the child suffered any organic brain damage during the event, as they may then require more specialised neuropsychological testing as part of the assessment. It should also be remembered that traumatic brain injury in children, in its own right, is associated with an increased risk for the development of subsequent psychiatric disorder (Max et al. 1998).

Details are also required regarding the nature of any continuing physical disabilities, the degree of restriction these place on their day to day life, whether these impairments will be permanent and whether any future physical treatment including surgery is planned. In particular, it should be noted if the child has been physically scarred as a result of the traumatic event and whether the scars are visible. Reference should be made to reports prepared by the plastic surgeon regarding the amount of scar maturation which may occur and the expected time duration. In addition to the main areas of psychological symptom enquiry outlined below, the child should be asked about their perceptions of, and emotional responses to, their physical disabilities. This should include the degree of embarrassment caused by their scars and whether this has resulted in the avoidance of certain activities where their disfigurements may be more visible, such as swimming or sunbathing. In the case of adolescents, enquiries should be made as to whether the scars have impaired their ability to form and maintain romantic relationships.

Symptom screening

It is important that the symptom enquiry covers the full range of PTSD symptoms and general child psychopathology. In order to screen accurately for these psychological symptoms in the child interview, leading questions must be avoided. This is particularly the case when assessing young children whose understanding is limited and in children who, as a result of their trauma, employ avoidance and denial in order to minimise their chances of reliving the event. One should therefore begin the symptom enquiry by asking open questions regarding current and previous difficulties, thereby allowing the child to provide a spontaneous report of the symptoms which they have experienced since the traumatic event. Thereafter, a more structured specific systematic screening of the other areas of psychopathology can be carried out.

For each symptom, information is required regarding its time of onset after the traumatic event, duration and subjective account of severity. Details should be obtained regarding the effect the symptoms have had on the child's family relationships, schooling, peer interactions, interests and activities.

The clinician must be particularly aware of the potentially adverse impact of the traumatic event on the child's education. Disruptive classroom behaviour, poor attendance, learning problems and academic failure have all been reported in children and adolescents with post-traumatic stress (McFarlane 1987, Kinzie et al. 1989, Sack et al. 1993, March et al. 1997). It is therefore important for the clinician to obtain specific information regarding the child's functioning in these areas via the child and parent interviews and school report covering the period following the traumatic event. This information can then be compared with the child's pre-event level of school functioning. Further details of the child's problem behaviours can be obtained from the Teacher's Report Form rating scale. However, it should be borne in mind that several of the symptoms, particularly those which are internalising in nature, may not be evident in the school setting. In addition, as in the case of parents, teachers tend to underestimate the level of children's post-traumatic psychological difficulties.

Wherever possible, there should be attempts to quantify changes in the child's psychosocial functioning by objective measures. These can include:

- number of days not attended at school
- specific deterioration in exam results and subject grades and any associated enforced changes in higher education or career plans
- decreased contact with friends
- reduced participation in organisations or clubs.

When assessing the development and change in symptom pattern over time, the clinician must bear in mind the period which has elapsed since the traumatic event. Psychological symptoms are not always present in the immediate phase following exposure to a trauma (McFarlane et al. 1987, Finkelhor 1990, Shaw et al. 1995). Hence early assessment of the child will miss the development of later psychopathology. By comparison, later assessments made months or years after the event may overlook the previous occurrence of symptoms which have since resolved. In addition, if a long time has elapsed since the trauma the post-traumatic symptoms may be wrongly attributed to another cause and condition (Eth 1990).

Attention should be paid to the child's emotional response to subsequent adverse life events, including anniversaries of the original traumatic event, as they may exacerbate the established post-traumatic phenomena and precipitate the development of new symptoms. As a result, the presenting clinical picture becomes contaminated and it is difficult to establish which symptoms and impairments are directly attributable to the original traumatic event. Further difficulties arise when the child has experienced chronic multiple traumatic stressors, particularly from a young age. In such instances, it may not be possible to 'track' accurately specific symptoms or identify clear changes in psychosocial functioning. In addition to detailing the child's reactions to subsequent adversities, it is important to document their response to any psychological treatments which have been implemented since the traumatic event.

In order to facilitate the child's and parents' recall of events and changes in symptoms or functioning over time, enquiries should be made with reference to key personal and family events, e.g. birthdays, school holidays. This is particularly helpful when there has been a lengthy passage of time since the original trauma.

Finally, to gauge the child's current level of emotional adjustment a detailed mental state examination must be completed. This should include specific reference to the child's level of engagement, verbal and non-verbal expressiveness, distractibility, distress, anxiety, range of affect plus any associated suicidal ideation and previous history of deliberate self-harm.

Post-traumatic phenomena

Although children and adolescents can exhibit all the core features of PTSD (re-experiencing, avoidance, numbing and hyperarousal phenomena), partial symptomatology occurs frequently (McLeer et al. 1988, Cuffe et al. 1998). In particular, 'numbing of general responsiveness' phenomena are less consistently reported by children (Terr 1985, Mirza et al. 1998). However, children with partial features of PTSD may still exhibit significant psychosocial impairments (Giaconia et al. 1995). These partial presentations may reflect difficulties eliciting some post-traumatic phenomena or a relative absence of certain symptoms in this age group.

In addition to PTSD, children who have been exposed to multiple stressors, such as child abuse, may exhibit other more enduring and pervasive clinical problems including affective changes, denial, psychic numbing, rage and relationship difficulties (Kiser et al. 1991; Terr 1991). The clinician should be alert to the possible presence of these features, particularly in children who have been subjected to chronic extreme stressors and who have shown clear changes in their psychosocial functioning.

In young children, the clinician should screen for the presence of developmentally based post-traumatic features. These details will be obtained predominantly via the parental report. The phenomena include repetitive re-enactments of the traumatic event via play, constricted play, day dreaming, withdrawn behaviour, generalised night-mares and sleep disorders including night terrors, somnambulism, initial and middle insomnia, loss of developmentally acquired skills including toileting behaviour and language abilities, aggressive behav-iours and separation anxiety (Eth 1990, Scheeringa et al. 1995, Stores 1996). However, these developmentally based features are not entirely discrete and there is a degree of overlap, with, for example, attachment difficulties also being reported in adolescents (Yule 1994).

Psychiatric co-morbidity

PTSD in children and adolescents is associated with a high rate of psychi-atric co-morbidity (Goenjian et al. 1995, Hubbard et al. 1995). A wide range of conditions has been reported. These include anxiety disorders, depression, grief reactions, conduct disturbance and substance abuse (Brent et al. 1995, Giaconia et al. 1995, March et al. 1997, Mirza et al. 1998).

It is therefore important that the clinician enquires about a full spectrum of internalising and externalising problems in order not to overlook any coexisting disorders. In addition it should be established whether these conditions predated the traumatic event or developed subsequently. In the case of pre-existing conditions, the clinician should attempt to clarify whether the traumatic event resulted in an exacerba-tion of the co-morbid problems, although in the case of chronic stressors and more enduring changes in personality development this temporal relationship may not be demarcated clearly.

Family reactions

Traumatic events can have an adverse impact both on the child and on other family members (Terr 1989). Associations have been found between parents' post-traumatic symptoms and those experienced by the child (Breton et al. 1993). Maternal PTSD and in particular avoidance phenomena may predict the presence of post-traumatic symptoms and level of adjustment in the child (Laor et al. 1997, Rossman et al. 1997). Information should therefore be obtained both from the parents and the child regarding any post-traumatic symptoms which the parents or other family members may have experienced as a direct or indirect result of the traumatic event. The child's perception of the psychological distress suffered by the family, and in particular the parents, is important as it may contribute to the child minimising their own post-traumatic symptoms and impair the child's symptom resolution.

A separate family interview may be required to further ascertain changes in family functioning since the trauma and any ongoing difficulties. This should include identifying factors such as discordant family relationships which risk retraumatising the child and parental overprotective behaviours towards the child which may result in continuing psychosocial impairments. In addition, changes in patterns of communication within the family, and in particular avoidance of discussion about the traumatic event and expressing accompanying emotional feelings, should be noted.

These factors should be weighed against the level of emotional supports which family members were able to provide for the child and each other following the trauma. These include the ability to discuss the incident openly and sensitively, the acknowledgement of and allowance for the child's distress and the provision of a safe environment with appropriate protective measures taken to prevent the child from being further unnecessarily traumatised.

Diagnostic formulation

PTSD diagnostic issues

The diagnosis of PTSD in children and adolescents can be made by application of the diagnostic criteria in DSM-IV or ICD-10. The DSM-IV system takes some account of the differences in clinical presentation found in these age groups. However, for very young children the current diagnostic systems may not be sensitive enough and, in the case of DSM-IV, alternative criteria for the diagnosis have been proposed (Scheeringa et al. 1995).

The diagnostic significance of partial PTSD presentations is still to be established. They may represent a continuum of severity rather than discrete sub-syndromes. At a practical level, it must be borne in mind that post-traumatic symptoms in children often reach their maximum severity within 12 months following the traumatic event (Clark et al. 1994, Mirza et al. 1998, Winje and Ulvik 1998), and therefore, as noted previously, early assessments will not capture delayed onset symptoms. The clinician should also check that the child's current partial PTSD is not the resolving picture of a previous full PTSD syndrome. However, even with partial presentations, the central issue for the clinician when establishing severity is to ascertain the level of personal distress which the child has experienced and the degree of adverse impact which these symptoms have had on the child's psychosocial functioning.

Differential diagnosis and psychiatric co-morbidity

PTSD must be differentiated from other post-traumatic and stress precipitated conditions such as acute stress disorder (DSM-IV), acute stress reaction (ICD-10) and adjustment disorders (DSM-IV and ICD-10). These conditions are shorter lasting, show differences in the pattern of presenting psychopathology and may be triggered by a less extreme stressor than that associated with PTSD.

The presence of PTSD in children should also be differentiated from other conditions which may share or mimic some of its clinical features. These disorders include anxiety, depression, conduct disturbances and attention deficit hyperactivity disorder. However, it should be remembered that these conditions and other psychiatric disorders can coexist with PTSD, and particular attention should be paid to establishing whether they preceded the traumatic event or developed afterwards, as the timing may have implications for later treatment and prognosis. Finally, when assessing the degree of psychosocial impairment produced by the PTSD, it is important to differentiate out the adverse effects on functioning due to any co-morbid psychiatric disorders and the restrictions on daily living imposed by any continuing physical impairments.

Prognostic issues

There is a marked variation in the duration of PTSD in children and adolescents. In some cases the condition can persist for several years. At a practical level, when assessing overall prognosis, attention should be paid to the amount of symptomatic and functional recovery which has taken place since the traumatic event, the child's response to subsequent adverse life events, the likelihood of the trauma recurring (e.g. the perpetrator still having access to an abused child) and the possibility of the child having to face future secondary associated stressors (e.g. further surgical treatment).

In addition, the presence of continuing adverse personal and family circumstances including physical disability, psychiatric co-morbidity, maladaptive coping style and parental psychological distress must be taken into consideration. These maintaining factors should be balanced by an evaluation of potential buffering and protective components such as the presence of positive family relationships, a supportive school environment and good peer friendships.

If required, on completion of the comprehensive assessment and diagnostic formulation, a treatment plan can be drawn up and implemented. The child's subsequent response to the therapeutic interventions can then be monitored at regular intervals with reference to changes in their symptoms and adaptive functioning. If necessary, a subsequent revision of the initial prognostic opinion and treatment plan can be made in light of the child's progress.

References

AACAP (1997) Practice parameters for the psychiatric assessment of infants and toddlers (0–36 months). Journal of the American Academy of Child and Adolescent Psychiatry 36(10) Suppl, 21s–36s.

AACAP (1998) Practice parameters for the assessment and treatment of children and adolescents with posttraumatic stress disorder. Journal of the American Academy of Child and Adolescent Psychiatry 37(10) Suppl, 4s–26s.

Achenbach, T. M. (1991) Integrative Guide for the 1991 CBCL/4–18, YSR and TRF Profiles. Burlington, University of Vermont: Department of Psychiatry.

Achenbach, T. M. and Edelbrock, C. S. (1983) Manual for the Child Behaviour Checklist and Revised Child Behavioural Profile. Burlington: University of Vermont, Department of Psychiatry.

Achenbach, T. M. and Edelbrock, C. S. (1986) Manual for the Teacher's Report Form and Teacher Version of the Child Behavior Profile. Burlington: University of Vermont, Department of Psychiatry.

Achenbach, T. M. and Edelbrock, C. S. (1987) Manual for the Youth Self-Report and Profile. Burlington: University of Vermont, Department of Psychiatry.

Achenbach, T. M., McConaughy, S. H. and Howell, C. T. (1987) Child/adolescent behavioural and emotional problems: implications of cross-informant correlations for situational specificity. Psychological Bulletin 101, 213–232.

Boris, N. W., Fueyo, M. and Zeanah, C. H (1997) The clinical assessment of attachment in children under five. Journal of the American Academy of Child and Adolescent Psychiatry 36, 291–293.

Brent, D. A., Perper, J. A., Moritz, G. et al. (1995) Posttraumatic stress disorder in peers of adolescent suicide victims: predisposing factors and phenomenology. Journal of the American Academy of Child and Adolescent Psychiatry 34, 209–215.

Breslau, N., Davies, G. C., Andreski, P. and Peterson, E. (1991) Traumatic events and post-traumatic stress disorder in an urban population of young adults. Archives of General Psychiatry 48, 216–222.

Breton, J. J., Valla, J. P. and Lambert, J. (1993) Industrial disaster and mental health of children and their parents. Journal of the American Academy of Child and Adolescent Psychiatry 32, 438–445.

Burke, J. D., Borus, J. F., Burns, B. J., Millstein, K. H. and Beasley, M. C. (1982) Changes in children's behavior after a natural disaster. American Journal of Psychiatry 139, 1010–1014.

Clark, D. C., Pynoos, R. S. and Goebel, A. E. (1994) Mechanisms and processes of adolescent bereavement. In Haggerty, R. J., Sherrod, L. R., Garmezy, N. and Rutter M. (eds), Stress, Risk and Resilience in Children and Adolescents, pp. 100–146. Cambridge: Cambridge University Press.

Cuffe, S. P., Addy, C. L., Garrison, C. Z. et al. (1998) Prevalence of PTSD in a community sample of older adolescents. Journal of the American Academy of Child and Adolescent Psychiatry 37, 147–154.

Dyregrov A. and Yule, W. (1995) Screening measures – the development of the UNICEF screening battery. Paper presented at Symposium on War Affected Children in Former Yugoslavia at Eleventh Annual Meeting of the International Society for Traumatic Stress Studies, Boston, 2–6 November 1995.

Earls, F., Smith, E., Reich, W. and Jung, K. G. (1988) Investigating psychopathological consequences of a disaster in children: a pilot study incorporating a structured diagnostic approach. Journal of the American Academy of Child and Adolescent Psychiatry 27, 90–95.

Eth, S. (1990) Post-traumatic stress disorder in childhood. In Herson, M., and Last, C. G. (eds), Handbook of Child and Adult Psychopathology – A Longitudinal Perspective, pp. 263–274. Oxford: Pergamon.

Finkelhor, D. (1990) Early and long-term effects of child sexual abuse: an update. Professional Psychology Research and Practice 21, 325–330.

Frederick, C. J. and Pynoos, R. S. (1988) The Child Post Traumatic Stress Disorder (PTSD) Reaction Index. Los Angeles, CA: University of California.

Garrison, C. Z., Weinrich, M. W., Hardin, S. B., Weinrich, S. and Wang, L. (1993) Posttraumatic stress disorder in adolescents after a hurricane. American Journal of Epidemiology 138, 522–530.

Giaconia, R. M., Reinherz, H. Z., Silverman, A. B., Pakig, B., Frost, A. K. and Cohen, E. (1995) Traumas and post traumatic stress disorder in a community population of older adolescents. Journal of the American Academy of Child and Adolescent Psychiatry 34, 1369–1380.

Goenjian, A. K., Pynoos, R. S., Steinberg, A. M. et al. (1995) Psychiatric comorbidity in children after the 1988 earthquake in Armenia. Journal of the American Academy of Child and Adolescent Psychiatry 34, 1174–1184.

Green, B. L., Koral, M., Grace, M. C. et al. (1991) Children and disaster: age, gender and parental effects on symptoms. Journal of the American Academy of Child and Adolescent Psychiatry 30, 945–951.

Greenwald, R. and Rubin, A. (1999) Brief assessment of children's post-traumatic symptoms: development and preliminary validation of parent and child scales. Research on Social Work Practice 9, 61–75.

Handford, H. A., Mayes, S. O., Mattison, R. E., Humphrey, F. J., Bagnato, S. and Bixler, E. O. (1986) Child and parent reaction to the TMI nuclear accident. Journal of the American Academy of Child and Adolescent Psychiatry 25, 346–355.

Horowitz, M. J Wilner, N. and Alvarez, W. (1979) Impact of event scale: a measure of subjective stress. Psychosomatic Medicine 41, 209–218.

Hubbard, J., Realmuto, G. M., Northwood, A. K. and Masten, A. S. (1995) Comorbidity of psychiatric diagnoses with posttraumatic stress disorder in survivors of childhood trauma. Journal of the American Academy of Child and Adolescent Psychiatry 34, 1167–1173.

Kashani, J. H., Orvaschel, H., Burk, J. P. and Reid, J. C. (1985) Informant variance: The issue of parent–child disagreement. Journal of the American Academy of Child and Adolescent Psychiatry 24, 437–441.

Kinzie, J. D., Sack, W., Angell, R., Clarke, G. and Ben, R. (1989) A three year follow-up of Cambodian young people traumatized as children. Journal of the American Academy of Child and Adolescent Psychiatry 28, 501–504.

Kiser, L. J., Heston, J., Millsap, P. A. and Pruitt, D. B. (1991) Physical and sexual abuse in childhood: Relationship with post-traumatic stress disorder. Journal of the American Academy of Child and Adolescent Psychiatry 30, 776–783.

Kovacs, M. (1985) The Children's Depression Inventory (CDI). Psychopharmacology Bulletin 21, 995–998.

Laor, N., Wolmer, L., Mayes, L. C., Gershon, A., Weizman, R. and Cohen, D. J. (1997) Israeli preschool children under scuds: a 30-month follow-up. Journal of the American Academy of Child and Adolescent Psychiatry 36, 349–356.

Lonigan, C. J., Shannon, M. P., Finch, A. J., Daugherty, T. K. and Taylor, C. M. (1991) Children's reactions to a natural disaster: symptom severity and degree of exposure. Advances in Behaviour Research and Therapy 13, 135–154.

March, J. S., Amaya-Jackson, L., Terry, R. and Costanzo, P. (1997) Post-traumatic symptomatology in children and adolescents after an industrial fire. Journal of the American Academy of Child and Adolescent Psychiatry 36, 1080–1088.

Max, J. E., Koele, S. L., Smith, W. L. et al. (1998) Psychiatric disorders in children and adolescents after severe traumatic brain injury: a controlled study. Journal of the American Academy of Child and Adolescent Psychiatry 37, 832–840.

McFarlane, A. C. (1987) Post-traumatic phenomena in a longitudinal study of children following a natural disaster. Journal of the American Academy of Child and Adolescent Psychiatry 26, 764–769.

McFarlane, A. C., Polikansky, S. K. and Irwin, C. (1987) A longitudinal study of the psychological morbidity in children due to a natural disaster. Psychological Medicine 17, 727–738.

McLeer, S. V., Debbinger, E., Atkins, M. S., Foa E. B. and Ralphe, D. L. (1988) Post-traumatic stress disorder in sexually abused children. Journal of the American Academy of Child and Adolescent Psychiatry 27, 650–654.

Mirza, K. A. H., Bhadrinath, B. R., Goodyer, I. M. and Gilmour, C. (1998) Post-traumatic stress disorder in children and adolescents following road traffic accidents. British Journal of Psychiatry 172, 443–447.

Pynoos, R. S. and Eth, S. (1986) Witness to violence: the child interview. Journal of the American Academy of Child and Adolescent Psychiatry 25, 306–319.

Pynoos, R. S., Frederick, C., Nader, K. et al. (1987) Life threat and posttraumatic stress in school-age children. Archives of General Psychiatry 44, 1057–1063.

Reynolds, C. R. and Richmond, B. O. (1978) What I think and feel: a revised measure of children's manifest anxiety. Journal of Abnormal Child Psychology 6, 271–282.

Rossman, R. B. B., Bingham, R. D. and Emde, R. N. (1997) Symptomatology and adaptive functioning for children exposed to normative stressors, dog attack and parental violence. Journal of the American Academy of Child and Adolescent Psychiatry 36, 1089–1097.

Sack, W. H., Clarke, G., Him C. et al. (1993) A 6-year follow-up study of Cambodian refugee adolescents traumatized as children. Journal of the American Academy of Child and Adolescent Psychiatry 32, 431–437.

Sack, W. H., McSharry, S., Clarke, G. N., Kinney, R., Seeley, J. and Lewinsohn, P. (1994) The Khmer adolescent project, I: epidemiologic findings in two generations of Cambodian refugees. Journal of Nervous and Mental Disease 182, 387–395.

Scheeringa, M. S., Zeanah, C. H., Drell, M. J. and Larrieu, J. A. (1995) Two approaches to the diagnosis of posttraumatic stress disorder in infancy and early childhood Journal of the American Academy of Child and Adolescent Psychiatry 34, 191–200.

Shannon, M. P., Lonigan, C. J., Finch, A. J. and Taylor, C. M. (1994) Children exposed to disaster, I: epidemiology of post-traumatic symptoms and symptom profiles. Journal of the American Academy of Child and Adolescent Psychiatry 33, 80–93.

Shaw, J. A., Applegate, B., Tanner, S. et al. (1995) Psychological effects of hurricane Andrew on an elementary school population. Journal of the American Academy of Child and Adolescent Psychiatry 34, 1185–1192.

Stores, G. (1996) Practitioner review: assessment and treatment of sleep disorders in children and adolescents. Jounal of Child Psychology and Psychiatry 37, 907–925.

Terr, L. C. (1985) Children traumatized in small groups. In Eth, S. and Pynoos, R. S. (eds), Post-Traumatic Stress Disorder in Children, pp. 45–70. Washington, D.C.: American Psychiatric Press.

Terr, L. C. (1989) Family anxiety after traumatic events. Journal of Clinical Psychiatry 50, 15–19.

Terr, L. C. (1991) Childhood traumas – an outline and overview. American Journal of Psychiatry 148, 10–20.

Winje, D. and Ulvik, A. (1998) Long-term outcome of trauma in children: the psychological consequences of a bus accident. Journal of Child Psychology and Psychiatry 39, 635–642.

Yuille, J. C., Hunter, R., Joffe, R. and Zaparniuk, J. (1993) Interviewing children in sexual abuse cases. In Goodman, G. S. and Bottoms, B. L. (eds), Child Victims, Child Witnesses: Understanding and Improving Testimony. New York: Guilford.

Yule, W. (1994) Posttraumatic stress disorders. In Rutter, M., Taylor, E. and Hersov, L. (eds), Child and Adolescent Psychiatry – Modern Approaches, 3rd edn, pp. 392–406. Oxford: Blackwell Scientific.

Yule, W. and Williams, R. A. (1990) Post-traumatic stress reactions in children. Journal of Traumatic Stress 3, 279–295.

Yule, W., Udwin, O. and Murdoch, K. (1990) The 'Jupiter' sinking: Effects on children's fears, depression and anxiety. Journal of Child Psychology and Psychiatry 31, 1051–1061.

Chapter 7
Individual treatments for children and adolescents with post-traumatic stress disorder: unlocking children's trauma

Rosie Shepperd

Traumatic events can be dealt with by an individual by using defence mechanisms of denial, splitting, repression and isolation. The traumatic incident can be isolated and held as ego-dystonic, but will remain unprocessed and can re-emerge as emotional and behavioural disturbance or psychopathology. Individual therapies using a psychodynamic understanding aim to allow the child to become aware of the experiences that previously have been unmanageable, to process the memories and reintegrate them into the child's world without being overwhelmed by the terror of traumatic memories.

Children coming to a child and adolescent psychiatry service following a traumatic experience will need an assessment within the family context with an opportunity to talk to parents alone, and the child alone; an assessment of family functioning; and an assessment of the child's level of psychopathology, the level of disturbance in other areas of the child's life, for example at school and in their social network, so that treatment can be planned to impact on the areas where help is most needed.

A psychodynamic understanding can be used in a variety of settings, from brief interventions, play therapy and observations in other settings than the clinic, as well as in individual therapy. Child psychotherapists are a rare resource but are often part of a multidisciplinary team in a child and adolescent psychiatric service, and can give supervision or consultation to the team's work.

Place of psychotherapies in helping traumatised children

Therapeutic interventions for children suffering post-traumatic symptoms may include the following approaches:

131

- pharmacotherapy
- psychotherapies (e.g. family therapy, group therapy, cognitive-behavioural therapy, psychodynamic psychotherapy including play therapy and art therapy)
- other therapies (e.g. hypnotherapy, eye movement desensitisation and reprocessing – see Chapter 11).

As PTSD is increasingly anticipated after disasters and recognised in victims, management strategies and therapeutic approaches continue to develop. Research for effective treatments of children and adolescents has always lagged behind that for adults, and this remains true for treatment of PTSD as well as other areas of therapeutic need. Udwin (1993) described much of the research to date on treatment of PTSD in children and stated the need for systematic, carefully controlled evaluations of treatments for PTSD symptoms in children.

This chapter describes treatments used in current practice, some of which have not been evaluated using formal research methodology, but have been shown to be helpful in reducing symptoms. Psychological treatments are being evaluated and no doubt in the next few years evidence-based treatment plans will be recommended.

Debriefing

Recommended practices have changed over the years, from the advice that if parents could stay calm in the face of disaster, children would cope better too. This can lead to emotional numbing in order to present a coping face to the child, and can reduce the possibility of talking about the traumatic experiences.

Early intervention is recommended, with debriefing by teachers, parents, health visitors or trauma counsellors. This should involve discussion of the facts around the event and clarification of any misconceptions. There should be encouragement of expression if the child is avoiding recognition of the trauma. The child may need to tell and retell, to play and replay the trauma. The family should be reunited as soon as possible after a traumatic event. Children will gain comfort that they are not alone with their feelings; parental involvement is very important (Yule and Canterbury 1994).

An evaluation of psychological debriefing (Robinson and Mitchell 1993) describes its value in a study of emergency services, welfare and hospital personnel in Australia. Psychological debriefing was reported to reduce stress symptoms in almost all personnel who reported a stress response. The effectiveness of the debriefing was found to derive from talking particularly with others who had experienced the same situation.

One child is not usually traumatised in isolation. Their siblings, parents, school friends and community may also be traumatised to a greater or lesser extent. Treatment approaches need to embrace the whole network of the child.

Pharmacotherapy

Black et al. (1997) describe the use of pharmacotherapy for symptom reduction to enable access to other therapies. The author proposes that evaluation of medication used as an adjunct to psychological therapy will enhance the treatment of PTSD over the next few years. They describe the possible use of beta-blockers for anxiety, and serotonin reuptake inhibitors and monoamine oxidase inhibitors – classes of antidepressant medication with particular efficacy on symptoms of anxiety with depression – as drugs worth considering for the treatment of co-morbidity in children and adolescents suffering symptoms after trauma. For example, a young person may be so disabled by depression and anxiety that medication is needed to improve their mental health to enable them to attend sessions for therapy and to begin normal social interaction with their peers.

McIvor (1998) reviews the use of drugs in PTSD and comments that the degree of symptom reduction with drug therapy is not as marked as with psychological treatments, although it is particularly beneficial with co-morbid depression. Ideally medication should be used in combination with psychotherapy in order that symptoms resistant to pharmacological treatments are tackled and issues of personal meanings and values are resolved.

Psychodynamic psychotherapies

Treatment of PTSD aims to reduce disabling symptoms following severe or life-threatening traumas. Not all survivors will require treatment. The symptoms experienced include re-experiencing phenomena, avoidance phenomena and symptoms of increased arousal. Survivors may experience a wide range of additional symptoms causing distress and significant interference in every-day functioning, such as poor impulse control, behavioural change and relationship difficulties. Co-morbid conditions such as depression and anxiety can complicate treatment and impede recovery.

The dynamics of traumatisation allow the traumatic event to be isolated and split off from the individual as a defence from overwhelming anxiety. This unprocessed memory needs to be accessed in a safe environment in small amounts, without the individual being overwhelmed, in order for them to assimilate, digest and process experiences that have previously been impossible to manage (Creamer 1993).

A variety of individual therapies is used for PTSD in children and adolescents; the choice depends partly on the development level of the child and also on the theoretical framework of the treatment. The developmental stage of the child will affect the assimilation and expression of the traumatic event, and the appropriate therapeutic approaches used. Gaensbauer and Siegel (1995) describe specific techniques they have found helpful in the treatment of post-traumatic stress reactions in infants and toddlers. They outline the various levels of disturbance that the child experiences:

- first, the direct impact of the trauma itself
- secondly, a range of emotional responses dependant on the resilience of the child and family
- thirdly, the effect on the accomplishment of concurrent developmental tasks
- fourthly, the impact of trauma on future development
- lastly, the impact of trauma and its symptomatology on the child's interactions with their family and peers.

The traumatised infant will have intensified needs for security, regressive behavioural and physiological functioning, and increased levels of hypervigilance and arousal will require heightened levels of sensitivity on the part of the caregivers. From the second year of life Gaensbauer and Siegel (1995) describe play enactment as the cornerstone of treatment for traumatised infants and toddlers. Until representational play emerges in the second year and the therapist can use play to convey empathy, holding and comforting the toddler is the most effective way of conveying empathic understanding. The parents would be present for this psychotherapeutic work.

Traumas to children may be short and single or long-standing, multiple traumas. Psychic trauma below the age of 28–36 months tends to leave behavioural or somatic memories rather than verbal memories (Terr 1988).The severity of exposure to the trauma, which can include the physical distance of the child from the traumatic event, affects the child's pattern of response to that event.

Saylor et al. (1992) describe 200 preschoolers' play and verbalisations in the year following a devastating hurricane. The children showed re-enactment of the hurricane in play, discussion of the storm and fears of storms. They describe high functioning, well-supported children as showing developmentally appropriate attempts to cope with their distress.

The criteria for diagnosis of post-traumatic stress disorder may not all be reached in medium- or long-term adverse reactions to trauma. Variations in the individual response may be dependent on several factors:

- **Characteristics of the stressor**: the more traumatic the experience, the greater the degree and duration of exposure, the greater the risk of traumatisation.
- **Personal characteristics**: the developmental stage of the child, cognitive style, coping resources, previous experiences of loss and trauma, pre-existing medical and psychiatric problems can all influence the extent of traumatisation.
- **Recovery environment**: the extent of support provided by family, peer group and community can influence recovery, as can the social and societal context of personal disaster (Terr 1991).

For example, Black (1988) describes how difficult it can be for a child who has witnessed the murder of his mother by his father and has effectively lost both parents, one by death and the other by committal to prison or psychiatric hospital. The child is likely to be placed with relatives, perhaps the maternal grandparents, who may be unable to help the child grieve because of their anger and grief over the death of their daughter at the hands of the child's father.

The child can show a variety of responses – adjustment reactions, complicated grief reactions, a range of anxiety symptoms. Major depression can arise, especially if secondary adversities accumulate as a result of trauma. There can be exacerbation of pre-existing vulnerabilities and disorders. For a child to be able to use an individual therapeutic approach to PTSD they must be able to symbolically represent or re-experience the event in bearable amounts within a safe and supportive context. This can be a challenge for the child and also the therapist.

Traumatic material is highly emotionally charged, and children's responses are often coloured by graphic memories based on direct sensory impressions. The clinician must be willing to discuss these matters without avoiding material that may be anxiety provoking for either child or therapist.

The clinician's ability to tolerate the pain and distress, and to hold those feelings – described by Fonagy et al. (1994) as **reflective self-function** – enables the child to come to terms with their experience, and to take back the traumatic memory in a digestible form. Reflective self-functioning can serve as a protection against adversity. This function arises out of the child's experience with their caregiver. Before a baby can make sense of its own experience it has to have repeated experiences of its caregiver trying to understand it. This requires the parent to tune in and be responsive to the baby's communications, and then to be able to think about what is being communicated and respond accordingly. The receptive parent's mind is described by Bion (1962) as a container for the baby's communications. The process of thinking or reflecting on these communications by the parent, which informs his or her response to the baby, is termed **containment**. Commonly used structures around individual therapy with children are a useful mechanism to allow the child and therapist to do their task. These include assessment of the child and family, and support for the family while the child has individual therapy, by the same therapist or by another if that is thought desirable.

The setting should be predictable and reliable, for example weekly sessions at the same time, in the same room, with the same toys and therapist, and the session protected from interruption. This will give the child a sense of containment, and the predictability will reduce anxiety for child and therapist. Some children will find a well-stocked toy room overwhelming and therapists may choose a few materials to bring into each session for that child. The provision of a box with dolls, animals, pens, paper, glue, scissors, string, can help a child feel they have a place in the therapist's mind, by bringing the same box each session and realising that no one else uses their box between the sessions.

The therapist should have access to regular supervision with a colleague who has had experience of individual therapy with children. There are few child psychotherapists working in general child and adolescent psychiatry, but more child psychiatrists are having training experiences of child psychotherapy cases, as are nurses, occupational therapists and psychologists in child mental health. The therapist should also be aware of their own psychopathology which may unconsciously interfere with the therapeutic process. This can be a function of supervision but the therapist may benefit from personal therapy before working with such vulnerable clients.

Within the context of the sessions the approach should not be overconfrontational; there is no need to extract the grisly details from the child. There also should be care not to avoid anxiety-provoking material; the child may need to re-experience or represent the trauma to gain mastery.

Most children will readily show material linked to their trauma, but some will avoid the feelings and thoughts associated with the trauma.

Case example

A 5 year old boy was referred for assessment as part of a personal injury compensation claim. He lived with his father and mother and one younger brother.

Two years prior to the assessment he had been walking to the park with his mother, holding a football. They were going to a play area behind their house, accessed by an alley. One of the houses adjacent to the alley had two Alsatian dogs in the garden, and the fence was broken. As the boy and his mother passed by the dogs attacked the 3 year old from behind, biting him in the back. The owner of the dogs and the boy's mother chased the dogs away, and the boy's father who had been at home with the baby heard the snarling and barking several houses away. The boy was taken home and the bites found after inspection of his torn shirt. He was very distressed at the time and was further distressed by the treatment of cleaning and dressing the wounds in the hospital accident and emergency department. He developed nightmares within a week of this attack, was clingy to his mother and more withdrawn at playgroup. He was very fearful of returning to the park and fearful of dogs. He would startle at hearing dogs bark. His mother was hypervigilant on his behalf, scanning the street for dogs before they went out.

The parents had received no counselling from the accident and emergency department or from the general practitioner or health visitor who were also involved. They did not talk about the attack as they feared enhancing the child's anxiety. After initial assessment, the boy had five sessions of play therapy, and the whole family attended two family therapy sessions. The play therapy consisted of unstructured sessions where the boy was allowed to choose his toys or activities and engage the therapist as he wanted. The therapist observed and commented on the themes of the drawing or play. During the sessions the therapist noticed an opening up of the child's play. He became more inquisitive and interactive, more animated in expression and more talkative. He spoke about the dog attack only once, describing his belief that the dogs had punctured his football, which they had not. He was able to describe his nightmares which were of dogs barking, a man shouting and waking up in a state of terror.

In the family sessions the parents were helped to talk about the dog attack and their fears of making their son worse. They decided to arrange to meet a relative with a 'friendly' dog and try to help their son differentiate between 'bad' dogs and safe dogs. This was successful. The nightmares reduced and were gone before therapy ended, and everyone was in agreement about the freeing up of the boy, with increased confidence at home and at nursery.

Post-traumatic responses

In the individual setting the therapist hopes to help the child to acknowledge the post-traumatic responses, whether rooted in the trauma or re-evoking memories of earlier difficulties. Children may be helped by being told that many children have reactions to traumatic events with a range of experiences that may help them not to feel isolated and gain reassurance that they are not 'going crazy'. The therapist's knowledge of the usual and expected responses to trauma can be helpful in reducing a child's anxiety. Knowledge that others have reacted in a similar way can allow the child a greater sense of inner control. In beginning to integrate feelings with post-traumatic symptoms the child can be reassured that they are not 'going mad'

Cognitive distortions

Children commonly misunderstand how traumatic events took place and their misinterpretations can prolong their anxiety. Children also readily take on blame for events happening, as if it were punishment for a misdemeanour. Their sense of guilt and responsibility can be addressed in an individual setting and reinforced with the family by discussion of the known facts around the traumatic event, and explanations, responsibility and guilt can be clarified and given a sense of perspective.

Post-traumatic play

Post-traumatic play may be allowing a child an alternative outcome, a happier ending, and therefore may be useful in reducing anxiety on a temporary basis. Post-traumatic play may also be ineffective in reducing anxiety. It can be a literal re-enactment of traumatic events, with themes being compulsively repeated. In this situation the connection between post-traumatic play and traumatic events remains unconscious. The therapist interprets the link and this can allow exploration of the feelings associated with the trauma. Children can then begin to explore the terror, rage, sadness or helplessness as these themes emerge in play, and develop a sense of internal control.

Case example

A 7 year old boy presented for treatment following a road traffic accident, when he ran out from behind an ice cream van and was hit by a speeding car. He sustained a head injury and leg and facial scarring. Along with nightmares, hypervigilance and increased clinging to his mother, he occupied himself in endless games of car crashes where a creature called Fred was the victim, usually smashed to pieces by the impact of the car. Fred did escape sometimes, however, and could also destroy the cars as well. The child had been stuck with these symptoms for over a year following the accident before receiving treatment.

Here the post-traumatic play is the boy's attempt to gain control of a situation where he was terrified and felt helpless. However, without some therapeutic input he was stuck in repetitive play with a narrow repertoire of imaginary games.

Revenge fantasies

It is important to acknowledge and allow for the discussion of revenge fantasies, which are very common in children and adolescents. They need to be able to express their anger in a safe environment. As the revenge fantasies are discussed and accepted, the obsessive preoccupation will diminish. The child may also need to look at their ideas of self-blame, guilt and helplessness from the time of their trauma. These memories may be accompanied by intense anxiety, obsessional repetitions, extreme grief and overwhelming need to flee the situation, in this case the therapeutic session. The therapist must be able to tolerate the emotions, contain the child in the setting and help them to integrate the experience as being located in the past.

Future concerns

The child may also express their distrust about the future, and concern about the survival of significant others in their lives (Yule and Williams 1990).

Trauma and grief

Children are often bereaved as a consequence of trauma. Pynoos (1992) emphasises the need to help the children distinguish their trauma–related responses from those related to grief. He suggests that the traumatic circumstances of the death may need to be addressed before the grieving process can begin. Klein (1932) and Freud (1945) described the use of observing children's play as a link to the child's feelings and anxieties. They did not use the traumatic play as a therapeutic medium but used observation of play to make a diagnosis.

Levy (1939) developed a structured play technique in which the child was presented with a play situation reconstructing the anxiety-provoking event. The therapist did not offer any direct interpretation to the child but allowed the child to play out their anxieties with the toy. Therapists following Levy's lead began to interpret the child's distress within the metaphor of the child's play and the children improved (Terr 1989).

Hopkins (1986) describes the effect of trauma on the individual as linking a specific external event with internal psychic conditions, and indicates the shattering, devastating and generally overwhelming effect of trauma on the ego. She describes spontaneous recovery as possible, but that subsequent development is pathological. Her paper describes the treatment of two children with analytic psychotherapy and discusses treatment issues for the child, family and therapist.

Terr (1989) describes how despite interpretation, post-traumatic play goes on and on. The therapist has to help the child detach from the compulsive repetitions, enunciating the feelings that are part of the trauma. She describes naming these feelings – terror, rage, sadness, shame, excitement – and both the child and therapist can apply the feelings to pieces of the old experience as the child plays.

The therapist may also link other repetitive behaviours, dreams, visualisations, actions, to the traumatic experience. They can offer the child new coping possibilities and integrate the trauma into a longer view of life by weaving rehabilitation and reward into the child's play.

Case example

An 8 year old girl was referred with aggressive outbursts at home following a sexual assault by an older male at the same time as a period of hospitalisation for her mother. The girl was described as having a difficult temperament, poor verbal skills and low tolerance for frustration. Her parents were unable to deal with her anger or aspects of the sexual abuse. She was experiencing temper tantrums with physical and verbal aggression, recurrent flashbacks from the sexual abuse, and night terrors. Because of the intensity of the behavioural difficulties she was admitted to an in-patient unit and part of her treatment was individual therapy twice a week with an occupational therapist.

The themes of the play were strictly set by the child mostly using role play. Initially the play involved conflict between friends, animals being asked to keep secrets yet threatened with death if they lied. Figures were drowned or buried in sand with rescue attempts making things worse. Disguises were used but she was desperate to be seen as the little girl before the trauma. As time moved on the play changed to crime and punishment themes where the therapist was the prisoner being given stricter sentences from the police (the girl). This 'cops and robbers' theme continued with friends giving false evidence, lifetime imprisonment, etc., until it began to have a humorous presentation, with funny voices being used. Then the child was able to move on. In her next sessions she wanted to make things for a dolls' house, for the first time bringing the home into the sessions. Then she made biscuits to take home, and it became clear that the issues had been dealt with and the child was looking to move on.

These individual sessions were part of an in-patient treatment and crucially important for this girl as they provided a space for her on a regular basis where she could explore her feelings, behave as she felt necessary without harming herself or the therapist, and receive some feedback or interpretations about the content of her play and the meanings behind it. She was able to process her trauma through play and the relationship with the therapist and move on to a freer style of interaction, with diminution of her behavioural problems.

Art therapy

Psychotherapists working with children tend to have art or play materials to hand, finding that the art process offers the child a non-verbal, symbolic language through which to tell their story. Arguile (1992) describes the art therapy process, with boundaries of time, staying within the session, the unacceptability of damage to the room, therapist or themselves. Children are free to draw, paint, make or say anything they like within these boundaries, this permission often sparking off the session. The therapist will accept a child's picture without judgement, and may enter the child's world with a question about the picture.

Children may use art as a way of avoiding difficult issues. It may be a way of conveying special or secret information. The therapist is careful in the area of interpretation as art objects can say all manner of things. The unconscious is given expression in art therapy and children can be surprised or shocked when they realise what they have produced. The process of doing art can help people become more aware of feelings previously hidden from them, and can be used to depict experiences which are hard to put into words (Liebman 1990).

Zambelli et al. (1989) describe the use of art therapy for bereaved children. Non-verbal activities allow the children to act out conflicts that they may be unable or afraid to talk about in traditional insight-orien-tated talk therapies. In an art therapy programme, these feelings are initially addressed through the safety of drawing or painting, and later through the child's direct verbalisations about his art work. Art therapy can assist development of a sense of worth, communication skills, social co-operation, problem solving and increased personal efficacy. The skills of an art therapist can be used to help a child unlock and articulate post-traumatic memories.

Family therapy

If an entire family has been traumatised in the same way, family therapy can be a helpful treatment approach in the first stages. Family treatment following trauma is most useful to the child if the therapist provides the child with adequate time and space for his own verbal expression. Traumatised children tend to be more reticent in talking about their experiences than adults involved in the same disaster.

Terr (1989) states her opinion that the most likely symptoms to subside using a family approach to PTSD are personality changes coming from habitual re-enactments, fears and trauma-related grief. The least likely symptoms to resolve would be those symptoms connected to the inner emotional life of the child, post-traumatic play, trauma-related fantasy, paranormal experiences and the sense of a limited future. Family therapy may not be helpful in situations where the trauma is occurring through incest or abuse. Children need to be able to express their rage and often cannot do so in front of their abusers.

Family therapy enables the family to open up and discuss painful areas which may have been kept silent for fear of upsetting the child, or the child's fear of upsetting the parent. Thus family members may all individually have been suffering greatly, but by sharing the fears and anxieties can reduce distress. Information about the traumatic event can be shared, and a sense of reality by correction of misperceptions, assumptions and guilt and blame can help the process of acknowledging and assimilating traumatic memories.

From an initial family approach the therapeutic needs of individual members which may need addressing in their own right will become apparent; however, a family approach remains essential to utilise the family's resources in helping the child, monitoring progress and addressing dysfunctional behaviours.

McFarlane (1987) describes post-traumatic symptoms in a population of Australian schoolchildren and finds that the mother's responses to the disaster were better predictors of post-traumatic symptoms in the children than the children's direct exposure to the disaster. One third of the children in the study were found to have a continuing preoccupation with their exposure to a bush fire 26 months after the disaster. The intensity of post-traumatic phenomena observed by the parents 8 months after the disaster was significantly correlated with symptoms 18 months later. McFarlane found that separation from the parents in the days immediately after the fire, continuing maternal preoccupation with the disaster, and changed family functioning were more powerful determinants of post-traumatic phenomena in the children than were exposure to the disaster or losses sustained. This provides some support for the observation that children's responses to traumatic events are determined more by the parents' attitudes than by the intensity of the danger experienced. McFarlane (1987) suggests that if a mother continues to experience intrusive and unwanted memories of the fire, she would find it very difficult to hear her child's anxieties and memories of the disaster. The children's preoccupation about the disaster may be determined by their awareness of their parents' recurring imagery of the event, independent of their own experience of the fire. Mothers with most post-traumatic imagery were also the most overprotective, and this maternal anxiety is likely to be easily perceived by children, making it more difficult for them to resolve their own anxieties and heightening their sensitivity to further trauma. This highlights the need for assessment of all the family and provision of treatment to other family members as well as the referred child if appropriate.

Case example

A family of two girls and their parents were referred with behavioural disturbance, oppositional attitudes and particular difficulties around bedtimes. The older girl, aged 7, had lost her best friend a year ago in a house fire. The fire had been across the road and all the family could recall the smell of the smoke, the sounds of the fire crew and the spectacle of the fire. They were all devastated to find that a child had been killed. The girls had four sessions as a sibling pair with an occupational therapist doing grief work and enquiring into post-traumatic symptoms, of which there were relatively few. The parents were seen by a psychiatric nurse to assess parenting issues and it became clear that mother was unable to adopt a behavioural approach to managing the girls, particularly at bedtime, as she was still so traumatised over the loss of this child. She could not instil a sense of authority at bedtime as she feared losing her children in the night and had to check on them up to 10 times a night. Individual work with mother was necessary before the family could make progress.

Case example

A 6 year old boy was involved in a car crash with his family, sustaining facial cuts and leg injuries. His mother had whiplash injury; the father was not injured. The boy was referred with nightmares and bed wetting, having previously been dry at night for over 2 years. He was also reluctant to leave mother in the mornings to go to school and was noticed by his teachers to be less confident. His play involved car crashes and also many references to damaged children, fatal injuries and disability. The mother was receiving antidepressant medication from her general practitioner. After the initial assessment, the boy was offered play therapy weekly and the parents seen every 3 weeks. The boy's symptoms settled over a few weeks, during which he spent much of his sessions engaged in repetitive play, with him describing a fox who was involved in accidents, sometimes being injured, sometimes escaping. The car drivers were also sometimes killed, taken to prison, or tracked down by the resourceful fox and attacked for revenge. The therapist allowed this play but began to help the boy to own the accident as something which happened to him, that it was an accident, and the driver was not prosecuted. His anger and distress were named and worked with, and his play expanded out of the set post-traumatic play.

The family were discharged, but about 7 months later they were re-referred with a recurrence in the boy's symptoms. On detailed questioning it became apparent that the boy's symptoms were not the same; he was not having nightmares, or post-traumatic play. His confidence at school was reasonably similar to what it had been at the end of therapy. He was talking about bad drivers, the dangerousness of cars and drivers going to prison. His mother believed he still had post-traumatic symptoms, and in an observed family play session the mother was noticed to be encouraging talk about accidents and damage and made reference to the facial scarring of her son, and how distressed he was about this. Shortly after this re-referral a request from the solicitor arrived for a psychiatric assessment for a compensation claim.

Group therapies

Group work can be a useful way of providing psychotherapy to traumatised children. Groups have been particularly used for victims of sexual abuse. Group therapy is described in Chapter 9 of this volume.

Behavioural therapy

Desensitisation therapy

Desensitisation can be an effective treatment of PTSD in children. It can be necessary as an emergency measure before any other treatments are started. This might occur in the situation where a traumatised child must first overcome a fear in order to go back to school or to venture outside the house after an overwhelming event.

Classical conditioning

Methods such as flooding, systematic desensitisation and relaxation, with holding, may be used but these approaches should be used by an experienced psychologist. Thompson et al. (1995) describe exposure therapy based on deconditioning for PTSD in adults, which showed statistically significant improvements on four assessment scales and considerable short-term efficacy in the management of PTSD.

Operant conditioning

Operant conditioning methods are commonly used to change behaviour. Reinforcement of wanted behaviours and extinction of undesirable behaviours can be affected by shaping the behaviour; rewards such as star charts can be used. Massed practice can be used to extinguish repetitive activities. Response prevention can also be helpful. Again, supervision by an experienced psychologist is necessary.

Cognitive therapy

Cognitive therapy is probably the most useful behavioural approach and is gaining research validation as a treatment of choice for older children. This is discussed in full in Chapter 8 of this volume.

Other therapies

Hypnotherapy

Everstine and Everstine (1993) describe the use of direct and Ericsonian hypnotic induction as being successful with children as young as 2 years to help with symptoms such as hypervigilance, sleep disorders and emotional blocking. The child is enlisted as an active participant and can achieve a greater feeling of mastery over their symptoms.

Treatment in this medium can be a positive experience in at least three ways:

- pleasant thoughts and feelings are paired with traumatic ones, thus diluting their impact
- in the same way that acquisition of a skill raises confidence, so does mastery of a symptom
- a beneficial interaction with an adult may make up for interactions that have become strained since the traumatic event.

The author also describes the use of audio tapes containing therapeutic messages which they describe as being generally effective in anxious or phobic children, or those with sleep difficulties.

Eye movement desensitisation and reprocessing (EMDR)

This new and exciting treatment approach is described in Chapter 11 in this volume.

References

Arguile, R. (1992) Art therapy with children and adolescents. In Waller, D. and Gilroy, A. (eds), Art Therapy: A Handbook. Philadelphia: Open University Press.

Bion, W. R. (1962) Learning from experience. In Seven Servants: Four Works by Wilfred R. Bion, pp.1–111. New York: Jason Aronson.

Black, D. and Kaplan, T. (1988) Father kills mother: Issues and problems encountered by a child psychiatric team. British Journal of Psychiatry 153, 624–630.

Black, D., Newman, M., Haris-Hendriks, J. and Mezey, G. (1997) Psychological Trauma, A Developmental Approach. London: Gaskell (Royal College of Psychiatrists).

Creamer, M. (1993) Recent developments in post-traumatic stress disorder. Behavioural Change 10, 219–227.

Everstine, D. S. and Eversteine, L. (eds) (1993) The Trauma Response. Treatment for Emotional Injury. New York: W. W. Norton.

Fonagy, P., Steele, M., Steele, H., Higgit, A. and Target, M. (1994) The theory and practice of resilience. Journal of Child Psychology and Psychiatry 35, 231–257.

Freud, A. (1945) Indications for child analysis: the evaluation of infantile neurosis and conclusion. Psychoanalytic Study of the Child 1, 131–149.

Gaensbauer, T. J. and Siegel, C. H. (1995) Therapeutic approaches to post-traumatic stress disorder in infants and toddlers. Infant Mental Health Journal 16(4), 292–305.

Hopkins, J. (1986) Solving the mystery of the monsters: steps towards the recovery from trauma. Journal of Child Psychotherapy 12(1), 61–71.

Klein, M. (1932) Psychoanalysis of Children, International Psychoanalytic Library series No 22, Strachey, A. (trans). London: L. V. Woolf-Hogarth Press, 1932, third edition, 1949, reprinted 1950.

Liebman, M. (1990) Art Therapy in Practice. London: Jessica Kingsley.

McFarlane, A. (1987) Post traumatic phenomena in a longitudinal study of children following a natural disaster. Journal of American Academy of Child and Adolescent Psychiatry 26, 764–769.

McIvor, R. (1998) Post-traumatic stress disorder: the role of drug therapy. Progress in Neurology and Psychiatry 2(5), 18–22.

Pynoos, R. S. (1992) Grief and trauma in children and adolescents. Bereavement Care 11, 2–10.

Robinson, R. C. and Mitchell, J. T. (1993) Evaluation of psychological debriefings. Journal of Traumatic Stress 6, 367–382.

Saylor, C. F., Swenson, C. C. and Powell, P. (1992) Hurricane Hugo blows down the broccoli: Pre-schoolers post disaster play and adjustment. Child Psychiatry and Human Development 22(3), 139–149.

Terr, L. (1988) What happens to early memories of trauma? A study of twenty children under age 5 at the time of documented traumatic events. Journal of the American Academy of Child and Adolescent Psychiatry 27, 96–104.

Terr, L. (1989) Treating psychic trauma in children: a preliminary discussion. Journal of Traumatic Stress 2, 2–20.

Terr, L. (1991) Childhood traumas: an outline and overview. American Journal of Psychiatry 148, 10–20.

Thompson, J. A., Charlton, P. F. C., Kerry, R., Lee, D. and Turner, S. W. (1995) An open trial of exposure therapy based on deconditioning for post traumatic stress disorder. British Journal of Clinical Psychology 34, 407–416.

Udwin, O. (1993) Children's reactions to traumatic events. Journal of Child Psychology and Psychiatry 34 (2), 115–127.

Yule, W. and Canterbury, R. (1994) The treatment of post traumatic stress disorder in children and adolescents. International Review of Psychiatry 6, 141–151.

Yule, W. and Williams, R. (1990) Post traumatic stress reactions in children. Journal of Traumatic Stress 3, 279–295.

Zambelli, G. C., Clark, E. J. and Heegaard, M. (1989) Art therapy for bereaved children. In Wadeson, H., Durkin, J. and Perach, D. (eds), Advances in Art Therapy. New York: John Wiley.

Chapter 8
Cognitive-behavioural therapy for post-traumatic stress disorder in children and adolescents

Tania Phillips

This chapter covers the rationale behind the use of cognitive-behavioural therapy (CBT) for treating post-traumatic stress disorder (PTSD), briefly reviews the research on the use of CBT to treat PTSD in young people and describes some of the techniques involved.

Definitions and models of PTSD

CBT is a psychological treatment intended to change maladaptive thoughts (cognitions) and behaviours. At its core lies an assumption that thoughts, behaviours and emotions are all interrelated so that changing one will exert an effect on the others. Usually the treatment is focused on aspects of behaviour which are unfavourable, or on the maladaptive thoughts. Sometimes adjunctive techniques are used to control directly those extremes of emotion, especially anxiety, which would otherwise interfere with the CBT.

PTSD usually consists, broadly speaking, of a triad of symptoms: hyperarousal, avoidance of reminders of the precipitating event, and re-experiencing of the event. One model which could explain the latter phenomenon is classical, or Pavlovian, **conditioning**. In this, otherwise independent stimuli, when occurring together by chance or design, can become linked in memory. So, for example, a person who has experienced a traumatic event may be reminded of that event by other stimuli which were linked with it at the time. The person may then re-experience the traumatic event, plus the associated emotions, as if it were happening all over again. In such a situation the trigger is acting as a **conditioned stimulus** and the imagery and emotions, often fear or extreme anxiety, form the **conditioned response**. Usually such links between otherwise unconnected stimuli are only forged through repeated pairings over time, and they fade if the stimuli then fail to be linked in the future, a process called **extinction**. In cases of PTSD a single, highly emotional, event seems to be enough in some individuals to create the links between mundane situations and objects, and the traumatic memories. It also seems enough to prevent the subsequent natural course of extinction which one would otherwise expect since the original trauma is not really being repeated each time the memories are triggered. It is as if the intrusive imagery and memories are themselves reinforcing the links because of their similarity in intensity to the original trauma.

The fear of re-experiencing the event, in memory or in reality, can then lead to phobic avoidance of situations and objects reminiscent of the original trauma. This avoidance of exposure prevents the sufferer from developing tolerance to the triggers and becoming less aroused, a process known as **habituation**.

With such a basis in learning theories, both phobic symptoms and intrusive imagery can be treated through behavioural components of CBT which encourage habituation and extinction. These rely on a controlled exposure to trigger stimuli such that the intrusive imagery and emotions are no longer actually reinforcing the original link.

Although many adult PTSD sufferers can recover with behavioural work alone, some benefit from cognitive work too. So far, the recognition of PTSD in children and adolescents, and so the evaluation of treatment, has lagged behind that of adults and they have usually received a combined approach.

PTSD has important cognitive components too. The impact of an event on an individual, and hence whether or not he develops PTSD, is dependent on many factors. Its meaning to that individual is particularly important and may cause some sufferers to reappraise their core beliefs about themselves, their efficacy and life in general. In particular, a sufferer may feel helpless, having failed to prevent or change the event itself, or may have a new sense of the fragility of their own life which could leave them feeling hopeless and short of time (McFarlane 1989). Such beliefs can be maladaptive to normal life, having been created in an exceptional situation, and so they can cause additional problems by decreasing the sufferer's confidence and drive (although they may also have the opposite effect in certain individuals, creating a greater hunger for experience). The cognitive aspects of CBT can be helpful in changing such maladaptive beliefs by exposing the faulty assumptions underlying them and replacing them with new, adaptive beliefs – a process called **cognitive restructuring**. It can be used directly to tackle internal attributions (self-blame) for the traumatic event; greater numbers of these attributions have been found to be associated with greater symptomatology in adolescents (Joseph et al. 1993).

Another relevant and alternative model for PTSD could be based on the theory of emotional processing (Rachman 1980). According to this theory, distressing events need to be 'emotionally processed' and so 'absorbed'. If this processing is incomplete, the individual is liable to re-experience the original emotional reaction on encountering relevant stimuli. Rachman postulated that factors which might facilitate processing included 'exposure to the disturbing material, habituation training,... vivid presentations of stimuli' and 'the evocation of controlled autonomic reactions', whereas factors impeding it included avoidance of reminders, and inability or refusal to talk about the disturbing event.

CBT outcome research

CBT has become well established as a treatment for PTSD in adults, and there are many protocols, case examples and handbooks describing the treatment according to different models. However, there is still little research evidence of its effectiveness in treating children and adolescents, partly because for a long time they were not thought to suffer from PTSD (Garmezy and Rutter 1985) and so went unrecognised and hence untreated.

The studies conducted with young populations so far can be categorised according to the types of trauma experienced. Some have looked at young people exposed to disasters at sea (Yule and Williams 1990, Joseph et al. 1993), or within the school grounds (Pynoos and Nader 1988); others have concentrated on victims of child abuse (Deblinger et al. 1997, Hyman et al. 1988, Farrell et al. 1998) or survivors of road traffic accidents (Canterbury et al. 1993) or natural disasters (Green et al. 1991). This is a relatively new field and much of the research to date has been investigating how children and adolescents react to traumatic events (Hyman et al. 1988, Yule and Williams 1990, Terr 1991, Udwin 1993), what factors predict this (Green et al. 1991, Joseph et al. 1993) and how much a very young child can remember (Terr 1988). However, more recently there has been increasing interest and research into treatment, and so the use of CBT in such populations is being evaluated and expanded, although randomised controlled trials are still lacking (Deblinger et al. 1997, Farrell et al. 1998, March et al. 1998).

Indications for CBT

PTSD is a categorical diagnosis based on the aggregation of certain symptoms after exposure to a traumatic event. The details of assessment and diagnosis are discussed elsewhere in this book. Children and adolescents may develop many non-specific additional symptoms following exposure to trauma (Yule 1991, Udwin 1993, Yule and Canterbury 1994), which do not bear a direct relation to the diagnosis, but which nevertheless may respond to treatment of the PTSD or to other CBT approaches. As already discussed, CBT is specifically indicated to treat avoidance behaviour and phobic symptoms but it can also be used for some intrusive imagery such as nightmares (Halliday 1987, Palace and Johnston 1989). Many of the other coexistent conditions (co-morbidity) may also respond to treatment with CBT, especially depression and anxiety disorders (Birmaher et al. 1996, Brent et al. 1998), which may occur particularly in adolescents (Yule and Canterbury 1994). The elements of CBT which will be useful for an individual case are determined by the type of trauma and the variety of symptoms suffered by that individual. Ideally a treatment package should be decided for each individual based on these variables, and this may include other forms of therapy (Yule and Canterbury 1994).

CBT has been used to treat groups of young people (Yule and Williams 1990) even when they have not all experienced the same type of trauma (March et al. 1998). This is because there are elements of the treatment which are useful in common to all cases of PTSD. Even so, there may be need for some individual sessions to tackle the specific thoughts and images troubling the young person (March et al. 1998).

Limitations of CBT

The main limitations of CBT are the ability and motivation of the young person. Cognitive abilities develop throughout childhood, and the ability for abstract thought does not develop until adolescence. Despite this, more concrete methods have been used to treat children with PTSD as young as 5 years old (Deblinger et al. 1997), still following the basic CBT principles. In place of abstract discussions of emotions and thought processes, the therapist and child use more practical techniques such as role play, drawings or even puppets, and may focus almost exclusively on exposure rather than understanding.

Motivation needs to be high as the process of CBT will involve the young person confronting the thoughts and images they have been fighting against and avoiding until now. It will also be particularly difficult, even impossible, for them to engage in the treatment if they are still genuinely unsafe in some way. For example, when PTSD follows child abuse, the young person should be safe from further abuse before treatment can begin.

Assessment

The general assessment of a young person suspected of having PTSD is covered in Chapter 6. The specific features of assessment before treatment with CBT are discussed here and are basically the same whichever model of CBT might be used for treatment.

It is important that the assessment includes an interview with the young person alone to gauge the level of distress. Children have been noticed to understate their symptoms in the presence of their parents if they perceive the parents also to be distressed about the precipitating event (Yule and Williams 1990). However, it can be useful for parents to be present at some stage in assessment as, by the same token, they may be underestimating the distress of their child. By seeing the child's problems explored by the therapist, parents may gain a better understanding of what their child is experiencing. It may also facilitate discussion of the trauma between parent and child, both within and outside the therapy sessions (Deblinger et al. 1997).

These first few sessions are vitally important as they provide the grounding for all the subsequent work. During these first sessions the therapist must win the young person's trust and motivate them to continue with the treatment despite the emotional effort and discomfort required. As a part of the trust-building process, it is advisable for the therapist to explain the likely difficulties and distress which may be aroused at the start of the treatment (Udwin 1993). However, by following this warning with emphasis on the potential gains in terms of improved mood, sleep and enjoyment once these difficulties are passed, the young person may be encouraged to work through the distress. In addition, since there may be advantages for the young person in continuing to be 'ill', such as spending more time at home with a parent, these should be identified early and explored so that they do not contribute to resistance to treatment later. If they are made explicit they can be compared and contrasted with the advantages and freedom which result from being 'well'.

The therapist must also be aware of the power differential which exists between him- or herself and the young person, as there is a risk of the therapist persuading the young person to participate in discussions against their will. The young person may also wish to please the therapist by giving answers he or she believes the therapist wishes to hear, but which may not reflect the true situation.

The therapist begins by explaining the need for treatment and the techniques to be used. These are explained in general terms initially, but can become more specific once the details of the young person's problems have been clarified.

The purpose of treatment is to relieve the young person of symptoms. In its simplest form this may be achieved by encouraging habituation to stimuli through exposure as outlined above. An alternative explanation would be the relief of symptoms through the reprocessing of emotions aroused during the event (Rachman 1980). Either way the young person is required to revisit the memories of the original trauma and experience the emotions and thoughts related to it. This is what people usually do following a personal trauma when they relate the events to friends, relatives and even strangers they may meet in passing. Such behaviour, as long as it is accompanied by the experience of emotion and is sufficiently prolonged, brings about adequate reprocessing of the events for most people, most of the time (Rachman 1980). This natural process can even be facilitated by informal meetings between groups of survivors of a disaster (Yule and Williams 1990).

Next, the facts of the event need to be established and then the symptoms clarified, including identification of symptoms other than those directly related to the diagnosis of PTSD, as some of these might respond to treatment with CBT techniques also. During this stage of assessment the therapist and young person should collaborate in identifying which symptoms to target and what the goals of treatment should be. As in all work with young people it may be better if the therapist approaches distressing subjects indirectly, or while engaged in an unthreatening activity such as playing or drawing. It is also advisable, if possible, to collect any collaborative information about the event from alternative reliable sources. Such information may then be useful within the therapy as a means of reality testing the young person's beliefs about the event.

Another possible means of identifying symptoms is through the use of instruments such as the Impact of Events scale (Horowitz et al. 1979) used by Yule and colleagues in children aged 8 and over (Yule and Williams 1990, Yule and Canterbury 1994), although originally designed for use in adults. There are many other similar scales which have been, and are continuing to be, developed and refined for specific use in children and adolescents (Greenwald and Rubin 1999). Their use as assessment instruments is covered in more detail in Chapter 6, but those scales which give severity scores for symptoms, such as the Child PTSD–Reaction Index (Pynoos et al. 1987), may also be useful for quantifying change with treatment. However, such scales are no substitute for a clinical interview (Yule and Canterbury 1994).

Many sufferers are afraid they may be 'going mad' because of their symptoms. They may be greatly relieved at this stage by the therapist's ability to suggest possible symptoms they might be experiencing, and then normalising these symptoms as being understandable in relation to the traumatic experience. This may also increase the young person's confidence in the therapist (Yule and Canterbury 1994).

Finally, the young person's support network needs assessment and consideration. The carers may need assessment themselves for PTSD which may have resulted from their also having been exposed to the trauma, or may have arisen vicariously (see Chapter 6). Their ability to support the young person should also be gauged as parental difficulties and irritability have been associated with higher risk of PTSD persistence in young children and adolescents (Green et al. 1991). They will certainly benefit from information about the condition and its treatment and from advice regarding the young person's needs (Udwin 1993). If the child is young they may also need to be involved in the identification of the child's target problems. Family involvement is discussed in greater detail later in this chapter.

Individual treatment of children and adolescents

There are several possibilities for treatment, varying from simple exposure techniques such as 'flooding' (in which the sufferer must stay with their anxiety-provoking situation, in reality or in imagination, until the fear subsides), or purely cognitive work, to a combined cognitive and behavioural package. The model described here is a CBT package based on Stress Inoculation Training (SIT) (Meichenbaum 1985). It would need an average of 10–20 individual sessions depending on the amount of trauma-relevant material to be processed. Multiple or repeated traumas, such as repeated physical or sexual abuse, might require more sessions than this.

SIT consists of three phases of treatment, here modified to:

- **Conceptualisation**: Assessment, trust building, identifying and labelling emotional states
- **Skills acquisition and rehearsal**: Relaxation training, cognitive strategies, educational aspects, rehearsal
- **Application**: Exposure, consolidation, termination.

The treatment may be tailored to suit the age of the sufferer. Children may benefit from greater use of techniques such as dramatisation and drawing during the conceptualisation phase, and from more rehearsal of skills through role play, than would be usual for adults. Such techniques are also more engaging and may help the young person to concentrate for longer than would talking alone. They are especially useful if related to the young person's own hobbies and interests, where possible (Deblinger et al. 1997). The treatment package for any individual will thus need to be decided with regard to the target symptoms, the young person's age and cognitive ability, the available resources and the presence or absence of co-morbidity. After every session the young person should be given something to do or practise as 'homework'.

Throughout the treatment there should be an encouragement of positive self-talk and reinforcement of personal efficacy. Self-talk consists of those thoughts one has as an internal monologue and which flavour one's feelings about events and situations and one's abilities within them. Positive statements regarding one's abilities, learnt and repeated in anticipation of stressful times, help improve one's sense of mastery. Examples given to a young person with PTSD might be:

- No matter how afraid I feel, it can't get so bad that I die
- I've done this before and been fine
- I handled that really well.

It is best if the young person develops their own positive statements, which have personal meaning. These should be recorded, and then only rehearsed when necessary so that they do not lose their meaning and impact.

Finally, as the treatment draws to a close, the skills and changes which have been achieved are summarised with the young person. As CBT is a brief and focused therapy, the end of the treatment should be discussed throughout the course whenever possible. This is especially important as the young person is likely to have already experienced loss, or threat of loss, during the original trauma; either due to friends or family dying, experiencing disability secondary to their own injuries, or because they now perceive their own life to be drastically foreshortened (Terr 1991).

Treatment of these young people, like assessment, should be accompanied by education and support for their carers or family. This may extend to include teaching staff, especially if the traumatic event involved a school party (Udwin 1993).

Finally, it is important to note that most PTSD sufferers have some degree of sleep disturbance due to their hyperarousal or to intrusive phenomena such as nightmares. Such problems should ideally be tackled early as lack of sleep can be demoralising and can undermine the treatment efficacy by interfering with attention and concentration. If the problem is one of difficulty in falling asleep, then use of distraction techniques such as listening to music, reading reassuring stories such as those they may have liked at a younger age, or relaxation training may be helpful (Yule and Canterbury 1994). If the sufferer is repeatedly woken by nightmares then these may be treated in a similar way to flashbacks using gradual exposure to the dream content, positive self-talk, and rewriting the dream endings as less traumatic and more under their own control (Palace and Johnston 1989).

Conceptualisation phase

Once the assessment has been completed, the next stage in treatment may be focused on helping the young person to find an emotional vocabulary (Deblinger et al. 1997, Farrell et al. 1998). This may be achieved through drawing expressions, or acting out emotions, which are then labelled by the young person. A list of emotions can thus be built up and discussed in relation to the young person's experiences. If the drawings or lists are kept for subsequent sessions they can also serve as a reference point when talking about the feelings the young person has experienced. These emotions associated with the trauma may also be acknowledged by the therapist as being an understandable reaction to such an event ('normalised') at this point.

Skills acquisition and rehearsal phase

Further preparation for the core work, that of reprocessing the traumatic event and mastering the emotions and beliefs associated with it, may include relaxation training and education about anxiety management (March et al. 1998, Farrell et al. 1998). These are useful skills for the young person to acquire, as not only does PTSD usually consist largely of anxiety symptoms, but also it is necessary during treatment for the sufferer to return in his imagination to the original, probably terrifying, traumatic event. The young person will not be able to think and work within the therapy if they are overwhelmed by this original terror. Relaxation exercises before and during the sessions may enable further exploration to be possible and so increase a sense of mastery. If the training includes the development of a relaxing imaginary place, this place may be returned to within sessions if the young person becomes too upset.

The relaxation training may consist of progressive muscle tensing and then relaxing while listening to a commentary provided by the therapist in a monotonous and calming voice. The commentary could be audio-taped for practice at home between sessions, and this may help with sleep problems or other anxiety-based symptoms. With practice the young person may become faster at reaching a state of relaxation and so feel more confident about tackling the sessions, but care should be taken to ensure they do not use it as a means of avoiding the later exposure work (Deblinger et al. 1997). Younger children may understand relaxation if it is described in visual terms, contrasting tension (dry pasta) with relaxation (cooked pasta) (Deblinger et al. 1997).

Anxiety management work could consist of education about the body's physical responses to danger and how one can recognise this. As with all education, it is best if this is 'discovered' or 'led out' of the young person rather than given to him as a piece of received wisdom (Spark 1965). It can be broached through encouraging the young person to think about how they recognise when another person is anxious, or how they know when they are anxious themselves. Once the physical symptoms of anxiety have been identified they can be linked with concurrent thoughts and beliefs. At this point the therapist can also explore symptoms of panic and help the young person recognise how false beliefs about the dangerousness of the anxiety symptoms, or the provoking trigger (for example, a flashback), can lead to a feedback loop culminating in panic. The young person may believe that the feelings of panic can grow indefinitely and eventually cause death 'from fright', so they should be reassured that the physical and emotional effects reach a plateau that they cannot exceed. Advice could also be given at this stage about managing panic by rebreathing air from a paper bag so that the physical symptoms subside. In the case of younger children this advice should also be given to carers.

Application phase

The next stage in treatment consists of exposure to the memories of the original trauma. It is usually performed following the principles of systematic desensitisation, which also includes preparation through teaching anxiety management techniques, as described above. The young person may be able to identify a hierarchy of memories which cause increasing levels of distress, or the therapist may begin by discussing the subject in the abstract, or indirectly, as if another person were experiencing the same trauma (Deblinger et al. 1997). With younger children it might be necessary to act out the trauma using dolls or puppets, or drawings, paintings or role play (Deblinger et al. 1997).

The exposure to memories should be gradual but persistent, and the therapist should maintain the focus as vividly and for as long as possible, until the young person is able to tolerate the memory quite calmly (Yule 1991). Although the therapist may begin by exploring the subject indirectly, it is important that the young person be encouraged to talk about the event to facilitate maximal reliving and exposure. Ideally this should be done in the first person (using 'I' statements) and present tense. It is important that the exposure is not too brief or, paradoxically, it may serve to further sensitise the sufferer rather than decrease the distress (Rachman 1980, Saigh 1986, Yule and Canterbury 1994). Saigh described using flooding to treat a 6½ year old boy with PTSD following a bomb blast (Saigh 1986). The therapist assessed the boy's limits by presenting a scene and encouraging him to focus on it until he was tired. The length of time this was possible, 25 minutes, was used as the guide for treatment. Each session of flooding was then made to last for 24 minutes.

With exposure to the memories of the trauma, and gradual lessening of the anxiety aroused by them, the young person gains a sense of mastery where before there was only a sense of helplessness and passivity (Udwin 1993).

Cognitive aspects

More internal, or self-blaming, attributions for negative disaster-related events have been associated with greater post-traumatic symptomatology (Joseph et al. 1993). Cognitive work may allow the young person to make some sense of what happened to them, and reconsider why it happened.

Cognitive therapy requires a certain degree of sophistication and ability to understand abstract concepts, so it is most likely to be useful for adolescents rather than younger children. The subject of links between bodily symptoms, emotions, thoughts and behaviour will already have been discussed with the young person when considering anxiety management. Now other thoughts could be identified which the young person associates with the memories of the event. Those which are negative and interfere with ability to cope should be identified and written down in the first person. A common example might be 'I am to blame for others dying', or 'survivor guilt' in which the young person feels unjustifiably responsible for other's deaths because they have survived when others did not.

Underlying such thoughts are dysfunctional assumptions and core beliefs. For someone who is old enough and able to think abstractly, these assumptions and beliefs might be identified and corrected by getting the young person to question them and look at evidence in their life which is contrary to them. This exercise might be more easily performed indirectly through stories and role play, so that the dilemmas are once removed from the sufferer and so more easily observed (Farrell et al. 1998). However, eventually the aim would be to personalise the young person's conclusions.

If the child is too young to explore underlying beliefs abstractly, the maladaptive thoughts might still be identified, changed to more positive statements, and then practised in role play or as homework. Such positive statements, which the young person can recite to himself when symptoms return or when faced with triggers, have already been explained earlier as 'self-talk'. They can be practised in a variety of ways, to aid their generalisation and to help replace the negative thoughts that might otherwise spring automatically to mind. Drawing cartoons with positive thought bubbles, making scenes by cutting out pictures from magazines and then adding the thought bubbles, or using role play are all methods which have been used to rehearse and reinforce these new thoughts (Farrell et al. 1998). However, it is important that the meaning does not get lost through mindless, parrot-fashion repetition of the statements or their usefulness and impact may be diminished.

Termination

The final stage of treatment consists of application and consolidation of the skills acquired, in conjunction with work on termination and loss. At this point the therapist could stress the young person's achievements during the treatment in order to increase their confidence in themself and their sense of mastery over the presenting disorder. This would also help the young person to cope with potential apprehension at the therapy ending and the possibility of symptoms returning. These are areas which should be explored before the last session (Deblinger et al. 1997, Farrell et al. 1998).

Family involvement

Children and adolescents should be considered in context; this usually means meeting with their families or carers, and liaison with their schools. A family assessment provides objective information about the young person's behaviour at home, and provides an opportunity to assess family functioning and beliefs. Although parents can inform the therapist of their child's observable behavioural changes since the trauma, and give feedback at subsequent sessions, they are much less able to guess the emotional state of the young person. This information is best gleaned from young people themselves.

The families of sufferers also have their own needs. These may be direct needs when the source of the index patient's PTSD was an event which directly affected other family members, for example when the family were in a road traffic accident, or when there has been incestuous child sexual abuse or domestic violence. If the parents themselves are suffering from PTSD, this may be associated with greater conflict and irritability within the family (McFarlane 1987). In such a situation it might be useful to treat the whole family as a unit using family therapy techniques combined with elements of CBT (McFarlane 1989).

Alternatively, the family may become stressed by the knowledge of what happened to one of their members, and so by the proximity of the trauma to their own lives. This is discussed in greater detail in Chapter 4. The family dynamics may also change as a result of living with the young person and their altered behaviour and moods, or coping with their new disabilities. Under such circumstances the family could benefit from help with communicating effectively amongst themselves and with the young person. They may also need educating about PTSD and CBT and what they should expect of the young person in view of this information. As part of this education the therapist should stress the normality of the reactions in face of the abnormality of the traumatic event (Udwin 1993) and should reassure them that the young person does not have a psychotic illness and is not 'going mad'.

Finally, the family have a role to play in the recovery process. Their involvement shows the child that they are committed to helping, especially important in cases of incestuous child sexual abuse where the offending relative may have been imprisoned (Deblinger et al. 1997). In such cases the young person may need this as reassurance that they are believed and accepted by the rest of the family. The family of a sufferer should also be encouraged to be prepared to listen if the young person wishes to discuss the trauma, or their feelings about it. If the family style is usually one of reticence and avoidance of painful subjects because they believe 'least said, soonest mended', this can prevent the normal reprocessing of the trauma. Such families may need advice about the importance for the child of ventilating feelings appropriately and having this accepted. Equally the parents may need permission not to hide their own feelings of grief from the child if they have been bereaved during the traumatic event.

Co-morbid conditions

There is a high degree of co-morbidity, especially with disorders of emotion and conduct (behaviour) in the younger children, and depression in adolescents. At all ages there is also an increased risk of anxiety disorders, phobias and sleep problems. CBT can be used to treat all of these and may even be the initial treatment of choice for depressive disorders in adolescents (Birmaher et al. 1996, Brent et al. 1998). Where necessary, troublesome symptoms which are not being tackled within the therapy, as described above, might be treated alongside the PTSD using similar techniques. Alternatively, they might be treated before commencing the PTSD-specific course, as in the recommendation that sleep disorders be corrected from the outset (Yule 1991). Such an approach may increase the young person's ability to do the work of reprocessing the traumatic memories, as exhaustion due to poor sleep, or concentration problems and pessimism as part of a depressive illness, would make engagement and motivation more difficult. However, it is beyond the scope of this chapter to deal with these areas in detail.

Working in groups with CBT

Groups in general are covered in detail in Chapter 9. CBT groups have often been used to treat PTSD in adults. This is partly because many disasters precipitating PTSD affect groups of people at one time, but also it is due to the therapeutic factors within groups being applicable to the target problems of many PTSD sufferers. Principally, the members can learn from each other, and through modelling others' successful behaviours, they discover that other people can have similar problems to themselves, they feel less isolated and withdrawn, and they get the opportunity to help others within the group and so feel less impotent (Yalom 1985). In addition to all these reasons, there are practical advantages; many of the principles of treatment with CBT can be performed in groups and it is cost-effective.

Much group work in this field and age range has been carried out shortly after a disaster or trauma affecting a community of young people, and has consisted of preventive work rather than treatment of established PTSD. These groups usually invite all those young people exposed to the disaster (Pynoos and Nader 1988, Yule and Williams 1990) and since such groups are often school parties or classes, they will consist of young people all about the same age who may already see themselves as part of the same community or school or group. Their similarity in age is particularly important as the group members' developmental level will determine the interventions used (Vernberg and Vogel 1993). The children all need to be able to understand and use the same material as each other, and progress at a similar pace.

When treating cases of PTSD, rather than working with high-risk groups to prevent it, the young people may be selected to join the group rather than being members of the group already. Yule and Williams (1990) held parallel groups for parents and children with PTSD after the *Herald of Free Enterprise* ferry disaster. The members were not part of the same community prior to the disaster. This was not a CBT programme but the group did some problem-solving exercises. One therapeutic aspect for the children seemed to be that they had shared an experience which was beyond the comprehension of their usual peers, but they were not under pressure to discuss it.

March et al. (1998) also brought a group of children together for treatment of PTSD but they devised a CBT package, covering anxiety management training, cognitive training, anger control and systematic desensitisation over 18 sessions. There was also one additional individual session to address each young person's cognitive and trauma-specific requirements. The treatment was apparently successful for most of the group, but numbers were small and there were several methodological weaknesses. They also found that the younger children required more 'storybook' metaphors', whereas older children responded to instruction and reasoning. This illustrates the principle that treatment groups for children and adolescents should consist of developmentally similar, and therefore similarly aged, members (Vernberg and Vogel 1993).

References

Birmaher, B., Ryan, N. D., Williamson, D. E., Brent, D. A. and Kaufman, J. (1996) Childhood and adolescent depression: A review of the past 10 years. Part II. Journal of the American Academy of Child and Adolescent Psychiatry 35, 1575–1583.

Brent, D. A., Kolko, D. J., Birmaher, B. et al. (1998) Predictors of treatment efficacy in a clinical trial of three psychosocial treatments for adolescent depression. Journal of the American Academy of Child and Adolescent Psychiatry 37, 906–914.

Canterbury, R., Yule, W. and Glucksman, E. (1993) PTSD in child survivors of road traffic accidents. Paper presented to Third European Conference on Traumatic Stress, Bergen, 6–10 June 1993.

Deblinger, E., Heflin, A. H. and Clark, M. (1997) The treatment of sexually abused children. In Session: Psychotherapy in Practice 3, 69–88.

Farrell, S. P., Hains, A. A. and Davies, W. H. (1998) Cognitive behavioral interventions for sexually abused children exhibiting PTSD symptomatology. Behavior Therapy 29, 241–255.

Garmezy, N. and Rutter, M. (1985) Acute reactions to stress. In Rutter, M. and Hersov, L. (eds), Child and Adolescent Psychiatry: Modern Approaches, 2nd edn, pp. 152–176. Oxford: Blackwell.

Green, B. L., Korol, M., Grace, M. et al. (1991) Children and disaster: age, gender, and parental effects on PTSD symptoms. Journal of the American Academy of Child and Adolescent Psychiatry 30, 945–951.

Greenwald, R. and Rubin, A. (1999) Brief assessment of children's post-traumatic symptoms: development and preliminary validation of parent and child scales. Research on Social Work Practice 9, 61–75.

Halliday, G. (1987) Direct psychological therapies for nightmares: a review. Clinical Psychology Review 7, 501–523.

Horowitz, M. J., Wilner, N. and Alvarez, W. (1979) Impact of event scale: a measure of subjective distress. Psychosomatic Medicine 41, 209–218.

Hyman, I. A., Zelikoff, W. and Clarke, J. (1988) Psychological and physical abuse in the schools: a paradigm for understanding post-traumatic stress disorder in children and youth. Journal of Traumatic Stress 1, 243–267.

Joseph, S. A., Brewin, C. R., Yule, W. and Williams, R. (1993) Causal attributions and post-traumatic stress in adolescents. Journal of Child Psychology and Psychiatry 34, 247–253.

McFarlane, A. C. (1987) Family functioning and overprotection following a natural disaster: the longitudinal effects of post-traumatic morbidity. Australian and New Zealand Journal of Psychiatry 21, 210–218.

McFarlane, A. C. (1989) The treatment of post-traumatic stress disorder. British Journal of Medical Psychology 62, 81–90.

March, J. S., Amaya-Jackson, L., Murray, M. and Schulte, A. (1998) Cognitive-behav-ioral psychotherapy for children and adolescents with posttraumatic stress disorder after a single-incident stressor. Journal of the American Academy of Child and Adolescent Psychiatry 37, 585–593.

Meichenbaum, D. (1985) Stress Inoculation Training. New York: Pergamon Press.

Palace, E. M. and Johnston, C. (1989) Treatment of recurrent nightmares by the dream reorganization approach. Journal of Behaviour Therapy and Experimental Psychiatry 20, 219–226.

Pynoos, R. S. and Nader, K. (1988) Psychological first aid and treatment approach to children exposed to community violence: research implications. Journal of Traumatic Stress 1, 445–473.

Pynoos, R. S., Frederick, C., Nader, K. et al. (1987) Life threat and post-traumatic stress in school-age children. Archives of General Psychiatry 44, 1057–1063.

Rachman, S. (1980) Emotional processing. Behaviour Research and Therapy 18, 51–60.

Saigh, P. A. (1986) In vitro flooding in the treatment of a 6-yr-old boy's posttraumatic stress disorder. Behaviour Research and Therapy 24, 685–688.

Spark, M. (1965) The Prime of Miss Jean Brodie, p. 45. London: Penguin.

Terr, L. (1988) What happens to early memories of trauma? A study of twenty children under age five at the time of documented traumatic events. Journal of the American Academy of Child and Adolescent Psychiatry 27, 96–104.

Terr, L. C. (1991) Childhood traumas: an outline and overview. American Journal of Psychiatry 148, 10–20.

Udwin, O. (1993) Annotation: children's reactions to traumatic events. Journal of Child Psychology and Psychiatry 34, 115–127.

Vernberg, E. M. and Vogel, J. M. (1993) Interventions with children after disasters. Journal of Clinical Child Psychology 22, 485–498.

Yalom, I. D. (1985) The therapeutic factors in group therapy. in Yalom, I. D., The Theory and Practice of Group Psychotherapy, 3rd edn, pp. 3–18. New York: Basic Books.

Yule, W. (1991) Work with children following disasters. in Herbert, M. (ed.), Clinical Child Psychology: Social Learning, Development and Behaviour, pp. 349–363. Chichester: John Wiley.

Yule, W. and Canterbury, R. (1994) The treatment of post traumatic stress disorder in children and adolescents. International Review of Psychiatry 6, 141–151.

Yule, W. and Williams, R. M. (1990) Post-traumatic stress reactions in children. Journal of Traumatic Stress 3, 279–295.

Chapter 9
Therapeutic group work

Deborah Glass and Susie Thompson

'I now realise I'm not the only one who has these feelings and has been through this'. Gemma, aged 10.
'I liked the games and being able to talk about my feelings without feeling bad about it'. Andrew, aged 9.
'It was good to meet with others who had been through a similar thing'. Sandra, aged 14.

All the above comments were made by children and adolescents following group attendance. These groups looked at specific traumatic events which had occurred in the young people's lives, and which they were having difficulty coming to terms with, such as bereavement, parental separation or divorce and bullying. Indeed, the authors, in their various experiences of group work with children and young people, have rarely encountered a child who did not report feeling as though they had benefited from the group experience. In addition, the authors have found that, in the majority of cases, parents and other professionals have been very supportive of young people attending such groups.

This chapter explores group work as a treatment option for children and adolescents with, or with a predisposition towards, post-traumatic stress disorder (PTSD). It aims to demonstrate that group work is an appropriate and effective treatment medium for this client group, and outlines practical ideas and examples of how standard group procedures can be adapted to meet the needs of this population. However, we first consider group work and its role in society today more generally.

The group is a very familiar environment for us as humans because we spend most of our lives in groups of some form or other. These include friendship groups, family groups, work groups, interest groups, etc. Indeed, it could be said that since human life began, people have

163

functioned in groups and recognised the benefits of them. We are, after all, what biologists describe as a social animal.

In recent years, there has been increasing interest in, and attention given to, the beneficial ways that groups can be used in many aspects of society. These include schools, public services, government and industry where the establishment of groups is now routine, as people acknowledge that they can be an effective way of achieving goals. People are realising the many possibilities and opportunities the group structure can bring, and how, as Dwivedi (1993) states, 'Since most human problems arise in the setting of group life, many can be solved in a group setting'.

Historical development of group work in mental health services

Group treatment in psychiatric services, in its broadest sense, first began to be used by American doctors such as Pratt, Marsh and Lazell at the beginning of the twentieth century. European psychiatrists and psychologists such as Moreno and Freud were also key pioneers in the group psychotherapy movement, which initially began in the 1920s and steadily grew in popularity from then onwards. Many other professionals, including Bion, Adler and Foulkes, contributed to the development of this work that continues today in the late 1990s (McGrath in Dwivedi 1993).

Much has been written about the efficacy of group work for a wide range of adult psychiatric disorders and group work continues to be offered as a much-valued, respected and researched treatment medium by a wide variety of professionals. The use of short-term group treatments in particular, as opposed to the more open-ended and long-term psychodynamic groups, has increased in recent years. Some relate this at least in part to 'the cost-cutting efforts of the country's managed healthcare system' (Lomonaco et al. 1998), but it is also linked to the efficacy of the treatment medium.

Group work with children and adolescents is a relatively recent development and at present it is much less well documented. However, this looks set to change if the increasing interest in this work continues. Indeed, Lomonaco et al. (1998) describe how 'this decade has witnessed a virtual explosion of time-limited group measures for troubled children'.

Written documentation regarding group work with children and adolescents in both inpatient, outpatient and community settings can be found from the 1950s onwards. The earliest groups documented include child psychotherapy groups, groups for children on paediatric hospital wards, and psychoeducational groups for children at risk, or under stress (Lomonaco et al. 1998). Today, a huge variety of group work is being undertaken in a diversity of settings facilitated by different people of various professional backgrounds.

Types of group work with young people

Open-ended longer-term psychotherapeutic groups for children are still in existence but it appears that most groups run today are more focused, shorter-term interventions. Some of the issues for children and adolescents that can be addressed through group work include parental separation or divorce, anxiety management, bereavement, sexual abuse, parents with a mental illness, peer relationship problems, anger management, young offenders, encopresis and acute trauma (e.g. road traffic accident).

Why groups with young people?

The ever-increasing interest in group work with children and adolescents suggests that many deem it an effective therapeutic tool for this client group. The question which will now be addressed is 'why this should this be so?'. All of the reasons are applicable to children and adolescents with, or with a predisposition to, PTSD. Specific reasons why group work is particularly appropriate for these young people will also be considered.

The familiarity of the group situation

Dinkmeyer and Muro (1971) describe how the group is a particularly effective approach with children because children are social beings and are generally interested in interaction. As they state, 'Children like to be part of a group'. In support of this Rickford (1998), writing about work with children who have experienced parental separation or divorce, states how 'the children seem to especially enjoy the groups, in particular the club aspect of the group setting'.

Dwivedi specifies how latency-aged children in particular (aged 8–11 years) are very 'group orientated' and how, as schoolchildren, they spend most of their time in group settings. They are taught in groups, play in groups and eat in groups. Therefore, group work is an effective therapeutic approach for them as it recreates the important social aspects of the child's life, which occurs among the siblings, with the parents, at school, in the neighbourhood and so forth. Indeed, 'for most children and adolescents, the small group is a natural and highly attractive group setting' (Dwivedi 1993).

Contrast with individual therapy sessions

Farrell (1984) states, with reference to the contrast of group work to individual therapy sessions, that whereas 'the group situation fits in with ease developmentally into children's' ordinary lives of school and family, the more traditional one-to-one relationship is an uncommon one for children of school age'.

In a group the number of facilitators is less than the number of children and it is therefore often perceived by the child as a less threatening environment than an individual therapy session. As a result, children are less intimidated or overwhelmed and feel less pressured to speak. It can also make children feel less inhibited and free to express themselves, compared with the often more intense individual therapy session. Dwivedi (1993) expands this idea further, stating that 'In individual settings, the huge disparity between the status of the adult therapist and that of the child or adolescent becomes too obvious'.

Children and young people who have experienced trauma can often feel singled out and different from their peers. Attending individual therapy sessions may further exacerbate such feelings and therefore may not be recommended if this was a particular issue for the young person concerned.

Use of different activities

Group work creates the opportunity for the use of many therapeutic procedures, games and exercises that are not possible in individual or even family sessions. These include drama, role plays, group games/pictures/creative projects and brainstorming exercises that can be of great benefit to the group process.

Treatment economy

In the current climate of financial cutbacks, there are increasing pressures to provide the most cost-effective services. Although more research is still needed, many believe that group work is an effective use of limited resources. Indeed, 'research work on adults has indicated much lower costs for similar results in group work than in individual work' (Dwivedi 1993). A recent 2 year study comparing group and individual treatment outcomes for young peopl found that 'groups were at least equally effective, and more economical in two thirds of cases making more individual treatment time for those who most needed it' (Skynner in Dwivedi 1993).

Peer support and influence

For children and adolescents, peer reinforcement is far more powerful than adult reinforcement and therefore the group can be a powerful influence in effecting change in a young person's life. It is the task of the group facilitator to enable the mutual sharing and support to occur and to help the group members help each other. In a group setting the young people can have the chance to think about their own experiences, and help others to manage things better. An unhealthy, but plausible self-absorption may result from surviving a traumatic experience, particularly one that others did not survive. Group-based therapy can provide a forum from which to look outwards, an opportunity to give to and receive support from a sympathetic peer group.

Children and young people can often trigger thoughts and ideas for each other in a way which a 'nice lady/man sitting in a room with them may not' (Skynner in Dwivedi 1993). In support of this, Ljubomirovic writes of group work with adolescent refugees from the former Yugoslavia and describes how the 'boys and girls are often able to give better advice than the therapist is' (Ljubomirovic 1999).

The group setting allows children and young people to develop empathy as they learn how the lives and experiences of others are not so different from their own (Dwivedi 1993). The group experience can reduce the common feelings of isolation, of 'I'm the only one who feels like this/to whom this has happened'. There is often a strong need to meet others who have been through a similar experience and share the same feelings. The opportunity to do so and to learn that they are not alone is often the first step they can take towards coming to terms with their experience, moving forward from it and ultimately recovering. Participation in a group with similarly suffering people who can truly empathise and have a genuine understanding of the feelings engendered by the experience can offer a feeling of reassurance and safety often missing from other interventions. Knowing that someone else has been through something similar can often be of great benefit in itself. As Rickford (1998) writes in regard to groups for children who have experienced parental separation or divorce, 'they seem to find it very helpful to have the support of other children in a similar situation'. Similarly, following a traumatic event, such as a war or a single large-scale incident, e.g. the *Herald of Free Enterprise* disaster in 1987, survivors often feel the need to share experiences, to express feelings with others who have experienced the same and to address the inevitable questions, 'why/why not me?'. Such discussions are appropriately and naturally facilitated in a group situation. The extreme feelings of negativity – the guilt, anger, disgust and unworthiness often felt by survivors of trauma – can be expressed with greater freedom and with less fear of being judged, and may receive more understanding support with and from others who share those feelings too.

In support of the above, Ljubomirovic (1999) further writes with reference to group work with adolescent war refugees from the former Yugoslavia, how the young people found it easier to open up with group members, how 'one story encourages another. Adolescents can comprehend in a group that they are not alone with their problems, that they can share them with other group members'.

Structure and format

For children and young people who have experienced trauma, group work can provide a clear structure and format to the therapy, which can give a reassuring sense of control and predictability in a world often turned frighteningly out of control and chaotic by the trauma experienced.

The logistics of group work

Facilitating and running therapeutic groups can be extremely rewarding for the therapist. Not only is the planned content material potentially therapeutic, but the very process of the interaction of the group members can be used therapeutically, as mentioned previously, almost despite the content!

This presents the most experienced therapist with a challenging opportunity, so it is vital that sufficient preparation is put in beforehand. Wherever possible, the therapist should ensure that the group does provide the safe, secure, consistent environment it promises, and so free up the therapist during the session to facilitate and support the group.

Settings for group work

Groups can be held in a variety of settings but clearly some locations are more suitable than others depending on the type of group being run. Groups can be run in schools (e.g. the Cambridge Family and Divorce Centre staff run groups for young people who have experienced parental separation or divorce in local secondary schools) (Rickford 1998), youth clubs, child and family guidance clinics, community centres, and in-patient units. Finding an appropriate location is of prime importance to the successful running of a group. It must be accessible, to allow the young people to get to the group, and also private. A room where the group will not be disturbed and has minimal distractions is key to a group's success.

Children and young people who have experienced trauma must feel comfortable, safe and secure in order to be able to gain the maximum benefit from the group. The importance of the environment must not be underestimated for group work, as for individual work. The associations a young person may have with a certain place, or the memories that certain environments can evoke, must also be acknowledged and considered. This is of particular importance if during the course of a group it is felt to be of benefit for young people to revisit the place where the traumatic event or incident took place. Such visits should be done with very careful planning and preparation.

Rather than a weekly group meeting, some groups take place over a residential weekend. For example, the Winston's Wish organisation based in Gloucestershire runs residential 'Camp Winston weekends' for children who have been bereaved (Bond 1998).

Group facilitators

Although there are always exceptions, it is generally thought that a group should contain 6–8 young people of a similar developmental level (e.g. 6–8 year olds, 13–15 year olds), with two facilitators. Group facilitators can be from a wide range of disciplines, e.g. occupational therapists (the development of group work skills is a key part of their training), social workers, psychiatric nurses, psychologists, teachers, child and adolescent psychiatrists or registrars. It is recommended however, that at least one facilitator has some group work training and experience.

Professionals working together from different disciplines can often enable sharing of professional skills, providing a richer and more diverse group experience for the young people involved. If available, a third group worker to observe the group (e.g. from behind a one-way screen) can be of great benefit in evaluating the group, improving the group facilitators' skills through constructive feedback and enhancing the group process, through reflection on interactions and activities within the group.

It is of key importance that group facilitators set aside regular time for planning of each group session. Running a group involves much more than the 1–2 hours that they meet with the young people. Time needs to be allocated for setting up the room, pre-group assessments, liaison with parents and other members of the multidisciplinary team, post-group evaluations and reports and many other tasks related to the successful running of a group.

It is essential that, as far as possible, the group facilitators ensure that they can commit to the number of sessions planned for the running of the group. Clearly, some situations cannot be avoided, e.g. staff sickness, but it is important that facilitators are aware of the importance of their regular attendance at the group sessions. Continuity of facilitators is very important for the young people so that they feel safe and secure within the group setting. This enables them to be more open and honest when talking about often-difficult feelings.

Who?

Wherever possible, for all groups, careful screening of the participants is essential to ensure that the greatest possible benefit is gained by all, both from the content and the process of the group experience.

However, in the treatment of trauma victims, choice of participants may well be out of the control of the therapist. If the group work is held at the site of a traumatic event, for example in the form of a debriefing session, the group is likely to consist of any survivors. Even so, it is worth bearing in mind compatibility of group members, for example by age, social situation, cognitive and emotional maturity or gender, if appropriate. These can greatly affect group cohesion: e.g. children under 8 years of age have a less well developed concept of time, and may find verbalisation more difficult than older children.

If the group work happens some time after the event, for example where children have experienced the traumatic separation or divorce of parents, or are survivors of sexual abuse, it may be appropriate to control for other possible variables. For example, ongoing, unresolved family issues or the age at which the trauma was experienced might affect the young person's experience of it and their ability to address it with others. As listed above, there are other variables that can impact on the group process and will affect its content.

Obviously, there is a need for some flexibility, to ensure that the group offered meets the needs of the clients, not the service, but the key to the appropriateness of potential participants must be the pre-group assessment.

Assessment measures

Measures of assessment can take a variety of forms. They may be formal or informal measures.

- Formal measures in relation to traumatic experiences and their impact are discussed in Chapter 6. Such ratings enable a more objective measure both of progress and efficacy.
- Informal measures may involve filling in a non-standardised questionnaire that is group-specific (Box 9.1). It can also be helpful to set objectives together with the client. Obviously these will vary

depending on the needs of the young person and the aims of the group (Box 9.2).

Box 9.1 Pre-group assessment sheet (child)

Name: Date:
Please tick the statement you agree with more, either A or B:

A: I sometimes feel that nobody understands (about my parents splitting up).
B: I feel that at least somebody understands (about my parents splitting up).
A: I sometimes feel that I'm the only one who feels like I do about my parents.
B: I feel that at least somebody feels like I do about my parents.
A: I have lots of complicated feelings about my parents splitting up.
B: I don't have any feelings about my parents splitting up.
A: I know other children whose parents have split up.
B: I don't know anybody whose parents have split up.
A: I never talk about my feelings about my parents.
B: I sometimes talk about my feelings about my parents.
A: I find it hard to tell my parents how I feel.
B: I can easily tell my parents how I feel.

Box 9.2 Things I'd like to gain from the group:

- To stop arguing with mum and dad.
- Not to be so confused.
- To tell all my worries.
- To feel better.
- Not to be angry any more.
- To learn that it doesn't matter if they are together or not.
- To understand that it is for our own good.
- Knowing that other people understand or have been through the same.

Planning and preparation before the group

Legal issues

It is vital that any legal issues, e.g. in a child protection case, are clarified before a young person commences attendance at a group. For example, if the criminal justice system is involved, discussions with the relevant people must be undertaken to ensure that the young person's attendance at the group will not be undermined in any way. If a young person discloses something important in the group, which sometimes does occur, clear procedures must be established and agreed with all involved, ensuring the young person's safety and notifying the appropriate people or services. Such procedures must be made clear to a young person before commencing attendance at the group.

Similarly, if a young person has witnessed a murder, or other such criminal act, the position with the investigating officers in regard to the young person's attendance at the group must be clarified from the start.

Obtaining information regarding the traumas the young people have experienced

It is advisable where possible to obtain as much information as possible regarding the facts of what actually happened to the young person, or what they witnessed. When someone has experienced a traumatic event they may experience a distorted perception of the event. If the group facilitators have some factual information about what did happen, they might be able to help the young person gain a better sense of things, obtain a more reality-based understanding of their experience.

Meeting with the young person and their parents or carers

Following an initial assessment to establish that it is appropriate for the young person to attend a group, it is important that they should have the opportunity to:

- ask questions about the group
- meet the group facilitators
- be given some basic information about the group
- find out what kind of activities they might be doing.

For some young people who have experienced a trauma, attendance at a group might be a frightening prospect, particularly if they are unsure of what it would involve. Reassurance and explanations are very important to allay possible fears, anxieties and misconceptions the young person may have about the forthcoming group. If such time is not spent before the group, perhaps no group members will turn up!

It is also very important to explain about the group to the parents or carers to ensure they understand the aims of their young person attending. It is particularly important to explain about the confidentiality rules of the group, to try to ensure that parents or carers do not pressurise the young person or group facilitators for detailed accounts of what occurred or was said in each group session. Such behaviour could undermine the therapeutic benefits of group attendance for the young person concerned.

Group content

The secret of a successful group is to have sufficient set agenda to be able to run the group with confidence, but to be flexible enough not to lose touch with the 'here-and-now' process. This may be predictable after the first few sessions, once the group dynamics are established and understood, but also unpredictable, because of the very nature of human interaction and the myriad events that are forever impacting on it.

A number of 'protocols' are worth bearing in mind:

- A basic, reliable recipe to follow in formatting the sessions is the 'introduction–warm up–main event–wind down–homework' structure. This allows for a gentle build-up to the subject matter, building on the feeling of cohesion and support that grows between group members from week to week, and acknowledges the importance of finishing properly (Ayalon and Flasher 1993).
- Obviously, a degree of flexibility is important, but consistency and familiarity provides a supportive, predictable and therefore less threatening framework in which difficult issues can be addressed.
- Start and finish times must be adhered to responsibly. Again, this ensures that everyone is clear about, and respects, the boundaries of the group.
- Before starting, decide on the duration of the group and whether it is to be open (members may join or leave at any stage) or closed (membership is set from the start and there is an expectation of full attendance). Practical help might be needed to ensure regular attendance, and it is worth establishing from the start that the time and venue are manageable for everyone.
- It is often useful to establish rules in the group, so that everyone is aware of a minimum expectation of and from members. It can be helpful to reframe these in the positive, wherever possible, i.e. as things to help good practice happen, rather than 'don'ts' that may have a restrictive, demanding feel to them. For example: 'Try to listen to others' views with respect', rather than 'Don't interrupt or argue with other group members'.
- Confidentiality is an important issue to address at this point, so that everyone is clear about, and happy with, what may be talked about outside the group sessions. This is particularly important if a trustful environment is to be established, where difficult emotions and experiences can be shared with the group.
- It is vital to get the endings right, both of each session and then of the last group. It is important to acknowledge the approaching end and the difficult feelings it can arouse – particularly where the trauma has involved loss, separation and premature ending.
- One cannot protect young people from painful loss, but one can offer a model of well-managed endings and a positive experience of them that can be extremely healing.

- Providing a support group for parents or carers, to run concurrently, increases the success rate of the work with the young people, as it enables them to transfer the skills learnt in the group more easily to the rest of their lives (Frankel et al. 1997).

Supervision

It can be very difficult to listen to young people as they share their very powerful personal experiences and talk about their feelings relating to them. In order to be an effective group facilitator, it is very important to take care of yourself and have regular clinical supervision. It is vital to have the opportunity to talk about the personal effects of working with young people in this way and explore ways of coping with this, often difficult, work. Supervision can also enable practitioners to gain added insight into the group process taking place and give possible ideas and approaches to use in future group sessions.

Evaluation

It is advisable to regularly take notes after each session about each young person's participation in the group plus general comments regarding the group session as a whole. This can assist with planning future sessions, increasing awareness of the group processes taking place and writing final reports regarding a young person's attendance at the group if required.

Meeting with the young people individually after the group has finished is also often recommended in order to obtain their feedback with regard to their attendance at the group and whether they achieved their goals. It may also provide the opportunity to complete more standardised post-group assessment procedures to enable more formal outcomes to be measured.

The individual young person in the group setting

It is vital for group facilitators to recognise each young person as an individual within the group and not assume that because all of them may have experienced a similar trauma they all have similar difficulties. Mayall (1999) writes in regard to his work with children who had been held hostage in the Gulf War of 1990. He states how 'the children talked about different aspects of the hostage situation and different issues came up for each of them, independent of their backgrounds, their personalities and their age'. He concludes that 'we must never forget the completeness and uniqueness of each of the individuals in any particular traumatic situation, and it should make us wary of too sweeping generalisations about children's reactions, keeping in mind that each may have their own special stories that they may need to tell'.

The challenges of group work

Group work with young people can be rewarding and enjoyable. However, it can also be extremely challenging and difficult. There can be times when it is difficult to know what to do next, times when the group seems out of control or when things are just not going according to plan. Indeed groups can, by their very nature, be unpredictable and ever-changing. The authors maintain, however, that if you are prepared for the challenge, prepared to have a go and learn from your mistakes, the rewards can be great.

Examples of group work with this client group

The importance and use of critical incident stress debriefing groups is discussed in Chapter 7 and is not covered here.

Issues to cover in 'trauma' groups

As stated earlier in this chapter, a number of the issues may well be addressed as specific content material in the groups, for discussion and analysis, such as the loss and regaining of control. They may well appear also as functions of the group process, to be experienced and worked through by the group members, aided and supported by the group facilitators.

Emotional expression

An opportunity for emotional expression is vital. Trauma victims may need space to express anger, despair, guilt, fear, elation, sadness, anxiety, depression, grief, numbness, relief, euphoria. Acknowledgement and acceptance of these feelings is important, as is help to contain them and provide some perspective to them.

Examples of techniques to encourage appropriate emotional expression

- A group shout – standing in a line at one side of the room, the group move slowly towards the opposite side of the room, repeating a pre-chosen word, at first in a whisper, building to the crescendo of a shout.
- A brainstorm of the physical sensations associated with the emotion and appropriate physical actions to release these emotions. Experiment with using them if appropriate, e.g. punching a cushion, hugging, crying.
- Use a large piece of paper as a graffiti sheet for anyone to write down an angry word or saying whenever they feel like it.

- Shaving foam is also a useful graffitiing tool, as it disappears without trace from any surface with the slightest of elbow-grease and a cloth. Just shake the can and spray like spray-paint. If young people get covered with it (the activity is renowned for getting out of hand in groups), sharing in the clearing up can be a remarkably supportive, nurturing experience.

Narrative recounting

The use of narrative recounting is a psychodynamic method of establishing the personal meaning each individual gives to their survival experience. As previously mentioned, the significance of each individual's unique experience and understanding of the traumatic event must be taken into account (Mayall 1999). Considerable patience and tolerance on the part of both facilitators and other group members is required, as time and space is given to each participant to reconstruct and describe the incident as they experienced it. It enables emotions to be expressed, facts to be verified, and possibly the first opportunity for the true horror of the experience to be acknowledged and come to terms with. Often survivors are tempted to spare relatives' and carers' own feelings by trivialising the significance of the traumatic experience.

Examples of techniques to encourage narrative recounting

- Younger children (generally of 8 years and under, though any age group may benefit from this activity) may well find it easier to depict their experiences pictorially. They may wish to contribute to a group picture or draw a 'diary' of their experience before, during and after the incident. Art is also an excellent medium to use to help make links between the physical experience and the powerful, though often difficult to describe, feelings associated with it. For example, three young children from the same family used art extremely dramatically to help describe the feelings associated with witnessing their mother knocked down and killed as she got out of the car in which they were sitting.
- Puppets, playmobile characters and other toys are also extremely relevant props or prompts here.
- The facilitator may encourage story-telling by reading out a story told by another trauma victim, or may use a familiar fantasy story, encouraging the group to think of themselves as the central character, and asking every so often what they would do next or how they might be feeling (Cattanach 1997).

Constructive exploration

At all times, the facilitator must bear in mind the impact of the traumatic incident on the group's past and future experiences, as well as those of the present. The sense of loss or abandonment and the guilt experienced by the survivor may revive the experience of previous losses – often taking the young person completely by surprise – and may seem to that person to be trivial and irrelevant, but should not be underestimated.

This is also why the well-planned management of the endings of each group is vital. They must be predictable, consistent, calm and anticipated (a 5 minute warning might be useful, or a particular activity used consistently to designate the end of the session).

Examples of techniques to encourage constructive exploration of past loss

- Group members may find it easiest to start with a brainstorm of past losses. The facilitator should encourage them to consider even the most seemingly insignificant event as relevant, e.g. changing schools, breaking a favourite toy. Participants should be encouraged to recall how they felt at that time and how they coped.
- The facilitator might prepare a list of possible past losses and use it as a discussion prompt. At all times the feelings associated with loss should be acknowledged, to remind the group that loss and the feelings it engenders, in differing degrees, are part of the process of life.
- A possibly less threatening way of introducing this issue is to explore the idea of change or loss in other, less personal, areas of life; e.g. the changing seasons; trees growing from seeds, maturing and dying.

Specific symptoms

It may well be appropriate to address specific symptoms in the group. Members may experience high levels of anxiety, intermittent panic or avoidance responses (see Chapter 8 on cognitive-behavioural therapy).

Examples of techniques to address specific anxiety symptoms

- Relaxation techniques of various kinds may be used as a wind-down at the end of each session. The group members should be encouraged to use them at home, whenever they feel dysfunctionally anxious, i.e. not just in relation to the trauma.
- It may be appropriate for the group to visit the site of the traumatic incident. If particularly traumatic, this may be done in previously identified stages.

Problem solving

Group and shared problem solving is a good technique to use, to focus the group on coping strategies and to re-empower individuals. Feelings of vulnerability and powerlessness may be very strong, as well as the 'if only I'd done more' regret. Again, previous experiences may come to the fore here, as the young people can be encouraged to share strategies they have used in the past. Together they may find it easier to come up with more inventive, creative solutions than they would alone. Problem solving may be used to address every-day scenarios, or issues specific to the trauma, e.g. how to tell a parent to stop being overprotective.

Examples of techniques to re-empower and encourage problem solving

- Again, brainstorming all the possible solutions to a problem, no matter how crazy-sounding, is a creative way to finding the individual solution that might just work for one particular person.
- Role playing enables group members to practise the suggested scenario in a secure, non-judgemental environment, increasing confidence and allowing various possible reactions to be identified and analysed, before the real-life situation is tackled. For example, different ways of going about owning up to a misdeed could be enacted in small groups, together with the likely responses in each case.

Addressing future plans

Establishing a realistic sense of future should be tackled at a later stage in the group process, once issues of loss and survival have been addressed. For some young people it may be difficult to contemplate any future, whereas others may have a grandiose feeling of immortality. For both, it is appropriate to take a day-by-day approach to future planning at first, until a sense of proportion is established.

Examples of techniques to address future plans

- Group members might be encouraged to keep a diary to share with the rest of the group. This might begin by describing the process of a single event – beginning, middle and end – including associated feelings such as anticipation and happy memory or disappointment.
- Individual goal setting, e.g. 'three things I would like to achieve in the next year'.
- Problem solving (see above) may be useful, in helping re-establish an appropriate, realistic sense of control over future events.

- The group may plan the agenda of a group together, or a group activity such as an outing.

Sources of support

The group can spend some useful time discussing quite concrete matters, such as support networks, and identifying where to go in times of crisis. The facilitator may find it easiest to do some preparation, to find out what statutory or voluntary organisations are available to provide further help, or it may be appropriate to set the group the task of finding this out for themselves.

The facilitator can also have an important educative role to play, by factually informing the group of possible difficulties they may yet face in the future and reassuring them of the normality of this.

Post-separation and divorce groups

Young people are usually referred to post-separation and divorce groups when the separation or divorce of their parents has so significantly afected their mental health that it is affecting their ability to function. The young people themselves can identify a number of reasons why they wish to attend such a group (see Box 9.2).

In the authors' experience, a typical group of six sessions, each lasting for $1^{1}/_{2}$ hours, on a weekly basis, runs as follows.

Pre-group interview

The pre-group interview enables the participants to meet the facilitators, to ask any questions, to find out more about what to expect and to fill in the pre-group questionnaire.

Session 1

- Introductions: reintroduce yourself. Use a simple game, e.g. throwing a beanbag from one to another saying your name as you throw, to introduce the young people to each other. Make simple name badges.
- Remind the young people why they are in the group. Explain the group format.
- Write a list of 'group rules', e.g. respect others in the group and what they have to say; join in as much as you can; attend each week. Phrase these as positively as possible – reframe if necessary.
- Introduce the idea of change as something that occurs often in nature and is a natural part of life. Use discussion and/or drawing as a means of illustrating change – how we change as individuals and how families change.

- End with a closing/wind-down game, e.g. 'pass the picture' – each young person has a large piece of paper and a colour (different for everyone in the group). They have one minute to start drawing a picture. After one minute the facilitator says 'pass' and their picture is passed on to the person next to them who continues it for one minute and so on, around the circle, until each person has their original picture back. A brief discussion may then be held around the changes and feelings associated with them.

Session 2

- Introduction: throwing the beanbag, say your name and something about yourself. The catcher has to repeat the thing about you and something about themselves.
- Each young person receives a folder in which to keep the various worksheets they complete. They may decorate it as they wish.
- Discussion on marriage: what is it? why do people get married? Young people may wish to draw what marriage means to them and list reasons for getting married, or why they think their parents got married. This may include a discussion about different kinds of love, but all sorts of other reasons why marriage happens. All are valid.
- Why might marriage go wrong?: introduce the idea and brainstorm.
- Closing game: In pairs, with one large piece of paper between two and a different colour each, each partner has a turn to take the lead in drawing a line pattern on the paper, followed by the partner. Briefly discuss leaders and followers, who prefers which role, who takes on which role in each family, what happens if both parents are leaders, etc.

Session 3

- Warm-up: throw the beanbag and tell the group something nice or not so nice that happened to you last week.
- Begin to talk more about feelings, e.g. brainstorm to identify different feelings ('positive' and 'negative') ; what sort of incidents make you feel them – may not necessarily be to do with their parents' divorce but often are, e.g. 'I get upset/feel guilty when mum and dad row'.
- How do we tell when people are feeling (e.g.) angry, guilty, excited, depressed, happy? Discuss and demonstrate tone of voice, body language, etc. The adverb game: someone goes out of the room. The group chooses a feeling from the list and when the person returns, answer questions in turn expressing the chosen feeling, until the questioner guesses the feeling.
- How do we feel or express different feelings? An opportunity to talk about somatic expression of pain, anxiety, appropriate or inappropriate expression of anger.

- Teach a basic relaxation technique that can be done where they are sitting, e.g. tense and relax different parts of the body in turn.

Session 4

- Warm-up: 'I went to market and I bought a ...' each time adding something with a feeling attached to it, e.g. an angry volcano, a frightened mouse, a happy clown, each person in turn adding their purchase to the things that went before (the last person has to remember everything).
- Feelings: how to express feelings appropriately. Recap last week's discussion and talk about appropriate ways of expressing the more difficult feelings.
- Use role plays to enact scenarios where anger needs to be expressed or to help overcome anxiety, e.g. how might you handle meeting a parent's new partner?
- Talk about the feelings associated with the parent's divorce and their living situation now. These may not necessarily be all bad – some children may feel an overwhelming sense of relief once the decision to live apart is finally made. Others can acknowledge (guiltily) enjoying having two houses in which to live.
- Parents have feelings too. Identify them, and how you know.
- Relaxation or a closing game.

Session 5

- Warm-up, e.g. share a favourite memory.
- Identify changes brought about by parental divorce. These may include both good things, e.g. less arguing, and more difficult things, e.g. less money.
- Read appropriate pages from *Dinosaurs Divorce* (Krasney-Brown and Brown 1986). (This book may be used throughout the group, if felt appropriate.)
- Help the young people identify what is different that they would like to, and can, change, what others may have in their power to change and what may be impossible to change, about their life.
- Use sections of the 'You're both still my parents' video (Prestige Health Promotions 1997). Discuss 'rights and responsibilities' and encourage the group to identify and role play questions they might like to ask their parents, e.g. 'why can't I see more of dad?', 'why is there one set of rules here and another there?'.
- Remind the group that it is the last session next week. Acknowledge how this makes people feel. They may wish to mark it with a 'farewell party' of some sort.

- Say something nice about someone in the group, e.g. something they've done or that you've learnt about them.

Session 6

- Warm-up: something new I've learnt/something good I've done/a new person I've met this week.
- Brainstorm: things I like to do that make me feel good. Things I like to do with mum/dad/a friend/on my own.
- Share ideas about support networks. Fill in a worksheet –'where I can turn for help'.
- Changes – past, present and future: each young person depicts events in their lives on a pathway that may wind through woods, dark caves, over bumpy terrain, through bright meadows, etc. What do they look forward to?
- Leave time for a 'farewell party' if they want one.
- Review the issues covered; acknowledge the work that's been done.
- End: each young person draws a gift for another person in the group. This may be quite concrete, e.g. a room of their own, or something more abstract, e.g. strength to ask a difficult question of a parent or bravery to contact an absent parent.

Conclusion

This chapter has explored group work as a treatment option for children and adolescents with, or with a predisposition towards, PTSD. We have argued that it is an appropriate treatment medium for this client group, and shown some practical examples of how it can be used.

However, it is important to recognise that group attendance may often be recommended in conjunction with other work, e.g. family and or individual work, as part of an overall treatment plan for a young person.

In addition, it is important to note that 'not all traumatised children require help from psychiatric services' (Ainscough and Telford 1998). This includes group treatment too. All young people must be seen as individuals and it may be that group work is not an appropriate intervention for some, for a variety of reasons.

This said, the authors firmly believe that group work has a key contribution to make in the treatment and prevention of PTSD with children and adolescents, for as Dwivedi (1993) so clearly states, 'Group work can reach parts that other modes of therapeutic work may not'.

References

Ainscough, K. and Telford, R. (1998) Child sexual abuse and the phenomenon of trauma. National Association of Paediatric Occupational Therapists Journal, Summer, 26–28.

Ayalon, O. and Flasher, A. (1993) Chain Reaction. Children and Divorce. London: Jessica Kingsley.

Bond, H. (1998) Bearing their souls. Community Care, 24–30 September, 28–29.

Cattanach, A. (1997) Children's Stories in Play Therapy. London: Jessica Kingsley.

Dinkmeyer, D. L. and Muro, J. J. (1971) Group Counselling: Theory and Practise. Itasca, IL: F. E. Peacock.

Dwivedi, K. N. (1993) Groupwork with Children and Adolescents – A Handbook, pp. 4, 9, 10. London: Jessica Kingsley.

Farrell, M. (1984) Groupwork with children: the significance of setting and context. Group Analysis 17(2), 146–155.

Frankel, F., Myatt, R., Cantwell, D. and Feinberg, D. (1997) Parent-assisted transfer of children's social skills training. Journal of American Academy of Child and Adolescent Psychiatry 36(8), 1056–1064.

Krasney-Brown, L. and Brown, M. (1986) Dinosaur's Divorce. Belgium: Proust International.

Ljubomirovic, N. (1999) Therapeutic groupwork with adolescent refugees in the context of war and its stresses. Psychiatry On-line: Internet address HYPERLINK "http://www.priory.com/psych/refugee.htm"

Lomonaco, S., Scheidlinger, S. and Aronson, S. (1998) Time-limited group treatment of children. American Journal of Psychotherapy 52(2), 240–247.

Mayall, M. (1999) Post-traumatic stress disorder – issues in child hostages. National Association of Paediatric Occupational Therapists Journal, Spring, 22.

McGrath P. (1993) Historical development of group psychotherapy. In Dwivedi, K. N. (ed.), Groupwork with Children and Adolescents – a Handbook, pp. 100–114. London: Jessica Kingsley.

Prestige Health Productions (1997) 'You're both still my parents' (Video).

Rickford, F. (1998) Damage limitation society. Guardian (London), Wednesday 22 July, p. 6.

Skynner, R. (1993) Foreword. In Dwivedi, K. N. (ed.), Groupwork with Children and Adolescents – a Handbook, pp. ix–x. London: Jessica Kingsley.

Chapter 10
All in the family: therapy for the families of traumatised children and adolescents

CLAIRE FREDERICK AND CONSTANCE SHELTREN

Every therapist who works with traumatised children and adolescents must deal in some way or another with their families. Those families may be scattered, absent, or even unknown; they may consist of a rapidly changing pattern of foster-caregivers; they may be inescapable trauma-tising and re-traumatising horrors of transgenerational abuse; or they may be physically present and available as resources of support and restorative soothing in the child's treatment and recovery. In this chapter we examine some ways in which therapy for the family may be vital to the healing of the child or adolescent who has been a trauma victim. We look at the special kinds of therapy issues that exist when the traumatiser is a family member. We also consider how models of family therapy can be modified in practical ways that are consonant with the traumatised child's or adolescent's developmental level so that they can become treatment modalities that are as meaningful to the child members of the family as they are to the adults.

Historical perspectives

Early diagnostic and treatment models of acute traumatic and post-traumatic stress disorders were born of wars and their accompanying catastrophes such as the Holocaust (Kardiner 1941, Watkins 1949, Krystal and Niederland 1968). That the trauma victim's family was not usually worked with therapeutically is not surprising, for family therapy itself only began to emerge as a treatment concept in the 1950s, and it was not until 1956 that several separate groups that had been working on concepts of family therapy gained knowledge of one another (Gil 1994).

One group, later identified as the Palo Alto, or MRI, group, studied the families of schizophrenics (Bateson et al. 1956). Eventually, Virginia

184

Satir (1983, 1988) joined this group. From their work emerged a view that the family constituted a system within which the identified patient could be located. They placed more emphasis on the dynamics of the system and less on those of the individual patient, and they developed the concept of **family homeostasis** (Jackson 1957). Family homeostasis was an energy system whose purpose was to keep the family unit functioning. It was maintained through the roles and interactions of family members. Another well-known concept to come from this group was that of the **double bind** (Bateson et al. 1956). A double bind communication occurs when two contradictory messages, one conscious and the other unconscious, are given simultaneously.

Another group converged at the National Institute of Mental Health (Bowen 1960, Wynne et al. 1958) and also focused on work with seriously disturbed patients and their families. At the Menninger Clinic, Ackerman (1958) radically changed the old child guidance rules that neglected the child's family and introduced humour, and later play (1970), into family therapy. With the passage of time various schools and systems of family therapy emerged (Griffin 1993, Gil 1994).

Models of family therapy

Family therapy is a form of group therapy. It is based on the assumption that the patient's relationship to his/her family is an inescapable part of his/her identity. Its emphasis is interpersonal and it focuses on relationships. Family therapy thinks of families as '... comprised of interlocking subunits that influence the presenting problem ...' (Griffin 1993, p. 51). Family therapy can be thought of as having three broad categories of orientation (Levant 1984).

- **Ahistorical process family therapy** identifies and tries to change family interactions in the present. It has no interest in what happened in the past. Within this orientation various models place emphasis on changing communication, on altering the actual structure of the family, on modifying the behaviour within the family, or on the psychoeducation of the family (Griffin 1993).
- The **historical orientation** forms of family therapy have strong psychoanalytic underpinnings. Their emphasis is on the individuation of the family and the growth of the identified patient. This therapy features a less overtly active therapist and is generally longer in duration. Here can be found the object relations model (Wynne et al. 1958) as well as Bowen's (1978) and Kerr and Bowen's (1988) multigenerational family therapy.

- Finally, there are **experiential models** of family therapy (Satir 1983, 1988, Whittaker and Malone 1953) that rely heavily on the interactions of the family with the active therapist.

Therapy with the families of victims traumatised by forces external to the family

The trauma field developed in a fashion almost parallel to the emergence of family therapy. Trauma specialists began to realise that families of trauma victims had their own set of difficulties, and that therapeutic involvement with the patient's family could help them heal. Peterson et al. (1991) compended a list of family characteristics that a number of therapists working with traumatised veterans reported.

The traumatised individual was invariably labelled as the 'identified patient', and the families often had problems coping with the veteran's poor impulse control, rage and violence, substance abuse, poor self-concept, emotional isolation or alienation from the family, and their disturbances of identity.

The wives of the veterans experienced difficulties in several areas. They were often the victims of abuse; they usually operated in the 'caregiver' mode as they responded to crises, and they frequently functioned as the principal breadwinner in the family. They felt helpless to change the problems and guilty that they might be causing them. They were often clinically depressed and suffered from low self-esteem. Stanton and Figley (1978) recommended that both the family of origin and the family of procreation be assessed.

Danieli (1985) described the families of another group of trauma survivors, victims of the Holocaust. She was able to identify the characteristics of families who were successful in their post-traumatic adjustments. These families created patterns of adjustment that allowed them to separate themselves emotionally from the traumatic experiences.

The momentum of emerging family therapy orientations within the trauma field helped call the attention of the community to the fact that 'Families that seek assistance need to be oriented to view the victimization as a family problem, not just a problem of the victimized member' (Figley 1988b, p. 96).

Figley (1988b) described certain stages of family therapy with victims of external forces. It is crucial for such families to confront the trauma of its victim-member and share its catastrophic effects. According to Figley (1988b), there are four phases to such treatment:

- building commitment to the therapeutic objectives
- framing the problem

- reframing the problem
- developing a healing theory, a metaphor that allows the family to heal.

Other approaches to family therapy with the traumatised appear to have value as well. For example, Glynn (1997) reported successfully using behavioural family therapy and family education with veterans and their families. Communication training, anger management, and training in problem solving were featured. A group working with veterans who had served in Europe during the Gulf War (Ford et al. 1998) used an eclectic form of family systems therapy to help the veteran-patient return to psychosocial function.

The literature suggests that families that are treated with various family therapy approaches appear to be able to develop better understanding and appropriately directed empathy for the patient, to integrate them and their traumatic experiences into the family, and to be able to cope with their remaining symptoms more suitably. Family members are no longer isolated from one another by the trauma, and family and individual growth occur.

Family play therapy: addressing the developmental level of the child

Children will probably not fare very well with Figley's and other models of family therapy if they are forced to lie on the procrustean bed of adult communication. The child's verbal and cognitive skills are not fully formed. Children tend to express their feelings and the meanings of their interactions metaphorically, through play and games, story-telling and art. Unless family communication is geared to the developmental level of the child, the child will neither hear it nor understand it. Without avenues of communication that are truly expressive for them, children may not be able to tell or say what is of the deepest meaning to them. Play was introduced into family therapy with children in the 1970s and 1980s (Gil 1994).

Fortunately, many family therapy models can be modified so that the family is able to learn to communicate feelings by sharing the language of childhood together in family play therapy (Gil 1994). The shared vehicles of communication are metaphoric and involve such activities that are designed to allow children to communicate. They utilise the play, story-telling, games, and artwork through which children naturally express themselves. They have the additional value of allowing less developed, more childlike aspects of the adults in the family group to be expressed. In the case of adolescents therapists may have to accommodate to the shifting developmental scene by holding some family therapy sessions as talk sessions and others in therapeutic family play. Family play therapy can be particularly useful with those families that are crippled by their tendencies to view and treat children as little adults and are at a loss as to how to communicate with their children.

Therapy with the families of victims whose trauma has occurred within the family

A fundamental purpose of the family unit is to protect its children from trauma. Yet, intrafamilial trauma became a focus of interest when the physical and sexual abuse of women and children was brought out of the closet by the women's revolution (Ross 1989) and other social changes in the 1970s and 1980s. Eventually, it became well known that a great deal of trauma occurs within the very caregiving environments that should have been affording protection. This kind of trauma is often unreported, and it is not uncommon for its victims to forget it (Williams 1995).

Figley (1988a) noted that families in which trauma has occurred within family boundaries face special problems. Their treatment may take more time and call for therapists with special skills. Such situations are usually quite complex, and frequently the trauma of physical or sexual abuse permeates the entire family system over several generations. It is not uncommon for there to be a number of victims within a single family. Such families frequently have pervasive intrafamilial trauma histories and are often entrenched within special complex, even byzantine modes of coping.

It is this kind of family that often enters clinics and consulting rooms, pushing its vanguard of traumatised child or adolescent victims of intrafamilial abuse before it. The issues are usually complex and often baffling, even to seasoned clinicians, and the existence of intrafamilial secrets of abuse may not be revealed until therapy is well under way. This can produce what Herman (1981) has called the 'crisis of exposure'. There are several protocols available for working with families in which the abuse has occurred (Gelinas 1988a,b, Kolko 1996, Gorham 1997).

Phase-oriented approaches to the treatment of trauma victims (Horowitz 1973, McCann and Pearlman 1990, Herman 1992, Phillips and Frederick 1995, Brown et al. 1997) have become the standard of professional care. These approaches allow the patient to establish personal safety and stability and to develop greater ego strength (Frederick and McNeal 1999). It is only when the patient is stable that he/she can begin to access and learn to master trauma material safely. We recommend a phase-oriented approach for all therapy with the families of trauma victims as well.

Families, like individual patients, need to become as safe and stable as they can, to develop a stronger, healthier family ego, to be able to deal with the trauma of its children in a healthy way, and to honour the healthy growth and differentiation of their members. Much of the therapy with families within which the trauma has occurred remains in the safety and stability stages. The emphasis here is education, ego strengthening (Frederick and McNeal 1999), the promotion of appropriate boundaries, and helping the members learn to identify, express, and modulate affect. Eventually some of these families are able to confront and master the trauma, deal with the inevitable grief connected with it, and transform and integrate the traumatic family experiences. At any time and for any reason that a family destabilises, the therapy must become refocused on establishing safety and stability.

It is vital that the family therapist should have training and experience in family therapy and have a true family therapy orientation. We agree with Putnam (1997) that the family therapist should be someone other than the individual therapist of any family member. However, we also recognise that the constraints presented by limited numbers of trained family therapists in certain geographical locations and by certain administrative restrictions within some healthcare agencies may make this, at times, an unrealistic ideal. When extremely chaotic families are in treatment, we strongly advise that family therapy be conducted by at least two trained co-therapists. This permits transference and countertransference issues to be sorted out more productively.

Below are some guidelines for the therapist working with families within which the child has been traumatised. It is the better part of wisdom to follow these or similar guidelines in all therapy with the families of traumatised children. Because there is no way of knowing what information and revelations may appear during the course of therapy, structure and education about the limits of confidentiality cannot be glossed over.

A phase-oriented approach to family therapy should always include within its structure 'rules' or guidelines that promote the formation, strengthening and appropriate management of boundaries within the family. This facilitates the kind of healthy differentiation of family members that can cause a family to become more integrated.

Roadmap for phase-oriented therapy with families within which children and adolescents have been traumatised*

A therapeutic or working alliance is essential in family therapy

This alliance allows the therapist and the family to work together towards commonly agreed therapeutic goals and to resolve transference problems. It must be formed with the entire family unit. Like alliances with individual patients it is based on such elements as respect, consistency, and empathy. In family therapy it is the family that is asked to share some common goals that the members can agree upon with the therapist.

Confidentiality and the limits of confidentiality

An open discussion of the rules of confidentiality and the need to report any child abuse must take place with all the participating family members before family therapy can begin. This discussion establishes certain boundaries as well as the safety of the child. With very complex families, social agencies, such as child protection services are frequently involved. The clarification of confidentiality is crucial. Appropriate forms for releases of information must be signed so that consultations with other therapists involved as well as with child protection services can take place. We also recommend that the children sign releases so they can be aware with whom the family therapy would be discussed. When court proceedings of any kind are involved, the family needs to be informed that a summary of the family therapy might be included in the court proceedings. Explaining the limits of confidentiality with regard to suspected child abuse may take a full session of treatment. Often multi-generational families of abuse have different definitions of what abusive and traumatic activities are, compared with how legal statutes define them and how professionals may regard them. It may be necessary to brainstorm with the whole family about 'What is abuse?'. It may be important to hear out their ideas and then explain what the law says.

Establishing boundaries

During the initial phase of treatment, each of the participants is asked to sign a copy of the rules of family therapy (see Box 10.1). This becomes an important tool in treatment. The therapist may have to reinforce the rules by reminding family members of them. All family therapy must take

---

*This section is reprinted from 'Roadmap for therapy with families within which children and adolescents have been traumatized', an unpublished manuscript by C. Frederick and C. Sheltren, with permission.

place within a framework that provides both safety and the positive expectation that growth can occur. Certain therapy rules that promote boundary creation, strengthening, and management encourage and facilitate these goals.

Box 10.1 The rules of family therapy

- Listen when someone else is speaking. This means that you do not focus on forming a reply or retort in your own mind to what is being said. Instead, you sincerely attempt to understand what is being said.
- Use 'I' messages. This allows you to say what you think and feel without becoming a 'universal judge'. Use statements like:
  - 'I feel', (feeling word)
  - 'When', (state what action affected you)
  - 'Because', (state why it affected you)
  - 'What I would like you to do next time is....'
  - 'Would you be willing to do that?'
- Don't use roadblocks to communication such as name-calling, putdowns, belittling and blaming.
- Accept and validate the rights of others and of yourself to have feelings. Feelings are neither right nor wrong, good nor bad. They just are.
- Become aware of your body language. For example, slouching in your chair could be a way of saying 'I am not really committed to this'. Sitting rigidly with your arms crossed rigidly could be a way of communicating 'Don't you dare say anything that might upset me!'.
- Be on time.
- No mood-altering substances are to be used within 24 hours before and after therapy. If there have been problems with substance abuse in the past, there now needs to be a commitment to abstinence. If there has been a relapse, this needs to be discussed at the beginning of the following session.
- Family therapy sessions should end when the session is completed. This means that it is not all right to continue actively working on issues discussed in therapy with family members as if the session had never ended.

Reporting child trauma revealed in family therapy

The safety of the child (or children) must be the primary concern of the therapist. This may mean reporting material that has been divulged in family therapy sessions. Difficult though this may be, it is an unavoidable step when intrafamilial physical or sexual trauma to a child is revealed. Although many therapists feel compelled to report because of the legal mandate to do so, there are psychodynamic reasons why reporting may be valuable to the healing process.

- First, the reporting usually stops the abuser from traumatising the child.

- Secondly, although other family members may object to the reporting on one level, it must be remembered that more vulnerable and child-like ego states or aspects of self in these family members are usually strengthened by reporting. In families where intergenerational abuse is a pattern this can be particularly important.

In our experience, therapists who fail to report intrafamilial abuse and trauma are usually 'fired' by the same family members who are overtly upset at the idea of reporting. Additionally, the reporting therapist becomes a model of strength and protection with whom all family members can identify in their growth process.

Developmental roads to communication

When family play therapy is contemplated, it is necessary to establish that sometimes the family would use talking as the major form of communicating while at other times we would be more child-centred through using stories, doing a family sandtrays or playing games.

The expression of feeling in therapy

The expression of feelings by family members is crucial to the success of the therapy. The appropriate expression of feelings is difficult for many people, but in families of incest and substance abuse skills in these areas can be particularly low. We continually gave the family basic information about feelings: 'Feelings are not good or bad, right or wrong – they just are'; 'some feelings are comfortable and some are uncomfortable'.

Discovering and utilising the values of the family

The term 'family values' has been all too often misused for political and moralistic purposes. Yet within almost every family, no matter how pathological its behaviour may be, resides a core of positive values, which, when recognised and vivified, can energise and guide the progress of the family. It is often challenging to the therapist as well as to the family to turn, momentarily, away from the current conflicts into the repository of their treasured ideals. To do so can strengthen families enormously.

Family therapy may have to proceed when important family members cannot be present

Frequently traumatised children and adolescents become separated from physically and sexually abusive family members. Nevertheless, the principles of family therapy can be used with the remaining family, with foster and adoptive parents, and with social agencies. They can actually be extended into individual psychotherapy (Kerr and Bowen 1988, Hay et al. 1995).

Internal changes in family members may bring about changes in the family dynamics

Many theorists (Watkins and Watkins 1997, Frederick and McNeal 1999) believe that the human personality consists of a number of dynamic ego states that operate in relationship with one another as if they were members of an internal family. Many of these ego states are introjects of family members. When individuals are able to change their internal dynamics and ego state relationships, the dynamics of the family change as well (Frederick 1995).

Clinical example: the Blakes

The Blakes were a multigenerational family within which incest, physical abuse and alcoholism were substantive issues. The grandparents were raising their five grandchildren:

- Lacy, age 5, had been removed from her mother's home at birth
- Timmy, age 7, was a drug-affected child with severe attention deficit
- Ryan, age 9, was typically a quiet child who had outbursts of anger and displayed a great deal of passive resistance
- Megan, age 11, was 'the good child and student' who was also emotionally withdrawn
- Rachelle, age 14, had a dissociative disorder. She had been sexually abused by various men and boyfriends who had lived at her mother's drug-infested house.

The Blakes had been referred to family therapy by the child protective services. The children were all in individual therapy, and the grandfather was being treated for depression by a psychiatrist. The family was seen by co-therapists; a marriage and a family therapist and a psychiatrist.

The Blake family lacked consistency and the home was fraught with chaos. Grandfather was a strict disciplinarian who had been warned by social services that physical punishment would not be tolerated. The enforcement of rules within this household was totally inconsistent. Rules might be rigidly exacted, could be dealt with reasonably or might be totally ignored. Thus we, the co-therapists knew that establishing clear boundaries initially would be critical to the therapy.

The family was involved with the child protection services on an ongoing basis. This made the clarification of confidentiality a priority in setting up treatment. Appropriate releases of information were signed by all the adults and children involved. A full session of treatment was devoted to explanations and elucidations about how suspicions of child abuse could limit confidentiality. During this session, we challenged the whole family to reveal old ideas and develop new ideas about 'what is abuse?'.

During this initial phase of treatment, we also went through the rules of therapy and had each of the participants sign a copy. This became an important tool in treatment, as we constantly needed to remind family members of the therapy rules. A decision was mad to utilise family play therapy techniques in the therapy of this family. Consequently, we established that although talking would be used as the major form of communicating, at other times we would be more child-centred through telling stories, doing a family sandtray or playing games.

The expression of feelings was difficult for this family. We gave the family fundamental information about feelings. We told them repeatedly that 'feelings are not good or bad, right or wrong – they just are' and 'some feelings are comfortable and some are uncomfortable'. In spite of this ongoing educational piece of work, we observed that the grandparents continuously discounted their grandchildren's feelings.

One day we brought in the story from *An Elephant in the Living Room* (Hastings and Typpo 1984) called 'Fuzzy's feelings'. This is the story of a caterpillar who 'stuffed' the feelings he had in his alcoholic home and became immobilised in a cocoon. A wise butterfly came to his cocoon and told Fuzzy he needed to recognise, accept and share his feelings in order to get out of his cocoon.

Another communication and feeling tool used in the Blake's family therapy was the 'stamp game' (Black 1984). In this game each family member picked up stamps that represented three feelings he/she had during the past week and shared them with the entire family. We also utilised Richard Gardner's (1998) 'talking, feeling, doing game' to facilitate communication, understanding, and the expression of feelings. Utilising these stories and games provided a way of integrating the child's developmental level within the therapy and helped the grandparents learn how to relate more appropriately.

The 14 year old in this family was very sexually active, and her behaviour was sexually suggestive. The grandparents typically responded to this with rage. They tried to humiliate her, and they threatened her. Our task as therapists became one of helping the grandparents express their values about the kind of sexual behaviour that they believed was appropriate within this family. We were able to discuss the discrepancies and contradictions between the values they learned as children and the ones acted out as incestuous child abuse within the family. The teenage girl was aware that her mother had behaved in very much the same way as she currently was. We talked about how the family therapy could now support her becoming someone different from her mother. With the rest of the family we wondered with her what strengths she might already have that would help her get the attention, love and acceptance she wanted without using her body in a way that caused her to feel dislike of herself. This allowed us to help the family focus more on how individuals in the family were able to get attention, love and acceptance.

The family gradually developed better communication, greater empathy for its members, and better coping skills. As they began to look forward to meetings they had once dreaded and found alien and confusing, they discovered that they were learning to pull together as a family.

Conclusion

Family therapy when children have been sexually abused is challenging both for parents and for therapists. Often these families are experienced as overwhelming for the therapist. This is an indication of how the situation feels for the entire family. It is often essential to instruct and to reinforce parenting techniques with these very complex families. Parents in these family groups need a great deal of encouragement and support because, even with their best efforts, the behaviour of sexually abused children is often slow to change, and treatment is typically long term. This often means that many families may not remain with family therapy until it is brought to the desired, positive conclusion. It is important to remember that families that have not been able to stay the course may, nonetheless, have gained some valuable tools in the family therapy they did have.

References

Ackerman, N. W. (1958) The Psychodynamics of Family Life. New York: Basic Books.

Ackerman, N. W. (1970) Child participation in family therapy. Family Process 9, 403–410.

Bateson, G., Jackson, D., Haley, J. and Weakland, J. (1956) Toward a theory of schizophrenia. Behavioral Science 1, 251–264.

Black, C. (1984) The Stamp Game. Denver: MAC Publishing.

Bowen, M. (1960) A family concept of schizophrenia. In Jackson, D. D. (ed.), The Etiology of Schizophrenia, pp. 346–372. New York: Basic Books.

Bowen, M. (1978) Family Therapy in Clinical Practice. New York: Jason Aronson.

Brown, D. P., Scheflin, A. W. and Hammond, D. C. (1997) Memory, Trauma, Treatment, and the Law. New York: W. W. Norton.

Danieli, Y. (1985) The treatment and prevention of long-term effects and intergenerational transmission of victimization. In Figley C. R. (ed.), Trauma and its Wake:

The Study and Treatment of Post-Traumatic Stress Disorder, pp. 295–313. New York: Brunner/Mazel.

Figley, C. R. (1988a) Treating traumatic stress in family therapy. Journal of Traumatic Stress 1, 1.

Figley, C. R. (1988b) Post-traumatic family therapy. In Ochberg, F. M. (ed.), Post-Traumatic Therapy and Victims of Violence, pp. 83–109. New York: Brunner/Mazel.

Ford, J. D., Chandler, P., Thacker, B. et al. (1998) Family systems therapy after Operation Desert Storm with European-theater veterans. Journal of Marital and Family Therapy 24(2), 243–250.

Frederick, C. (1995) The internal family and the external family: perspectives on family systems aspects of ego state therapy. Presented at the Annual Meeting of the American Society of Clinical Hypnosis, San Diego, California, March.

Frederick, C. and McNeal, S. (1999) Inner Strengths: Contemporary Psychotherapy and Hypnosis for Ego-Strengthening. Mahwah, NJ: Lawrence Erlbaum.

Gardner, R. (1998) The Talking, Feeling, Doing Game: A Psychotherapeutic Game for Children. Cresskill, NJ: Creative Therapeutics.

Gelinas, D. J. (1988a). Family therapy: critical early structuring. In Sgroi S. M. (ed.) Vulnerable Populations. Vol.1, Evaluation and Treatment of Sexually Abused Children and Adult Survivors, pp. 51–76. Lexington, MA: Lexington Books.

Gelinas, D. J. (1988b). Family therapy: characteristic family constellation and basic therapeutic stance. In Sgroi S. M. (ed.) Vulnerable Populations. Vol.1, Evaluation and Treatment of Sexually Abused Children and Adult Survivors, pp. 25–49. Lexington, MA: Lexington Books.

Gil, E. (1994) Play in Family Therapy. New York: Brunner/Mazel.

Glynn, S. M. (1997) Behavioral family therapy for chronic combat-related PTSD. National Center for PTSD Clinical Quarterly 7, 34–38.

Gorham, E. L. (1997) Sixteen-step strategic family therapy for the treatment of child sexual abuse: a treatment adaptation and case example. Psychotherapy in Private Practice 16, 211–237.

Griffin, W. A. (1993) Family Therapy: Fundamentals of Theory and Practice. New York: Brunner/Mazel.

Hastings, J. M. and Typpo, M. H. (1984) An Elephant in the Living Room: The Children's Book. Minneapolis: Compcare Publications.

Hay, J., Leheup, R. and Almudevar, M. (1995) Family therapy with 'invisible families'. British Journal of Medical Psychology 68, 125–133.

Herman, J. L. (1981) Father Daughter Incest. Cambridge, MA: Harvard University Press.

Herman, J. L. (1992) Trauma and Recovery. New York: Basic Books.

Horowitz, M. J. (1973) Phase oriented treatment of stress response syndromes. American Journal of Psychotherapy 27, 506–515.

Jackson, D. D. (1957) The question of family homeostasis. Psychiatric Quarterly Supplement 31, 79–90.

Kardiner, A. (1941) The Traumatic Neuroses of War. New York: Hoeber.

Kerr, M. E. and Bowen, M. (1988) Family Evaluation: An Approach Based on Bowen Theory. New York: W. W. Norton.

Kolko, D. J. (1996) Individual cognitive behavioral treatment and family therapy for physically abused children and their offending parents: a comparison of clinical outcomes. Child Maltreatment 1, 322–342.

Krystal, H. and Niederland, W. G. (1968) Clinical observations on the survivor syndrome. In Krystal, H. (ed.), Massive Psychic Trauma. New York: International Universities Press.

Levant, R. (1984) Family Therapy: A Comparative Overview. Englewood Cliffs, NJ: Prentice-Hall.

McCann, I. L. and Pearlman, L. A. (1990) Psychological Trauma and the Adult Survivor. Theory, Therapy, and Transformation. New York: Brunner/Mazel.

Peterson, K., Prout, M. and Schwarz, R. (1991) Post-Traumatic Stress Disorder: A Clinician's Guide. New York: Plenum Press.

Phillips, M. and Frederick, C. (1995) Healing the Divided Self: Clinical and Ericksonian Hypnotherapy for Dissociative and Post-traumatic Conditions. New York: W. W. Norton.

Putnam, F. W. (1997) Dissociation in Children and Adolescents: A Developmental Approach. New York: Guilford Press.

Ross, C. J. (1989) Multiple Personality Disorder. New York: John Wiley.

Satir, V. (1983) Conjoint Family Therapy, 3rd edn. Palo Alto, CA: Science and Behavior Books.

Satir, V. (1988) The New Peoplemaking. Mountainview, CA: Science and Behavior Books.

Stanton, , M. D. and Figley, C. R. (1978) Treating the Vietnam veteran within the family system. In Figley, C. R. (ed.), Stress Disorders among Vietnam Veterans: Theory, Research, and Treatment, pp. 281–290. New York: Brunner/Mazel.

Watkins, J. G. (1949) Hypnotherapy of War Neuroses. New York: Ronald Press.

Watkins, J. G. and Watkins, H. H. (1997) Ego States: Theory and Therapy. New York: W. W. Norton.

Whittaker, C. and Malone, M. (1953) The Roots of Psychotherapy. New York: Blakiston.

Williams, L. M. (1995) Recovered memories of abuse in women with documented child sexual victimization histories. Journal of Traumatic Stress 8, 649–673.

Wynne, L. C., Rykoff, I. M., Day, J. and Hirsch S. I. (1958) Pseudomutuality in the family relations of schizophrenics. Psychiatry 21, 205–220.

Chapter 11
Eye movement desensitisation and reprocessing*

RICKY GREENWALD

Eye movement desensitisation and reprocessing (EMDR) is arguably the most effective and efficient psychological trauma treatment available. The efficacy of EMDR in trauma treatment is supported by more controlled studies than any other psychotherapy approach (Shapiro 1996a) and has gained mainstream acceptance (Chambless et al. 1998) despite a history of controversy (Greenwald 1996a). Direct comparisons with other recommended treatments have shown EMDR to be at least equal in effect and far more efficient (e.g. Marcus et al. 1997, Lee et al. 1999).

EMDR is a complex method which combines cognitive-behavioural and client-centred approaches in a unique manner. To oversimplify, it features having the client concentrate intensely on the most upsetting part of the traumatic memory while moving the eyes from side to side (by following the therapist's moving hand or other object) at the rate of about 1 round trip per second, for a variable duration of about 20–60 seconds. Following a set of eye movements, the client is asked to report whatever 'came up', possibly including changes in the imagery, thought, emotion or physical sensation (all are common). This report becomes the focus of the next set of eye movements. For example, if the client reports, 'Now I'm feeling more angry', the therapist may say, 'Concentrate on that' for the next set. This procedure is repeated until the client can identify no further distressing elements of the memory and can embrace a more positive or adaptive perspective regarding the memory. For full effect, related memories may also require similar treatment, as more than one traumatic memory may be driving the presenting symptoms. Detailed procedural information is beyond the scope of this chapter, but is available elsewhere (Shapiro 1995, Greenwald 1999a).

*This chapter is a modified version of a paper first published in the *Clinical Child Psychology and Psychiatry* 1988; 3(2):279–287.

History and current status of EMDR

EMDR's brief history has been marked by considerable excitement as well as controversy. Shapiro's (1989a,b) initial reports, which included step-by-step instructions, presented 'EMD' as a rapid treatment for traumatic memories, sometimes even curing post-traumatic stress disorder (PTSD) in a single session. When Shapiro observed that practitioners of her new technique were not doing as she was, she came to appreciate the complexity of the method, including the 'reprocessing' element, which was added to the name (Shapiro 1991b). She expanded her workshop to include more detailed instruction as well as small-group supervised practicums, and suggested this supervised training as a minimum requirement for responsible practice (Shapiro 1991a).

Meanwhile, outcomes in published reports of EMD and EMDR varied considerably, probably because of variations in the quality of the intervention. This led to a division between appropriately trained clinicians and academicians, who knew from experience that EMDR worked (Greenwald 1994b), and appropriately sceptical clinicians and academicians who had not been convinced by the empirical data (Acierno et al. 1994). This gap was magnified because EMDR-trained clinicians had greater access to positive reports before they were published, as well as a better understanding of the flaws which figured prominently in those studies that seemed to show EMDR in a less favourable light (Greenwald 1996a).

A number of more recent studies featuring a higher fidelity to the revised EMDR protocol have been quite positive, consistent with Shapiro's initial findings. In fact, EMDR's efficacy is supported by more controlled studies than any other psychotherapy treatment for trauma (Shapiro 1996a). EMDR has become widely recognised as efficacious in the treatment of trauma (Greenwald 1996a, Shapiro 1996a, Chambless et al. 1998, Feske 1998, van Etten and Taylor 1998) and is considered by many to be the treatment of choice for traumatic memories and related applications. At this writing, controversy does continue, with some die-hard EMDR opponents straying ever farther from the data to make their points (Greenwald 1999b).

The need for formal, supervised training in EMDR has been strongly endorsed by those therapists who have undergone such training (Lipke 1994). The emergence of treatment fidelity as a key factor determining outcome (Greenwald 1996a, Lee et al. 1996, Shapiro 1996b) has further highlighted the importance of training. Indeed, some now question whether the currently dominant model of training is sufficient for mastery of the method (Greenwald 1996a, 1997). The responsible clinician who plans to use EMDR is urged to pursue the most comprehensive training opportunity available. (Note: The EMDR International

Association is the independent professional organisation which sets standards for EMDR training. Their list of approved trainers is available on line at www.emdria.org.)

Although after EMDR a memory may become less vivid, during treatment the EMDR process seems to facilitate enhanced recall of memory details. Caryl McBride (personal communication, 12/94) studied EMDR's utility in enhancing recall of abuse memory details for children who had been identified as victims of abuse. Following the standard interview given by the state agency, EMDR was used to elicit numerous additional details, many of which were then independently corroborated. This well-designed study showed very strong results with the first 20 children, but then funding ran out and it was not completed or reported. McBride's findings are consistent with the results of Lipke's (1994) survey of 442 EMDR-trained clinicians, in which 86% described EMDR as more likely than other methods to lead to the emergence of repressed material (Note: Although there is no evidence that EMDR influences the accuracy of accessed memories, memories in general cannot automatically be assumed to be completely accurate.)

The underlying mechanism of EMDR is not known. Shapiro has suggested that the procedure somehow induces accelerated information processing, whereby dysfunctionally stored traumatic material can be accessed, rapidly integrated and thereby depotentiated. Along these lines, some have speculated that the purported accelerated information processing effect may be related to REM dreaming (e.g. Greenwald 1995, Stickgold 1998). Taking a different tack, and not addressing the possible effect of the eye movements, others have pointed out that the EMDR procedure is quite comprehensive in incorporating virtually every element believed to be effective in trauma therapy (Sweet 1995, Hyer and Brandsma 1997). The question of how EMDR works is far from resolved, and in particular the role of the eye movements remains a mystery.

Although most studies have focused on trauma or PTSD, EMDR has been applied to numerous conditions, including dissociative disorders, grief, somatic problems, anxiety, depression and addictions (Shapiro 1995). Generally the approach is to locate and reprocess the distressing memory or memories at the root of the disturbance. However, some applications also rely on the apparent enhancement effect of EMDR on other techniques, including hypnosis, visualisation, affirmation and learning. This range of application is consistent with Shapiro's (1995) proposition that EMDR facilitates accelerated information processing. Although we await further reports on EMDR's possible range of applications, its stature as a trauma treatment can no longer be denied.

EMDR for children and adolescents

The use of EMDR with traumatised children and adolescents also appears to be viable, although the documentation specifically relating to this population is more limited. Hundreds of cases have been informally reported, with generally positive results (Greenwald 1993). Published case reports on EMDR for children have been uniformly positive and consistent with findings on analogous treatment of adults, except that child treatment may be even more rapid (Shapiro 1991a, Mendoza-Weitman 1992, Cocco and Sharpe 1993, Greenwald 1993, 1994a, 1998a, b, Grosso 1996, Cohen and Lahad 1997, Pellicer 1993, Rodriguez 1997). For example, Greenwald (1994a) reported that all five children treated with 1–2 EMDR sessions several months after a hurricane recovered to their pre-trauma symptom levels, with gains maintaining at 1 month follow-up.

Controlled studies are also beginning to be reported; since most of them have not yet been published, they are briefly reviewed here.

Chemtob and colleagues (in press) reported very positive results in using EMDR with children traumatised by Hurricane Iniki in Kauai, who had already failed to respond to a generally effective small-group treatment programme. The design featured a delay control group, independent assessment with several standardised measures, and five therapists with varying levels of EMDR training and experience (level 1 minimum, plus specialised child EMDR training). The treatment protocol was clearly specified, and a number of efforts were made to ensure fidelity. Participants averaged a 58% reduction on the primary trauma measure following three sessions, with results holding several months later. Significant reductions were also found on anxiety and depression measures as well as visits to the school nurse.

Puffer et al. (1998) reported on a study of 20 children and adolescents aged 8–17 who were non-randomly assigned (according to convenience of scheduling) to EMDR treatment or delayed treatment groups. Treatment was a single session; the focus was a single trauma or loss. The first author conducted all treatment and assessment, using several measures at pre, post, and 1–2 month follow-up. There was no change during the 1 month no-treatment delay, and significant improvement between the first and last scores on all measures. On the best measure of trauma symptoms (Impact of Events Scale), of the 17 participants starting in the clinical range, 11 moved to normal levels, and 3 others dropped 12 or more points, whereas the other 3 stayed the same. Problematic design features include lack of independent assessment (although no subjective scoring was involved) and use of a therapist with only partial EMDR training. Also, 3 participants had ongoing sources of distress, making recovery unlikely. Still, the results were quite positive, although somewhat more variable than in other studies.

Wilson et al. (Sandra Wilson, personal communication, 6/98) have completed data collection on 70 participants in a study of a 3-session trauma-focused EMDR treatment with 70 children diagnosed with PTSD ($n = 27$) or PTSD symptoms ($n = 43$), aged 8–11. This study features a randomised design with a delayed treatment group, multiple well-trained therapists, and blind, independent assessment using multiple standardised measures. Although statistical analysis has not been completed, preliminary review of the data is extremely favourable for EMDR. Wilson noted that the occasional EMDR 'failures' were consistently diagnostic of ongoing sources of distress.

Rubin et al. (in press) reported on a randomised study in a child guidance centre, with EMDR being added to the eclectic treatment for the experimental group. Participants (N = 39, ages 6–15) had a variety of diagnoses, and all had a trauma history. Therapists were social work interns with the full EMDR training who received monthly supervision by an experienced EMDR-trained child therapist. Independent fidelity ratings ranged from adequate to good. The single outcome measure (Child Behaviour Checklist) does not assess post-traumatic stress, and is known to be relatively insensitive to change. This study found only non-significant trends favouring EMDR. It is unclear whether this reflects actual small-to-nonexistent effects, or the insensitivity of their assessment.

Weinberg and Caspers (1997) reported on a pilot study in which EMDR was applied in an innovative way to children with learning disorders. They randomly divided 6 boys (grades 3–4) from the same resource room into 2 groups. Participants in both groups received a 10 minute individual treatment session twice a week for 8 weeks, focusing on recent difficult or upsetting situations which occurred during school. The experimental group was given EMDR during these sessions, whereas for the control group, the situations were simply discussed. All 3 of the children in the EMDR group, as well as 1 in the control group, made rather dramatic gains on various measures of reading and writing skills; the 2 others in the control group showed little change. Their follow-up study (Weinberg and Caspers 1998) reported similar findings except that in the second study, not all of those receiving EMDR responded as positively as in the first one. These studies included serious limitations such as small nuber of subjects and use of children with untreated major trauma, who might not, therefore, reasonably be expected to respond fully to the treatment intervention, which was focused on more minor school-related experiences.

Several researchers have targeted traumatic memories with EMDR in the hopes of reducing criminal or acting-out behaviours. Soberman et al.

(in press) reported on the EMDR treatment of 22 pre-adolescent and adolescent boys adjudicated to residential treatment for a range of criminal offences. This study featured random assignment to wait-list and treatment groups, multiple trauma-focused and behavioural measures and a fully trained EMDR therapist. Design problems include use of a single therapist and lack of independent assessment (although only objectively scored measures were used). Following 3 EMDR sessions focused on the primary identified traumatic memory (or memories), both the memory-specific trauma measure (Impact of Events Scale) and the problem behaviours showed significant reductions. Global measures of post-traumatic symptoms showed a trend of reduction that did not reach significance, probably indicating that other traumatic memories remained untreated.

Datta and Wallace (1996) reported on the EMDR treatment of 10 incarcerated adolescent male sex offenders who themselves had also been sexually abused. Following an average of 3 EMDR sessions focused on their own trauma history, in addition to standard care, participants showed significantly increased empathy for victims of abuse – such empathy presumably being incompatible with further abusive behaviour. At 1 year follow-up, the empathy gains were maintained, as well as the reduced distress (SUDS) and increased self-esteem (VoC) related to the targeted traumatic memories. Similar gains in empathy were not shown by control groups. Design problems include lack of independent assessment as well as the fact that the empathy measure's validity has not been fully established. Additional data on individual participants indicate that many showed objective behavioural gains, including spontaneous attempts at victim restitution, increased scores on IQ tests, improved school performance and exemplary behaviour in the community.

Scheck et al. (1998) reported on the EMDR treatment of a high-risk acting-out community sample including both adolescent (aged 16–19, n =18) and young adult females (ages 20–25, $n = 42$). All reported a trauma history, and over $3/4$ met criteria for PTSD. Participants were randomly assigned to the EMDR group or the active listening (AL) control group, each of which received 2 treatment sessions focused on the traumatic memory. Independent, blind assessment of 5 standardised measures at pre- and post-treatment indicated that both treatments were helpful, but EMDR much more so. In fact, following treatment, those in the EMDR group fell within the normative (non-clinical) range for all measures, whereas only 1 outcome score fell in that range for the AL group. Three month follow-up of a sub-sample showed maintenance of gains. This study found no differences in the responses of the young adults compared to the adolescents (J. Schaeffer, personal communication, 11/96), in that EMDR was equally effective.

In summary, the main findings are:

- EMDR seems to be about as effective with children and adolescents as with adults, but may be even quicker
- the EMDR treatment of traumatic memories can affect a wide range of behaviours.
- a somewhat different technical repertoire is required to use EMDR with children. As with adults, supervised training and practice is required for client safety and for more consistent effectiveness. Those working with children and adolescents should additionally master the age-appropriate technical repertoire (Greenwald 1999) for optimal results.

Case examples

Case 1: PTSD

EMDR may be used in a variety of trauma treatment contexts, from single-session treatment following a disaster or critical incident, to frequent or occasional use in the context of long-term treatment with a chronic trauma victim. Individual response can vary, not only from one person to another, but from one session to the next. The following case is presented as an example to illustrate the procedure as used in clinical practice. This is not intended as a demonstration of efficacy, nor as an invitation for those untrained in EMDR to attempt the techniques incompletely described herein. Also, since the EMDR protocol includes a number of possible variations, the case also represents the judgement and personal style of the author.

'Jennie' was a 10 year old girl who, at age 6, had been raped and tortured daily for a week by a small group of older boys in school, until she finally told her mother. When the school failed to respond, Jennie was removed to prevent recurrence, and tutored at home. She developed PTSD, with numerous symptoms including intrusive memories, bedwetting, nightmares, social withdrawal and poor personal hygiene. Since the torture experience had involved orders to read aloud and perform in certain ways, Jennie later had a very hard time with structured academic activities, which triggered the torture memories. She received 2 years of psychotherapy, but made only slight improvement. She continued to experience an appropriate and supportive family environment.

Four years after the trauma, with symptoms unabated, Jennie's mother enrolled her in a pilot study involving EMDR. Just prior to EMDR treatment, she was assessed with the Parent Report of Post-traumatic Symptoms (PROPS) and the Child Report of Post-traumatic Symptoms

(CROPS), covering a broad spectrum of post-traumatic symptomatology (Greenwald and Rubin 1999). She was also assessed with the Subjective Units of Distress Scale (SUDS), a self-report of current reactivity to the traumatic memory (Wolpe, modified by Shapiro 1989a), and the Problem Rating Scale (PRS), a parent rating of the present severity of the problems which the parent has identified as being of greatest concern (Greenwald 1996b). She had 1 introductory and 5 treatment sessions over a 2 month period, and was reassessed at 2 months after the end of treatment.

Jennie expressed considerable discomfort at the prospect of deliberately facing her traumatic memories. Therefore, the therapist practised having Jennie call out 'Stop!' to make the therapist's hand stop moving, to emphasise that Jennie could be in control in this situation. Then the therapist helped Jennie to select images which might help her to begin to gain some sense of mastery over the memory (Greenwald 1999). She chose to imagine herself as more powerful, first by wielding a baseball bat, and then by becoming a bear. With each image in turn, she was asked to concentrate intensely on the image ('Notice how heavy the bat is, how you feel when you hold it ...') while moving her eyes back and forth as described above. Following this exercise, she did indeed report feeling stronger and more confident – and finally willing to begin to face the memory.

She was asked to select the most upsetting segment of the memory that she was willing to think about. She was asked to concentrate on the visual image (being held at knife point), along with the associated cognition (I'm helpless), emotion (scared), and physical sensation (sick to her stomach). She was instructed to maintain this focus during about 20–30 seconds of eye movements – but also to allow spontaneous changes in focus, should any occur. Then she was asked to take a deep breath, rest a moment, and report on anything she may have noticed. This routine was repeated perhaps a dozen times, with her previous response generally serving as a starting focal point for the new set of eye movements. Although at first she reported that the image became more vivid, along with a stronger sense of terror, after a few sets she began to report a steady decrease in the potency of the image. Using the SUDS, the image began at 7 (on a 0–10 scale with 10 being the highest level of distress), moved up to 9 and eventually went down to 5.

After about 35 minutes, Jennie said she felt very tired and wanted to stop. Before completing the session, she was asked to concentrate again on the positive images (with eye movements), and then, also with eye movements, asked to imagine packing the memory into a secure container where it could stay until the next meeting. This type of exercise is often done at the end of a session, to consolidate gains and facilitate recomposure (Greenwald 1999).

The next two sessions generally followed this routine and lasted about an hour each. The same positive images were routinely introduced, and sometimes Jennie would spontaneously inject the positive image into the memory, for example by imagining beating the boys up with the bat. She was able to master several disturbing parts of the memory in each session.

On a technical note, even when the SUDS goes down to 0, work on that memory segment is not over. The client is then asked to select an adaptive reframe related to the memory, such as, 'I'm safe now', or 'It wasn't my fault'. If she cannot endorse this view wholeheartedly, the obstacles to that endorsement are identified and treated with EMDR until no obstacle remains. Finally, the client is asked to notice any residual body tension or discomfort, which must also be treated to full resolution.

Once the memory itself appeared to be worked through, EMDR was applied to related targets, such as the location of the trauma and the faces of the perpetrators. EMDR was then applied to current triggers, such as seeing one of the perpetrators on the street, or being told by her tutor to read aloud. Jennie was also able to fully endorse, at this and later sessions, the following statements: 'It's over now', 'I can keep myself safe', 'It wasn't my fault', 'I'm a good person', and 'I'm pretty'.

The fourth EMDR session was only 15 minutes, and involved reviewing previously addressed material and applying EMDR to anything that still seemed to carry any degree of distress greater than 0. There was an additional memory segment that had been missed before, and there was more work done on current triggers related to personal attractiveness as well as educational activities. The fifth and final session was also short, and involved additional work on a few targets which still carried minuscule reported levels of distress.

Jennie's pretreatment combined score on the CROPS and PROPS (broad-spectrum post-traumatic symptoms) was 54, way over the suggested 'clinical' cutoff of 36 (Greenwald and Rubin 1999). At the 2 month post-treatment follow-up, her combined score was 26, well below the cutoff. The SUDS (current reactivity to the memory) began at 7 and was 0 at follow-up. The PRS (parent rating of biggest problems), using a similar 0–10 scale, included the following items: refusal to learn on command; self-worth (posture, dress, hygiene); and sleep problems (nightmares, wet bed). The pre-treatment PRS scores were, respectively, 10, 9 and 5; at follow-up, the respective scores were 1, 1.5 and 0.

Jennie's responses to this course of treatment were fascinating. On the physiological level, her mother reported that Jennie experienced a severe face rash for a couple of days following the fourth session (the memory included her face having been pressed on to concrete); and that she grew several inches taller within the 4 months following the beginning of treatment. Her mother also reported occasional emotional volatility between sessions, and then generally improved mood and functioning, as well as some turbulence and confusion in the family as Jennie was apparently 'suddenly catching up on 4 years of her development'. She worked with her tutor with increased comfort, and also began venturing outside her home for education, by attending a course at the local community college. Jennie herself, who only grudgingly participated in the treatment, later made a work of art for a community exhibit on the theme of interpersonal violence. Her piece featured the following statement: 'If you are raped, try EMDR. I did, and I feel good now'.

An informal follow-up occurred 2 years later, when Jennie and her mother read a draft of this report. Jennie is still occasionally bothered by the memory, but seems to cope well when it comes up. She is also able to discuss it with ease. Jennie has been very active in her Girl Scouts group and has won several awards for athletics, in addition to continued academic success. Her mother stated, 'I don't think you [the author] conveyed how much of an impact [EMDR] had. She's done so many things she could never have done otherwise. It has opened up all of our lives – she's no longer a handicapped child'.

Case 2: Disruptive behaviour disorders

EMDR has also been used to treat trauma and loss memories in children and adolescents with oppositional defiant disorder (ODD) or conduct disorder (CD). There is growing evidence that post-traumatic symptoms make a substantial contribution to the impaired empathy, aggression, anger and impulsive acting-out which is characteristic of this population (Greenwald 2000). Whether the primary diagnosis is trauma-based (PTSD) or behaviour-based (ODD, CD), treatment for traumatised acting-out children is likely to involve trauma resolution as well as enhancement of consistency and security in the child's environment (Greenwald 1999).

'Bryson' was a 12 year old boy in the fifth grade. About 2 years previously, a close family friend had died in a car accident, and soon after that Bryson's parents separated, leaving him only infrequent and irregular contact with his father. His mother also had an irregular lifestyle and he frequently stayed with his aunt. Soon after the separation Bryson was placed in a highly structured special education classroom owing to his non-stop disruptive behaviour. He was described as an 'angry' boy who was constantly moving around, making noise, provoking peers, arguing with teachers, and getting into fights. His diagnosis was ODD with possible attention deficit hyperactivity disorder (ADHD) as well. He acknowledged missing his father and feeling sad about the friend's death. He said that he wanted to do better in school so that he could rejoin his regular class again.

Treatment began with a parent consultation which led to a series of occasional meetings among Bryson's mother, father and aunt over the next several months. The outcome of these meetings was increased stability for Bryson, who was placed consistently with his aunt and had regularly scheduled visits with both father and mother. This was not a simple matter, as the father and mother were not particularly reliable people, but they did make an effort and it made a difference.

Individual treatment began rather typically with a general discussion of the purpose of treatment, along with rapport-building through playing a game together. By the second session, Bryson was willing to try EMDR on a recent minor upsetting memory: getting fish slime on his hands during a recent family fishing outing. This was a relatively simple chore and after only about 15 minutes he felt no further distress regarding the memory. Once he had experience with the relatively rapid relief EMDR brings, he was willing to try it on the memory of his traumatic loss.

The next two sessions were spent doing EMDR, processing the death of the family friend until no further distress was reported. Compared to Jennie, Bryson was more willing and able to face difficult material, but less articulate. The EMDR proceeded without the support of the extra positive imagery that was used in the first case. Bryson simply ploughed through the material until it got easier.

The two sessions after that focused on self-control skills. By then the teacher reported that Bryson was doing much better in school, no longer seemed angry, did not fight or provoke, was co-operative and responsive to discipline, and got his work done much of the time. However, he still had significant difficulty in staying focused, quiet and still.

With successful resolution of trauma and loss as well as increased environmental stability, the remaining problems seemed almost certainly due to ADHD. Previously the parents had been justifiably reluctant to medicate their child, because they understood that post-traumatic symptoms can mimic ADHD symptoms and they wanted the most appropriate treatment. Now that other recommended treatments had already been tried successfully and the ADHD symptoms remained, the potential value of medication became more evident. Stimulant medication was tried with great success and Bryson rather suddenly became an exemplary student. Within a month he was moved back to the regular (mainstream) class setting, and one year later was still successful there.

Discussion

In a very few years, EMDR has grown from a bizarre-sounding new technique to an experimentally validated, effective treatment for adults with PTSD. It is unclear to what extent downward age extension of a method's effectiveness can be presumed following preliminary supportive research to that effect. As the recent studies including children and adolescents are entirely consistent with earlier case studies, and with comparable adult studies, it is likely that EMDR will prove to be about as effective with children and adolescents as with adults. However, EMDR with children and adolescents will not be widely accepted until more high-quality studies targeting this population are completed, assuming results consistent with current data.

Clinicians appropriately trained in this method may now legitimately try EMDR as a first-line treatment for children and adolescents suffering from the effects of trauma. It should be clearly understood that EMDR is not a stand-alone technique, but a tool judiciously used by a qualified clinician in the context of an overall treatment plan (Greenwald 1999). Therefore, if EMDR should prove ineffective in a particular case, this will quickly become apparent, and other methods can be tried. Furthermore, as long as therapists are appropriately trained to use EMDR, it may actually have fewer side-effects than other therapy methods (Greenwald 1993, Lipke 1994), with the potential for intensely distressing sessions more than balanced by speedy resolution of the upsetting material. On the other hand, the traditional therapy approaches for traumatised children entail extended treatment and variable effectiveness (Finkelhor and Berliner 1995, Saigh et al. 1996). Whereas the empirical data on EMDR and children can only be considered supportive at this point, not definitive, the benefits of this potentially rapid and effective treatment already far outweigh the risks.

Although this discussion has focused on trauma, children often react to major loss in a very similar manner (Newcorn and Strain 1992), except that the hyperarousal effect may be absent. Child trauma and loss is so widespread as to be normative (e.g. Ford et al. 1996), yet potentially severely detrimental to psychosocial development and quality of life (Terr 1991). As we increasingly recognise the prevalence and consequences of child trauma and loss, much more effort is being devoted to helping children cope. Because EMDR appears to offer both effectiveness and efficiency, it may afford new hope for children and adolescents suffering from trauma or loss. Further controlled research on EMDR for children and adolescents is under way.

References

Acierno, R., Hersen, M., Van Hasselt, V. B., Tremont, G. and Meuser, K. T. (1994) Review of the validation and dissemination of eye-movement desensitization and reprocessing: a scientific and ethical dilemma. Clinical Psychology Review 14, 287–299.

Chambless, D.L., Baker, M., Baucom, D. et al. (1998) Update on empirically validated therapies, II. Clinical Psychologist 51, 3–16.

Chemtob, C. M., Nakashima, J., Hamada, R. and Carlson, J. (in press) Brief treatment for elementary school children with disaster related PTSD: a field study. Journal of Clinical Psychology.

Cocco, N. and Sharpe, L. (1993) An auditory variant of eye movement desensitization in a case of childhood post-traumatic stress disorder. Journal of Behavior Therapy and Experimental Psychiatry 24, 373–377.

Cohen, A. and Lahad, M. (1997) Eye movement desensitisation and reprocessing in the treatment of trauma. In Lahad, M. and Cohen, A. (eds), Community Stress Prevention, Vol. 2, pp. 160–165. Kiryat Shmona, Israel: CSPC Publications.

Datta, P. C. and Wallace, J. (1996) Enhancement of victim empathy along with reduction in anxiety and increase of positive cognition of sex offenders after treatment with EMDR. Paper presented at the annual meeting of the EMDR International Association, Denver.

Feske, U. (1998) Eye movement desensitization and reprocessing treatment for posttraumatic stress disorder. Clinical Psychology: Science and Practice 5, 171–181.

Finkelhor, D. and Berliner, L. (1995) Research on the treatment of sexually abused children: a review and recommendations. Journal of the American Academy of Child and Adolescent Psychiatry 34, 1408–1423.

Ford, J. D., Saxe, G., Daviss, W. B. et al. (1996) Post-traumatic stress detection and intervention in pediatric healthcare. Paper presented at the annual meeting of the International Society for Traumatic Stress Studies, San Francisco.

Greenwald, R. (1993) Using EMDR with children. Available from EMDR Institute, PO Box 51010, Pacific Grove, CA 93950–6010 with formal training.

Greenwald, R. (1994a) Applying eye movement desensitization and reprocessing (EMDR) to the treatment of traumatized children: five case studies. Anxiety Disorders Practice Journal 1, 83–97.

Greenwald, R. (1994b) Eye movement desensitization and reprocessing (EMDR): an overview. Journal of Contemporary Psychotherapy 24, 15–34.

Greenwald, R. (1995) Eye movement desensitization and reprocessing (EMDR): a new kind of dreamwork? Dreaming 5, 51–55.

Greenwald, R. (1996a) The information gap in the EMDR controversy. Professional Psychology: Research and Practice 27, 67–72.

Greenwald, R. (1996b) Psychometric review of the Problem Rating Scale. In Stamm, B. H. (ed.), Measurement of Stress, Trauma, and Adaptation, pp. 242–243. Lutherville, MD: Sidran.

Greenwald, R. (1997) A better approach to training: why you should teach EMDR in your home town. Eye–2–Eye. Internet address: http://www.geocities.com/HotSprings/Spa/1999/

Greenwald, R. (1998) Eye movement desensitization and reprocessing (EMDR): new hope for children suffering from trauma and loss. Clinical Child Psychology and Psychiatry 3, 279–287.

Greenwald, R. (1999a) Eye Movement Desensitization and Reprocessing (EMDR) in Child and Adolescent Psychotherapy. Northvale, NJ: Jason Aronson.

Greenwald, R. (1999b). The power of suggestion is still powerful: response to EMDR and Mesmerism: A comparative historical analysis. Journal of Anxiety Disorders, 13, 611–615.

Greenwald, R. (2000) A trauma-focused individual therapy approach for adolescents with conduct disorder. International Journal of Offender Therapy and Comparative Criminology 44, 146–163.

Greenwald, R. and Rubin, A. (1999) Brief assessment of children's post-traumatic symptoms: development and preliminary validation of parent and child scales. Research on Social Work Practice 9, 61–75.

Grosso, F. C. (1996) Children and OCD: extending the treatment paradigm. EMDRIA Newsletter 1(1), 10–11.

Hyer, L. and Brandsma, J. M. (1997) EMDR minus eye movements equals good psychotherapy. Journal of Traumatic Stress 10, 515–522.

Lee, C. W., Gavriel, H. and Richards, J. (1996) Eye movement desensitisation: past research, complexities, and future directions. Australian Psychologist 31(3), 168–173.

Lee, C. W., Gavriel, H., Drummond, P., Richards, J. and Greenwald, R. (1999) Treatment of PTSD: A comparison of stress inoculation training with exposure and EMDR. Manuscript submitted for publication.

Lipke, H. (1994) Eye movement desensitization and reprocessing (EMDR): a quantitative study of clinician impressions of effects and training requirements. Reprinted in Shapiro, F. (1995) Eye Movement Desensitization and Reprocessing: Basic Principles, Protocols and Procedures, pp. 376–386. New York: Guilford Press.

Marcus, S. V., Marquis, P. and Sakai, C. (1997) Controlled study of treatment of PTSD using EMDR in an HMO setting. Psychotherapy 34, 307–315.

Mendoza-Weitman, L. (1992) Case study. EMDR Network Newsletter 2(1), 11–12.

Newcorn, J. H. and Strain, J. (1992) Adjustment disorder in children and adolescents. Journal of the American Academy of Child and Adolescent Psychiatry 31, 318–327.

Pellicer, X. (1993) Eye movement desensitization treatment of a child's nightmares: a case report. Journal of Behavior Therapy and Experimental Psychiatry 24, 73–75.

Puffer, M. K., Greenwald, R. and Elrod, D. E. (1998) A single session EMDR study with twenty traumatized children and adolescents. Traumatology, 3(2). Internet address: http://www.fsu.edu/~trauma/v3i2art6.html

Rodriguez, G. (1997) Medical conditions in children and EMDR. EMDR Association of Australasia's Saccades Newsletter, 2(1).

Rubin, A., Bischofshausen, S., Conroy-Moore, K., Dennis, B., Hastie, M., Melnick, L., Reeves, D. and Smith, T. (in press) The effectiveness of EMDR in a child guidance center. Research on Social Work Practice.

Saigh, P. A., Yule, W. and Inamdar, S. C. (1996) Imaginal flooding of traumatized children and adolescents. Journal of School Psychology 34, 163–183.

Scheck, M. M., Schaeffer, J. A. and Gillette, C. S. (1998) Brief psychological intervention with traumatized young women: the efficacy of eye movement desensitization and reprocessing. Journal of Traumatic Stress 11, 25–44.

Shapiro, F. (1989a) Efficacy of the eye movement desensitization procedure in the treatment of traumatic memories. Journal of Traumatic Stress 2, 199–223.

Shapiro, F. (1989b) Eye movement desensitization: a new treatment for post-traumatic stress disorder. Journal of Behavior Therapy and Experimental Psychiatry 20, 211–217.

Shapiro, F. (1991a) Eye movement desensitization and reprocessing: a cautionary note. Behavior Therapist 14, 188.

Shapiro, F. (1991b) Eye movement desensitization and reprocessing procedure: from EMD to EMD/R – a new treatment model for anxiety and related traumata. Behavior Therapist 14, 133–135, 128.

Shapiro, F. (1995) Eye Movement Desensitization and Reprocessing: Basic Principles, Protocols and Procedures. New York: Guilford Press.

Shapiro, F. (1996a) Eye movement desensitization and reprocessing (EMDR): evaluation of controlled PTSD research. Journal of Behavior Therapy and Experimental Psychiatry 27, 209–218.

Shapiro, F. (1996b) Errors of context and review of eye movement desensitization and reprocessing research. Journal of Behavior Therapy and Experimental Psychiatry 27, 313–317.

Soberman, G. S., Greenwald, R. and Rule, D. L. (in press) A controlled study of eye movement desensitization and reprocessing (EMDR) for boys with conduct problems. Journal of Aggression, Maltreatment and Trauma.

Stickgold, R. (1998) Sleep, memory, PTSD and EMDR. EMDRIA Newsletter 3(3), 16.

Sweet, A. (1995) A theoretical perspective on the clinical use of EMDR. Behavior Therapist 18, 5–6.

Terr, L. (1991) Childhood traumas: An outline and overview. American Journal of Psychiatry 148, 10–20.

van Etten, M. and Taylor, S. (1998) Comparative efficacy of treatments for posttraumatic stress disorder: A meta-analysis. Clinical Psychology and Psychotherapy 5, 126–145.

Weinberg, R. and Caspers, S. (1997) Using EMDR with students who have a learning disability to improve reading skills. Presented at the annual meeting of the EMDR International Association, San Francisco.

Weinberg, R. and Caspers, S. (1998) Using EMDR with students who have a learning disability to improve reading skills. Presented at the annual meeting of the EMDR International Association, Baltimore.

Chapter 12
Refugee children and their families: theoretical and clinical perspectives

JEREMY WOODCOCK

Many refugee children endure extreme events as a result of violent warfare and human rights violations (Zwi and Ugalde 1989, UNICEF 1996, Loretti 1997) This chapter demonstrates how the clinician works with the multidimensional effects of trauma on refugee children and their families that are compounded by forced uprooting, massive losses and the myriad changes brought about by migration.

Debate in the arena of refugee mental health has polarised into two camps. There are those who eschew the medicalisation of distress and the use of psychological models of trauma, including post-traumatic stress disorder (PTSD). Then there are those who find the medical and psychological models extremely helpful in formulating interventions in this complex area of work. This chapter attempts to chart the middle ground. It draws on the critique of western models of mental health; it reflects on some indigenous healing practices and it also makes use of thinking about trauma from western psychological medicine.

The chapter shows how an approach that is integrative, which draws on systemic and psychoanalytic practice and makes use of narrative ideas and clinical thinking drawn from attachment theory, is uniquely well placed to attend to the 'broken social world' of survivors. It maps out how the clinician can work collaboratively with the child and family to make it possible to work simultaneously with intrapsychic material, family dynamics and socio-political factors.

Warfare and western models of mental health

The circumstances of political violence and the culture and ethnicity of survivors raise profound questions about the application of western models of mental health and family life. Some proponents are deeply sceptical that refugees can benefit from western psychological models

(Bracken et al. 1995). Others presuppose that trauma is a culturally neutral event that only requires the application of technically valid and value-free models of psychological intervention in order to make amends.

Bracken argues that people mediate their experience through culturally syntonic ways of living in which Western explanations are redundant. Bracken's chapter in *Rethinking the Trauma of War* (1998) sharpens the understanding of this redundancy. Western thought is characterised as dualistic and its scientific method is validated by virtue of its ability to be objective. As a result, medicine is based on a model that individualises illness experience. However, people in other societies do not prioritise or even live through individual experience and the nascent western trauma discourse does not make sense of extreme experiences that are mediated through communal ways of living. Therefore, if western methods are used imperialistically and unthinkingly in other societies, the likelihood is that the communal bonds, which provide resilience in situations of adversity, may be undermined. On these grounds, Bracken argues that the application of western psychological medicine, psychiatry and psychotherapy to other societies is both ethically dubious and clinically unsound.

This thinking is no less relevant to refugees settling in western societies. However, in the west the social context of survival is complicated by the experience of displacement. Refugees have to contend with the loss, or at the very least the weakening, of familiar ways of life and forms of support. Furthermore, they may find that the host society is explicitly hostile to their ways of living. In addition, despite being very resourceful, for some refugees lack of adaptation may be a form of protest against the world they have lost.

Extreme events or trauma?

Despite these reservations, it would seem that experiences inflicted on refugee children and families are accurately captured by the symptoms described in the DSM-IV definition of PTSD. Axis 'A' of DSM-III-R (APA 1987) describes that:

> The person has been exposed to a traumatic event in which *both* [writer's emphasis] of the following were present: (1) the person experienced, witnessed, or was confronted with an event or events that involved actual or threatened death or serious injury, or a threat to the physical integrity of self or others (2) the person's response involved intense fear, helplessness, or horror.

It is noted that, 'In children, this may be expressed instead by disorganised or agitated behaviour'. However, the term traumatic event is not defined. It is a tautology. Through the lens of western medical practice there may be broad agreement as to its meaning but in other contexts what may be regarded as traumatic (that is causative of trauma) may be experienced as integral to a way of life at a particular time. For instance, during the *intifada*, the Palestinian struggle for self-determination, Palestinian children maintained good mental health despite the almost daily infliction of extreme events (Punamaki 1990, 1993). Evidence from children exposed to similar levels of hardship in the political climate of South Africa before the ending of apartheid makes the same point that when extreme events have a context that makes their endurance understandable and worthwhile, trauma tends not to emerge (Dawes et al. 1992).

For these reasons **extreme events** is a preferable term to trauma. Used in this context the term extreme events is similarly self-referential but not tautologous. There is room for negotiation as to the meaning of what may be an extreme event in different contexts. Furthermore, to experience an extreme event does not imply that one will suffer trauma although, as with all life events, it often profoundly affects and reshapes life.

The self-referential nature of PTSD can reach absurd limits in particular clinical situations. For instance, on making a diagnosis of the disorder the clinician may reassure the patient that their symptoms are to be expected. This normalisation may relieve their secondary anxiety but what then? How does one advance from this tautology to primary symptom relief?

In the two sections that follow we first consider how indigenous healers in south-east Asia and Zimbabwe respond to extreme events. Then an example is taken from South Africa of how western and indigenous healing practices can be integrated. The chapter then moves on to look at how narrative can be used to integrate therapeutic practice with refugee children and families.

Indigenous responses to war and atrocity

Among young Cambodian refugees who were survivors of atrocity, Eisenbruch (1991) found that the intrusive phenomena of PTSD were considerably relieved in those who had access to indigenous priests and healers who were able to interpret their symptoms in terms that were syntonic with their culture. This led Eisenbruch to debate whether PTSD is an adequate diagnosis, or whether the concept of cultural bereavement is more appropriate.

Similar corollaries can be drawn from Reynold's (1996) study among Zimbabwean children affected by the *Chimerenga*, the native term for the armed struggle for independence. There was a belief that war upset the natural order. This explained how children were affected. When *nyangas*, that is native healers, were sought for consultation, negotiations ensued between the family and the *nyanga* in order to test their skill at forecasting what was wrong. First, less critical symptoms would be offered to see if an accurate forecast could be made. If this was satisfactory to the family they would open up to the *nyanga* and give him the full picture. The *nyanga*'s forecasts often revealed that the sufferer had transgressed the given order in some way which then had to be propitiated. The striking thing about Reynold's study was that the *nyangas* represented a benign authority. They sanctioned parents to treat affected children with care rather than discipline.

Integrating indigenous and western healing practices

Similarities between indigenous and western healing practices have encouraged some clinicians to attempt the integration of these practices. Characteristic of these attempts is that the therapist uses a reflexive cultural stance to interpret the culture of the patient or family through the lens of their own culture. Therapeutic curiosity is used as a means of accessing the patient's own understanding of their affliction. Ultimately the patient's own meaning systems and ways of healing are considered as ways of restoring their well-being, but the therapist uses their own principles of interpretation to guide them through the process. Straker (1994) offers a striking example of this approach with three teenage daughters of a chief murdered in the violence of the South African civil war. Within a conventional western framework they would have been considered to have been suffering from PTSD. However, Straker read their symptoms within the more holistic framework of traditional African beliefs. These encompassed the social significance of their father's death which led to the need to ritualise his untimely passing. They also derived meanings from the supernatural realm which led the young women to interpret their dreams and other intrusive phenomena as messages from the ancestors who sought propitiation for his death through ritual means.

Narrative and psychotherapy

The following sections extend the integrative thinking demonstrated by Eisenbruch and Straker with an outline of how therapy can make use of narrative ideas. Narrative is used as a theme to integrate thinking from anthropology, systemic practice and psychoanalytic psychotherapy. Narrative as an idea has come to be owned within the systemic tradition by a form of psychotherapy developed by the Australian family therapist

Michael White. His elegant therapy makes use of ideas from linguistics. He notes how people essentialise experience so that characteristics which they develop appear to be an immutable part of themselves. These characteristics can tyrannise when they are symptoms of illness. White uses notions of deconstruction to enable people to detach and externalise those tyrannical parts of themselves and thereby to 're-author' their experience (White and Epston 1990). These are helpful ideas when working with settled children and families. However, they need to be extended when working with refugees who inhabit a world that has been torn apart. Thus the task of therapy is more one of sorting and locating themes of identity, resilience, tradition and the story of one's life against a backdrop of persecution and dislocation.

Narratives of resilience and endurance

Survivors' use of their own resources is a notion which Eastmond, an anthropologist, emphasises in reference to the communal nature of the refugee experience. Exile is liminal, ambiguous, open-ended, complex and non-linear. It is disruptive of the social order itself and as such creates ontological insecurity. However, she notes from her work with exiled Chileans in the United States (1989, 1993) and Bosnian refugees in Sweden (1998) that refugees are not passive victims but interact and negotiate with the host society. Furthermore, referring to Myerhoff (1986), she writes 'one of the most persistent ways that people make sense of themselves is to show themselves to themselves, through multiple forms: by telling themselves stories ... recreating themselves in an historical narrative' (Eastmond 1989).

Stories recognise that life is radically discontinuous. At the same time stories provide an experience of endurance and wholeness. This may be an illusion but it is an illusion that is not a trick. Rather it communicates something very powerful and psychologically true about the resilience and continuity of life itself (Gersie 1997).

Narrative as a transitional space

Narrative ideas can be linked to important thinking by Winnicott about how the growing child develops a coherent grasp of internal and external realities. He believed that 'the child has a primary wish to be understood' (Phillips 1988); that the developing child and its mother are a unity; and that the child collaborates with the mother in gaining self and identity. The role of the parent is to enable this through 'appreciative understanding' (Phillips 1988) and by relating external and internal experience. As child and mother interact they create a 'transitional space' through literal and symbolic communication out of which language and play emerge (Winnicott 1971). Similarly, through attunement to the patient's inner world the therapist provides a similar transitional space in which conflicts can be contained and worked through so that a more coherent identity emerges. Stories and narratives can enable attunement and coherence to develop. Furthermore, what needs special emphasis is that, more than in any other psychotherapy setting, often what makes the real difference when working with refugee parents and children is just the actual therapeutic attachment itself. This provides a regular reliable appointment and the presence of a form of parental care and adaptation – very often without the need of interpretation – just being there: listening, understanding, bearing witness and validating experience.

Narrative and continuity

Many different approaches can be used to create narratives that provide a safe transitional space in which to engage and transform life experiences and difficulties. Linking psychotherapy to seasonal and religious festivals is a way of creating a transitional space that encompasses both the therapeutic setting and the external world of a refugee family's culture and traditions that is also affirmative of cultural identity. Aspects of the rituals can also be taken up within the psychotherapy to transform and carry away stuck and difficult feelings (Woodcock 1995a). Genograms, or kinship diagrams, are enormously helpful in mapping out families whose members may be scattered across the world. With children, the use of life story books, which embody both reality and fantasy and which enable them to sort out muddles of what is real and fantasy (Cattanach 1992), are very effective and powerful ways of creating healing narratives.

These ways described should make effective use of protective factors: explaining and making sense of experience; providing continuity; providing opportunities for mastery; and finally rendering experience syntonic with a world view, which will need to expand to encompass extreme events. Naomi Richman's work with war-affected children and refugees exemplifies the need to make not only symbolic but real connections with the communities of children and families; to practically track interactions and issues between generations; and to work to support refugee children's identities through practical methods. Good work with refugee children who have survived extreme events will only be effective when the practical groundwork is given proper attention and work is done to literally find the child's place in the world (Richman 1998).

Narrative and reflexivity

Reflexive questions are a good starting point for a process that sets out to make sense of what has happened in the external world and to link that to thoughts and feelings in the internal world of both refugee and psychotherapist. Unconscious feelings can be made more accessible as the inner story of what has happened is externalised. Children externalise readily through drawings and play. Adults externalise through narratives that situate inner experience 'out there'. For instance, a man who found it hard to face the anguish of his family often recounted the complex and anguished politics with which he had been involved. These were reflections of his inner world. As we talked and made links he was gradually able to make sense of the fact that the connection went back and forth between his internal and external world. We reached a point where talk of politics and human rights was enriched by this understanding, and when seeking metaphors for interpretations of psychological processes we made use of the rich fund of political stories to make our points.

The obvious truth is that refugees are persecuted by outside forces. However obvious, it is nevertheless actually helpful to make the point that the persecution they feel inside (and may act out in the family) comes from persecution inflicted on them by an external force or person or regime. That truism, strategically offered, can enable them to modulate feelings and sort out the muddle of emotions that come about as a result of human rights abuse. This is particularly important for young children who may muddle enraged fantasies that they feel towards their parents with actual events.

Narrative and self-determination

It is singularly important for psychotherapists to maximise refugees' capacity for self-determination. This is because one of the defining aspects of refugee experience is that they suffer massive and multiple losses, terror and coercion by authorities that intentionally persecute as well as coercion by agencies who try to help. As a consequence of lack of civil rights and loss of external trappings of identity they are often dazed and confused. As Parkes (1997) remarks in relation to extraordinary events, the whole assumptive framework is challenged by the psychosocial transitions that are forced on survivors. For refugees the tremendous disruption in the assumptive framework is amplified by the sensation that ultimately they are expendable. Their experiences are actually embodiments of terrifying psychic fears: nightmares that have become realities.

Psychotherapy with refugee survivors can help to overcome the sensation of complete loss of personal autonomy by situating the work within a reflexive historical narrative. In other words, psychotherapy that prefaces work with the question, 'What brings us together to work on these issues at this point in time?' directs curiosity not only at refugee children and their families' dilemmas, but also at the therapist's place in the world. That is, our culture, history and social and political relationship to the human rights violations that have caused the upheavals that caused the family to flee. This process of reflection does not yield easy answers, but it needs to be done if effective psychotherapy is to be achieved with refugee survivors. This is because, as noted above, work with refugees is a form of globalisation and questions of therapy cannot be limited to the intrapsychic and interpersonal domain but also have to yield to questions about what produces and sustains identity within the tensions and disruptions of this new and increasingly complex world order.

Racism and xenophobia: resistance to refugees

Whenever refugees seek asylum in a country there is resistance from the host community, which may manifest as outright rejection and xenophobia or may take more subtle forms. In health and social care agencies there may be resistance to engaging with refugees' needs because they seem overwhelming and do not easily fit in with prescribed care packages. Institutions may also unconsciously resist engagement with the disturbing and atavistic nature of the refugee experience. These responses tend to displace the responsibility for direct help on to voluntary organisations, which has the effect of marginalising refugee health care. Clinical experience suggests that this discrimination contributes to poorer social integration and ultimately to inferior health care. Lack of referral to specialist secondary services is borne out by health care studies among ethnic minorities (Nazroo 1997). Racism places refugees in double jeopardy because of its inherently damaging effects that echo the experience of persecution. This requires that issues of racism and discrimination and its effect on the internal and external world must be brought reflexively into the therapeutic work so both therapist and child or family are freed to make a positive exploration of identity rather than one that is suppressed and essentialised by racism (Fernando 1991, Thomas 1992, Krause 1998).

Social constructionist therapy

The following sections illustrate how social constructionism can be used in order to harmonise systemic and psychoanalytic practice.

The assumptions of social constructionism may be summarised as being that we do not live in a world in which the facts of our existence are stable scientific realities but one in which reality is mutable, socially constructed and constantly under negotiation (Anderson and Goolishian 1988). As a consequence, how one views and responds to reality will change, for example according to one's position as an insider or outsider to a culture (Merton 1973), or one's position in the life cycle, or one's gender (Gorel-Barnes 1998). Accordingly, this opens up the possibility that therapy can enable families to elaborate narratives, as detailed in the sections of the chapter above, which are ultimately freeing and healing.

The important feature of social contructionist therapeutic work with survivors of extreme events is its efficacy when combined with thinking from attachment theory. What the therapist sets out to do is to enable the child or family to understand and re-internalise what has been inflicted on them in a narrative that is congruent with their experience and valid in relation to their beliefs about themselves and the world around them. This may mean having to extend their beliefs about themselves and also having to accept that not everything is explicable. However, these narratives are effective, not when they are simplistically palatable, but when they struggle to make sense of the grittiness of experience. Furthermore, the child or families' clinical experience of having a therapist working alongside them, thoughtfully providing safety (Dolan 1991) while unpacking and making bizarre and troubling experiences coherent, offers not only a cognitive map of what has happened, but a relationship that can begin to overcome the intense psychological and existential loneliness of extreme experiences. This is an absolutely vital part of the healing experience. It may be thought of as akin to Winnicott's model of psychotherapy and parenting described earlier. The thinking of Byng-Hall (1995) is also very pertinent here. As is common in most forms of psychotherapy, the therapist sets out to provide a secure base from which the child and family can explore new scripts that transcend patterns of interaction inculcated by extreme experience, loss and the savage disappointment of exile.

Systemic therapy

Because of the co-development of later systemic approaches to psychotherapy with constructionism, the two are somewhat conflated nowadays. Constructionism can be used to deconstruct and relativise any psychotherapy; however, the strength of systemic therapy is that it inherently lends itself to constructionism because its underlying epistemology is based on an open systems approach. This presupposes that causality is circular and that all living systems are open-ended and mutually influence each other (Jones 1993). The notion of punctuation is used to denote the idea that nothing can be described as essential, that is absolutely having to be in a particular way, because any description is dependent on the view one takes and therefore from which it is punctuated. For instance, if two boys are climbing and one falls out of the tree and breaks his neck, trauma in the boy who witnessed the event is not an absolute entity. It will depend on how the event is punctuated factually, cognitively and emotionally. Was the broken neck fatal or disabling? Were they brothers? Were they forbidden to climb trees or were their adventures encouraged? Was non-judgemental help easily on hand? – and so forth.

The strength of this open, negotiable, narrative approach when applied to refugees and extreme events is that it can be used to bring into view all the mutually influencing factors in their life story which shape their response to what has been inflicted on them. The family may view, or punctuate, what has been inflicted on them through the lens of their affiliation to a resistance culture. Another family may view what has happened through the lens of being helpless victims of political events outside their control. Naturally, different views may compete for attention in one family and very often within the individual parent or child. Here the notion of intertextuality is useful (Papadopoulos and Hildebrand 1997). This emerges from ideas current in narrative therapy, which as we have seen has made use of concepts drawn from Foucault (1972) and other social theorists that individuals, societies and by extension families construct reality through competing discourses. This produces discourses which are either marginal or dominant. For instance, in some families the experiences of children may be marginalised in favour of the dominant experience of the adult males in the family. Or the adaptive responses of women may be seen as a challenge rather than an opportunity for the family as a whole. Work with refugee families can make use of these narrative ideas in order to unpack, reframe or re-punctuate family interactions so as to illuminate the perspectives of family members that have been overlooked. The therapist attunes themselves to family scripts and attachment patterns and draws forth scripts and patterns that may be more inclusive, adaptive and resilient.

Psychoanalytic approaches

Because the psychoanalytic approach is included in this analysis of working with refugee children and families, the implication may be drawn that ultimately trauma is an intrapsychic event. However, the approach to psychoanalytic knowledge taken here is to regard its underlying precepts as guiding metaphors, that are socially constructed, rather than regarding them as immutable and universalisable scientific facts. Nevertheless, this observation does not set out in any way to diminish the hard-won experience of psychoanalysis, awakening people to the instinctual drives and the unconscious and how we mediate these – ways of thinking that have reshaped western consciousness and permeated all forms of psychological thinking.

It is important that both external and internal experiences are validated and that unconscious processes are understood. With this in mind it is apparent that the most affected clinic population is helped by understanding the intrapsychic corollaries of extreme events. For instance, children internalise relationship schemas that include observed and felt reactions of peers and adults to fear, repression and extreme violence. Thus we know if adults model robust coping, children are more likely to respond in a similar fashion (Freud 1965, Rutter 1985, van der Kolk 1987). At a deeper level responses to extreme events may resonate negatively with the child's or adult's internal working model of relationship with self and others. These may be complicated by the developmental stage and needs of the child. The young child's innate difficulty in distinguishing reality and fantasy may interfere with their ability to meaningfully process extreme events that in any case overwhelm their cognitive and emotional schemas. For example, a 5 year old boy who witnesses the violent rape of his mother in front of his arrested and helpless father may confuse this with the acting out of his own oedipal desires.

Because extreme events may overwhelm the individual's psychological defences, that is their ability to modulate incoming stimuli, the psyche responds by attempting to repress memories of the event. This leads to a phenomenon by which the event is both known and not known (Laub and Auerhahn 1993). Aspects of an event may be completely repressed. For example, an aid worker saw me after a breakdown, which followed a terrifying ambush on a convoy in which he had been travelling. He had a serious but medically unexplained weakness of his ankle. Our shared anxiety had deterred us from some of the central aspects of his narrative. However, in one session I intuited that one of the guards had stood on his ankle while returning fire and suggested this to him. That was indeed true. The realisation was co-constructed from our conversation in which I attuned to his emotional state and listened very carefully to how the emotional tone and the facts hung together, while looking for key psychological experiences such as overwhelming fear, loss of control and shame (indicated by their absence in the narrative as much as their presence). This sensitivity to cues of what may have happened enabled us to unpack the story that when their truck was ambushed he was thrown out and into a roadside ditch by one of the guards who courageously fought off the attack. He had been in a state of acute fear and had soiled and wet himself. At the same time the guard had pinned him to the ground out of harm's way by standing on his ankle. As he recovered the memory his ankle recovered spontaneously. This illustrates that powerful associations to extreme events are sometimes 'stored' in the body (Scarry 1985). This can be particularly true of survivors of violence (Callaghan 1998): unbearable things that cannot be faced are very often somatised.

The particular attunement to his inner state described above is counter-transference. What occurs is that the unbearable things, which the sufferer cannot face, put the therapist in touch with their own experiences of pain and desperation. Unlike the sufferer, the therapist can make use of that experience on the sufferer's behalf and thereby offers a way of transforming their unbearable experiences. Counter-transference is often intuitive but as the therapist develops experience there comes an understanding that it is a form of knowing that can also be developed and trusted and put at the service of the sufferer. Systemic therapists would identify this process as making use of experience of the self.

In children, memories which are either repressed or more consciously forbidden can often be enacted and externalised through play. For example, I worked with a boy and his father in conjoint play sessions. The father had been severely tortured and continued to be terrified. The 6 year old son had become anxious, bedwetting, defiant and unruly. My understanding was that despite the father's attempts to hide his experiences from his boy the son had both consciously and unconsciously experienced his father's terrorisation by the secret police. In the play work the boy symbolised the hated leader of their homeland with a caricatured Plasticine figure. He also modelled snakes with flames coming from their mouths. Towards the end of a session we entered a process of naming each of the more recognisable figures. When the boy named the dictator his father went into a paroxysm of fear. The boy then took one of the snakes and curled it around the dictator in a motion of entrapment. With this the father visibly relaxed. Later he recounted how at that moment he had realised how the son had been living with his terror, but they had no shared language with which to process their sensations of that experience. The son's play provided them with a repertoire of symbolic language with which to communicate about their experiences.

Defences

Defences need to be respected because they constitute effective ways of coping. They should only be challenged if the therapist has the skill and time to work things through to a resolution. For instance, a family with whom a colleague and myself worked had a very rigid set of defences based on their religious beliefs that allowed them to cope, but at some cost to their overall well-being. They were under threat of deportation by the immigration service and we did not believe it ethical to challenge and dismantle their defences, which enabled them to cope with this very difficult situation. This point leads to a further observation that refugees often have strong religious beliefs. These comfort and rationalise an often cruel world. These beliefs must be worked with and respected. Sometimes direct parallels can be drawn between religious beliefs and attitudes and psychological understandings. For instance, a child who witnessed violence against his father and mother later became very delinquent and was taken into care. When he eventually returned home his older sibling resented the care and attention he attracted. We talked with the parents about the return of the prodigal son. This biblical story with its cogent metaphor of rivalry in family life helped them to communicate about family relationships and to mediate the conflicts that had emerged.

By contrast, to regard psychological conceptions as rigorous and scientific and the religious beliefs as forms of reification will almost certainly confound therapy. Differences in world view become creative when brought into the open and discussed and negotiated. Furthermore, when a social constructionist position and therapeutic knowledge are taken as being a set of guiding metaphors that enables us to negotiate realities, to arrive at insight and to enable change, then the insights of Cox and Theilgard (1981) that 'metaphor is our means of effecting instantaneous fusion of two separated realms of experience' become very pertinent.

Attachment theory

The following sections consider how attachment theory can help in our understanding of reactions to extreme events and how interventions may be modelled that make use of this approach. This understanding of attachment theory also integrates thinking from psychoanalytic and systemic practice.

Attachment theory explains how parents transmit their attachment patterns from childhood to their own offspring. It is suggested that children with difficult attachments have parents who have internalised attachment patterns that are coercive, neglectful, ambivalent or unpredictable (de Zulueta 1993). Attachments between parents and children who have endured extreme events are often very strained. This can be because parents are distracted, preoccupied, depressed or traumatised (Melzak 1993). Equally, children who have endured the same events may be irritable, distracted, preoccupied or demanding and less rewarding to parents' and this can also strain attachments (Woodcock 1995b).

Attachment schemas and extreme events

However, attachment theory explains more than the interpersonal schemas of attachment behaviour, in fact it goes to the heart of how extreme events are internalised and how traumatogenic symptoms are set in motion.

Main (1991) suggests that before the age of 3 children are unable to be metacognitive. In other words, they are unable to think about their own thinking or, by corollary, their own feelings. To use her language, they are unable to 'dual code' events. Therefore, people, things and events are understood concretely as being a particular way. For instance, a grandfather cannot be simultaneously 'grandad' and 'mummy's father'. Between 3 and 4 children do begin to dual code. However, before this the child's development is helped if they experience relationships that are both emotionally congruent and cognitively coherent. This may explain why the cognitive and emotional development of children who suffer abuse is affected because children cannot dual code relationships and this leads to incoherence and confusion when, for instance a 'daddy' who loves them is also abusive. Similar confusion can occur for refugee children who experience figures of authority in their society abusing and terrorising their parents and even themselves.

During extreme events people report being 'lost' in the moment and being unable to process what is happening to them cognitively and emotionally. This may be because the event is so bizarre, or threatening or sudden that it overwhelms their ability to internalise it in a meaningful way. There is a loss of the ability to dual code the event. It is internalised as a set of very concrete gestalts – sometimes re-experienced as intrusive iconic images and possibly physical sensations of the original experience. Furthermore, what is felt as particularly devastating is the sense that they are alone with the experience: that no one can attune themselves to what has happened to them. This is experienced as a terrifying existential loneliness. This is made worse because they feel unable to maintain relationships with others. Their attachment nexus is disturbed and in its place are highly charged indigestible fragments of experience. This disturbed attachment to one's own internal representations of self and others suggests why many individuals find it hard to socialise in the aftermath of extreme events and how previously gregarious, pro-social people become withdrawn and socially anxious.

Intrusive phenomena, such as nightmares and flashbacks, represent successive attempts to recreate and metabolise extreme events. However, extreme events are likely to be too far beyond the scope of a person's cognitive or emotional range to be accommodated. Simultaneously, avoidance emerges because the person does not wish to recall the event either consciously or unconsciously, both because it is too ghastly and also because it challenges the basis of their earlier psychic development and as such represents an unsurpassable problem of assimilation.

Parents with coherent explanations of their childhood attachments (gained through direct experience or through therapy) are more likely to attune to their children's needs for proximity and thereby provide an experience of attachment that is emotionally congruent and cognitively coherent. The process of attunement between parent and child creates a zone described as a **third area** in which symbolic interaction such as play springs forth. This is exactly the same as the transitional space discussed above in relation to Winnicott's work. It is surmised that this forms the crux of the creative nexus. This third area can also be described as the epistemic space of the person. It is the cognitive and emotional space in which thoughts and feelings are processed and brought into consciousness through metacognitive action. In fact, the term 'metacognitive' does not go far enough because feelings are also modulated in this space. One could say that feelings recognise each other and meta-emotional processing also occurs.

The concretisation of extreme events is the opposite of the creative symbolising experience that arises in the transitional space or third area. This contrast throws into focus the central task of therapy which is to provide a basis on which the extreme event can be symbolised cognitively and emotionally and thereby assimilated. This is inherently a creative process. As such, it makes sense of why practices which enable people to participate and witness performances from theatre through to political protest and religious ritual, which promote symbolic realisation and so enable alternative views to arise, are likely to enable healing. Furthermore, it explains why indigenous healing practices are effective because they bring into play similar creative and symbolising functions (Englund 1998). It also speaks to the efficacy of play and play therapy as media for enabling both children and adults to process extreme events.

Working with children and parents

Extreme events unsettle, disturb and displace parents' own internal representations of their own parental attachments laid down during their own development. In brief, it is as if the parent has 'lost' their own internalised parent. They in turn are incapacitated in the parenting of their own children. However, the child's healthy impulses towards development mean that the parent is challenged to respond. Sometimes they are unable to do so and the child complains of a father or mother who looks and smells the same as their original parent but is just a shell or shadow of their former self. When the parent is unable to take up the child's challenge for attachment, therapy can be helpful.

The therapist should hold in mind that through the process of projective identification they can enable the parent to assimilate parts of themselves that they find repugnant or otherwise indigestible. Projective identification is the process by which the parent (or child) unconsciously projects parts of themselves which they cannot assimilate into the therapist who then identifies with or acts out the projection. The therapeutic task is to accept the projections, metabolise them and symbolically represent them back to the parent (or child) in a way they can then assimilate. As the therapist works with the interpersonal relationship between parent and child through the process of projective identification, the parent can experience the supportive parenting of the therapist. Simultaneously, through the relations between themself and the child, supported within the therapeutic experience, the parent may be able to re-internalise at a real and symbolic level a healing version of their previously shattered attachment schema and thereby re-experience a recovery of their own 'internal parent' through the responsive and attuned attention to the needs of their own child. Very often this involves a great deal of supportive work – sorting and validating experience through quite robust observations and interventions.

When parents are very disturbed the therapist can act as a container of the family's experiences and interactions and as 'digester' for the family working with both parent and child's projections until such time as healthier family patterns can emerge. This is demanding work but understanding how these levels of experience interact and mapping the child's, parents' or family's experience into a constructed narrative of their real world experience can enable the therapist to cope with the demands of the projections.

Clinical descriptions

There follow two case descriptions. The first exemplifies work with a family, which illustrates the process described above of working with a parent's damaged inner self through family work that is focused on parent and child dynamics. The second illustrates direct work with a refugee child who has survived an enormous personal atrocity.

Work with a family

The first case to be discussed is that of a Sudanese Catholic family. They were referred by the father David's psychotherapist, who continued to work with him. This proved to be very fruitful.

David had received a very harsh upbringing. His wife, Elizabeth, was warm, capable and strong, although overwhelmed by her husband's periodic violence towards herself and children. She was also haunted by a sense of isolation which, at times bordered on despair. They had four children. Zeph, the 2 year old, had been born in exile. The others were Hannah aged 9, Benjamin, 8 and Maria, 6. David had been the organiser for an aid organisation. The organisation had been set up to provide succour to Christian refugees fleeing from the war in the south. His work led him to believe that the regime wished to destroy Christians moving into the north. Differences of outlook and policy conflicts led him into being imprisoned and severely tortured by the regime. After he was released his life remained under threat and the family fled into exile.

Clinical issues

The immediate clinical issues that emerged were David's violence towards his wife and children. He seemed to be mentally and emotionally rigid and emotionally disconnected from the children. He had very high academic expectations of the children and they were all fearful of him, particularly Benjamin. The children had various somatic symptoms – Hannah and Benjamin were bedwetting. Benjamin also had very sore and poorly managed eczema. We noticed the particularly conflictual nature of the relationship between David and Benjamin and the fact that Hannah, of all the children, seemed to be able to get away with a lot more. We saw Elizabeth's dilemma as being how to position herself in relation to the children's needs and David's behaviour.

I worked with this family with a colleague who is a child psychotherapist. Work in a partnership that represented the genders was pertinent to this family. David's brittle and rigid set of mind caused a gulf in the gender roles which he imposed on himself and his wife Elizabeth. She had a freshness of mind and the adaptability and opportunities in exile to study, develop and work, which apparently were not available in their homeland. Unsurprisingly these qualities were experienced as threatening by the rigid David. It can be hypothesised that his rigidity of mind came about because his inner representations of relationships and attachments had been engulfed by extreme events. It seems that he retained a cognitive map of intimate relationships but lacked the epistemic space and empathy to mediate the emotional information that came his way within relationships. Thus his relationships were mapped out on to a moral and cultural framework, but without the empathy to mediate cultural norms, his position was experienced as very rigid. For men accustomed by former cultural norms to fulfil authoritative roles, the rigidity that emerges when authority is asserted without empathy, backed by anxiety and fear because they can no longer 'read' the emotional map of the family, can lead to terrifying violence.

David was understandably in a very poor mental state after torture, because of the many losses inflicted on the family and the dilemmas of exile. He was anxious about the family's future. He was jumpy about just about everything that came his way. He ground his teeth at night and had frequent epileptiform fits in his sleep, which seemed to be triggered by tension. He also had terrible, frightening dreams filled with horror and violence. During the day he had intense flashbacks that often developed into fugues. He got into rages with the children's playfulness and noise. He attacked them for jeopardising their future by not doing their homework. Elizabeth tried to soften him towards the children but she was cowed into silence.

Interventions

We set out to understand the family attachments. They can be described as the 'royal road' for understanding family dynamics after extreme events. Our way of achieving this was to seek out the family's stories about itself. In doing this we were interested in both their declared or overt stories and their undeclared stories. We also listened out for whatever narratives were suppressed or repressed. For instance, the extent of David's violence was initially denied and also the pain of Elizabeth and the children's suffering. We had to choose the moments carefully to challenge this denial. The family system as a whole, which included them, ourselves and the community of support around them had to be able to cope with the potential for discomfort and change this would invoke.

Building trust and the therapeutic alliance

Understandably, the undeclared narratives emerged more readily as the family began to trust us and as we attuned ourselves to their style of relating to themselves and others. We discovered that David had always been a tense man. His childhood had been fraught with neglect and violence. The intense loneliness and physical and mental pain of the torture concatenated with his experiences as a growing child. It seemed that he had only the most brittle emotional template against which to rebuild relationships with his family. However, Elizabeth was a great therapeutic ally. We wondered what had led this warm, generous woman to marry this evilly ill-tempered and violent man who terrorised her and their lovely children. We discovered she had responded to a man who was singular, intelligent, idealistic and thoughtful: qualities which only seemed to appear during this period of their life in brief flashes. In their exhausted relationship we had to appeal to those aspects of his character: for instance, his belief in fairness which, for the reasons described above, manifested itself rather rigidly. We were also able to map the family's experiences on to their wider social and political circumstances. These aspects provided sufficient frame of reference to hold together a workable therapeutic alliance. Simultaneously, we also had to be mindful of David's possible fury at the gratifying role that Elizabeth had hewn for herself as the thoughtful carer, which so conveniently split the good and bad between them.

As described earlier it was a reasonable hypothesis to assume that extreme events had caused a breakdown in David's ability to make and maintain attachments. Because his internal representations had been overwhelmed with violence all attachments were fraught with the potential for being triggers to the extreme experiences of torture or an earlier layer of childhood neglect and violence. Furthermore, as he tried to participate in the interplay of intimate relationships they seemed to mock this proud man's inability to connect emotionally. As psychotherapists we had to see if it was possible for attachments to be made more coherent and therefore more safe.

One of the positive benefits of working with survivors where there had previously been workable relationships in the family is that once small bits of progress are made these are often amplified by positive feedback from the family to the survivor. Restored aspects of relationships are refracted through family relationships in general and a sense of hope is generated. Throughout the work of this depth it was important that we identified strengths and the normality of how difficult it was to cope with extreme events while simultaneously working with the difficulties thrown up by their experiences.

Making use of attachment

At the same time we offered ourselves as attachment figures to the family, becoming as it were 'good enough parents' to both parents and children. Thus we were as if parents to a pre-logical child, to the confused and emotionally incoherent aspects of David. Simultaneously, we were the same to the rumbustious 2 year old Zeph, whom Elizabeth had to keep physically separate from David because he aroused his father dangerously. At the same time we were parental to the older children, seeing their need for warm, involved and contained parental experience. The firmness this required also suited the setting down of certain rules of conduct for David; for instance, the explicit requirement that he should not be violent to the family. Work on insight was required to arrive at an understanding of this injunction. It fitted David's sense of duty and moral responsibility but his violence was not experienced by either himself or Elizabeth as rational and this made it more frightening. The lack of emotional connection between himself and the family when he was violent was terrifying for them. It felt as if they could not appeal to the inner person of David; he was beyond reach, emotionally cut off.

The detail of this work involved unpacking interactions within the family sessions of family therapy. We examined current themes and linked those with patterns of family life before exile. One of the family memories was of the older children playing in the Land-Rover and starting it up. The vehicle lurched forward and stalled. Luckily no harm came of it but David was incandescent with rage out of proportion to the incident. He read the situation as children being intentionally naughty. By degrees he was able to compare their behaviour back then with little Zeph's behaviour in the present. Zeph was a responsive child, full of curiosity and play. This gave the impression to David of a child who was knowing and deliberately annoying in an adult sense. But this was the behaviour of a bright, imitative child seeking attachment to his father. After a series of interventions which worked on elaborating an understanding of Zeph's play as seeking a relationship with his world (in which his father played an enormously significant part) David was able to read it as that, rather than having a more paranoid vision of a child deliberately setting out to naughtily provoke him. To begin with his acknowledgement was rather rueful, a sort of, 'So I have to put up with the brat because this is good for both of us!'. But this was a significant breakthrough that enabled him to appreciate his child at play, and gradually he was able to engage playfully and with enjoyment himself.

The ability to play is an important marker in understanding the inner world of survivors of extreme events. The space between people at play or people and objects at play is composed of epistemic space. It is a space of possibility and imagination. To be able to make use of it is a sign of an intact attachment nexus. As David engaged in Zeph's play he began to internalise through his son an internal working model of attachment that offered reparation for the damage done to him during torture and his own deprived childhood.

Enabling resilience and coherence

This work was enriched by being anchored within the matrix of the beliefs and myths passed down through past generations of the family. We looked for strengths in their families of origin that could be adapted to their situation in exile as well as ways of being that were redundant in their new circumstances. We also understood the family's experiences within the political and social context of what had been inflicted on them and their experiences, good and bad, within Britain as a host society. The purpose of all this work was to create coherent narratives for the family that made sense of life and their interactions at different levels of context. This created a scaffolding through which the therapeutic work was systemically linked. From the broadest, that is most socio-cultural to the most intimate, that is intrafamilial and intrapsychic, this conceptualisation of the work is isomorphic with the model of parent–child coherence that has been noted in experimental work about attachment outlined earlier in the chapter. The notion of projective identification also came into play. This enabled us as therapists to inter-nalise the unbearable parts of David's experience and behaviour that he projected into us, to absorb, dwell on it in consultation with each other and re-present it back in less toxic forms. For instance, we took the frightening violence that he projected at Elizabeth and the children. We struggled to absorb its impact and bring into our consciousness an understanding of the emotional currents that ran through it. Elizabeth also participated in this struggle on a daily basis during the early part of treatment as she sought to lessen the impact of David's violent internal world on the children. She was grateful for our partnership in the emotional enterprise and they were a delightful couple with their children as David came back to life.

Work with a child

When Simon was 6 his father, a political activist in an opposition party, went into hiding because of threats against his life. Police and army units raided the farmstead to search for him. They brutally interrogated Simon's mother, his paternal grandmother, a paternal aunt and Simon himself. They got no information from the family (sensibly, Simon had been told nothing of his father's whereabouts). In revenge – perhaps also in the desire to get information through terror and also to provide an exemplary case of what is inflicted on dissident families – the family was brutally terrorised. His grandmother and aunt were burned to death in a wing of the farmstead. His mother was raped. In a state of terror and agitation Simon hit out at the police. He was dragged into an adjoining room and anally raped by three police.

At the age of 12 he was referred for psychotherapy by a paediatrician who had seen him because he was regularly soiling. This had been thoroughly investigated but had not been resolved with prophylactic care.

Simon was a well-presented, bright boy, precocious in his attitudes and very articulate. In the first assessment meeting he and his mother wept silently as we went through the terror they had both endured. Apparently, he had no sensation of being 'full'. He did not have any other sensations that signalled when he needed to empty his bowel. Nor did he have any sensation when he soiled himself. To combat what amounted to a lack of feeling control over his bowels he had developed an elaborate routine of regularly visually checking himself to see if he had soiled. This was done anxiously every hour in the school lavatories. At home he was more relaxed but nevertheless still anxious enough to check himself frequently. He was academically able and did well in school but was a little remote from his peers. Throughout the work I was able to draw on his many strengths and to foster his self-esteem while simultaneously working with his difficulties.

Interventions

Simon was a charming and articulate child, who described flashbacks that regularly occurred in school. One occurred during a history lesson on mediaeval warfare. Some of my work consisted of helping him to manage his flashbacks. We set out to understand them as 'memories of the past that had not been fully digested'. This relieved him of the worry that they were signs of a sinister and permanent mental disorder. However, this sort of reassurance, which reframes a mental phenomenon, is of small value unless the phenomenon can be brought under control. This was more slowly achieved over the course of the therapy by bringing into consciousness the associations that triggered the intrusive phenomena and teaching relaxation. Unsurprisingly, in as complex an experience as anal rape and murder these associations existed at many different levels and emerged over time as Simon gained confidence that I listened and absorbed his experience. Furthermore, they emerged as his own tolerance and consciousness of the associations developed. Forcing the pace would not have been helpful. Thus the initial work was largely successful in diminishing their occurrence but I remained alert to other associations that emerged as our work progressed.

Work with anger

Other work focused on Simon's feelings of anger. He modelled Plasticine figures of police and ran them down with a Lego-built truck, but he remained muted in his verbal expression of anger. He had no return of sensation or control in his bowel. I wondered if when wishing to open his bowel he could imagine 'shitting on the police who had raped him'. This worked a little and Simon was gleeful when reporting back to me, but the lasting benefits were marginal. Meanwhile he had run away from home over the evening several times and had become angry towards his mother and father. This seemed like progress, although the parents had to be helped through consultation to see the benefit of their mild-mannered son expressing such obvious aggression. The father was more able to cope with this than the mother who remained symbiotically attached to Simon and the extreme events both had endured. In fact both Simon and his parents found it very difficult to deal with their guilt at Simon's exposure to such terror and the fact that initially they had to flee without him leaving him in the company of a trusted family friend. Sessions were spent tracking Simon's feeling about these matters and gradually enabling him to verbalise his experience.

Work with autonomy and identity

Despite his parent's affection and attention, Simon was a psychologically lonely child. This loneliness, in the theory outlined above, was a consequence of the disturbance of his own internal attachments during the extreme events. This was complicated because he also had to contend with the impact on his psychological development of the simultaneous rape of his mother and his own sexual assault. This was evidenced by his continued struggle to separate what had happened to himself and his mother literally and symbolically. This 12 year old, entering puberty, felt a huge degree of fusion with his mother. Within a safely conducted therapeutic relationship he was able to construct a strong narrative of the events, but there was often an elision of the facts and his psychological state: he had difficulty in holding the reality of who was inside whom.

Work was conducted on several fronts: to enable the oedipal 6 year old part of Simon to symbolically work through an attachment to his mother that was confounded by their extreme experience, to tackle his sense of psychological loneliness, and to improve his sense of autonomy.

Issues of sexual identity

Simon's oedipal confusion was taken up simultaneously with thinking with him about his current sexual identity. We spoke frankly about sex and relationships in a manner appropriate to his age and development. He was very eager to demonstrate interest in girls. He said they often importuned him for romantic friendships, although the stories were very unlikely. At the same time he evidenced worry that he had somehow been made homosexual by the rapes. He veered between bravado and self-doubt, seeking reassurance from me. He was eventually able to verbalise his worry that because the policemen had been inside him this had forcibly altered his sexual identity. We then spent some time considering the meaning of coercion and consent. He understood that at different levels of his being he had to consent to his sexuality. It was about what he was drawn to, not what was forced on him.

Boredom, distraction, defensiveness and play

Cognitively Simon had a fairly clear narrative, although his dreams, flash-backs and anxieties revealed a more confused and less assured picture. The extreme events had seriously interfered with his sense of autonomy. His symbiotic attachment to his mother revealed itself in his transference relationship to me as the therapeutic work deepened. For instance, he was enormously sensitive to my moods to the extent that I felt he had an uncanny ability to detect my underlying feelings. Sometimes, he spoke of my moods as if they were his own. His observations were often spiced with mildly deprecating comments about his feelings about himself. For instance, while struggling against my own sleepiness (a sure sign of avoidance of the intense feelings evoked by Simon's experiences) Simon noted that he was sleepy and bored. It was too threatening for him to be boring, which would add up to me being bored by him. Putting this directly into words resulted in a flat denial that this was the case. However, putting my own feeling state forward for examination was more productive. For example, 'You know, I'm feeling rather sleepy now. Sometimes I think it's so hard to think about what happened to you and your mum that it's easier just to sleep, then the pain, and everything, fades away'. This offer of my own feelings legitimised his own sensations of wanting the horror to go. But then I wondered, 'How can we be more thoughtful about what has happened without being sleepy?'. 'Well', said Simon, 'we could play with my yo-yo'. This was an attempt at distraction of which I could approve if it is being used creatively. I wondered to myself, does he focus on his beliefs and feelings and then shift into distraction or does the need for distraction come on him (like the sleepi-ness) too defensively, before the issue from which he is seeking distrac-tion emerges into consciousness? Gradually, by judicious offerings of my own reactions to him and noticing and interpreting his feelings and sensations he gained a greater sense of insight and autonomy. Together with the work on his sexuality this enabled him to get free of the oedipal hold of the extreme events on his inner world.

The work here presented is very contracted into a fluency often missing from the spikiness of the sessions. There were sessions when he deterred me with charming defensive strategies and we got little further than playing with his latest toy. It felt initially as if here was a boy who had to please. The index of success was the gradual resolution of his soiling.

My guiding hypothesis was that Simon's lack of sensation in his bowel was a psychological blocking off of the physical and psychic pain of the rape. My hunch was that when he could feel and work through that, full bowel control and sensation would return. Gradually this was so. He was able to accept his feelings; he was able to conceptualise his beliefs and re-order them positively, and as time passed he was able to experience what had happened to him in the past, rather than as a continuous present.

Conclusion

Work of this nature is often horrifying. With David and Elizabeth's family and with Simon it was important to delineate the external world because it provided a structure which made sense of what had happened. This was as equally important as a container for my sense and emotions as it was for them. This was done by understanding the political story; the story of the family in its homeland with all the connotations of culture and differing family patterns and also the story of exile. Understanding their strengths, defences and coping mechanisms provided a structure that enabled their vulnerabilities and the effects of the horror they had endured to be explored. Recognition of their resilience also helped in the establishment of a workable therapeutic alliance.

Finally, it is the complexity of the experience of extreme events that requires a multidimensional model. Therapeutic notions were helpful constructs that enabled me to engage in the work. They are guiding metaphors. The ultimate task was to attune to the experience of David and Elizabeth and their children and to Simon: to close the gap between sensation, experience, language and understanding and enable a more coherent version of the self in the world to come forth. Ultimately, the challenge of this chapter and this work is for us to find ways of clinical thinking that contribute to social and political justice.

References

Anderson, H. and Goolishian, H. (1988) Human systems as linguistic systems: preliminary and evolving ideas about the implications for systemic therapy. Family Process 27, 371–393.

APA (1987) Diagnostic and Statistical Manual of Mental Disorders, 3rd edn, revised (DSM-III-R). Washington, D. C.: American Psychiatric Association.

Bracken, P. (1998) Hidden agendas: deconstructing post traumatic stress disorder. In Bracken, P. and Petty, C., Rethinking the Trauma of War. London: Free Association Books.

Bracken, P. Giller, J. and Summerfield, D. (1995) Psychological responses to war and atrocity: the limitations of current concepts. Social Science and Medicine 40, 1073–1082.

Byng-Hall, J. (1995) Rewriting Family Scripts: Improvisation and Systems Change. London: Guildford Press.

Callaghan, K. (1998) In limbo: movement psychotherapy with refugees and asylum seekers. In Dokter D. (ed.), Art Therapists, Refugees and Migrants: Reaching Across Borders. London: Jessica Kingsley.

Cattenach, A. (1992) Play Therapy with Abused Children. London: Jessica Kingsley.

Cox, M. and Theilgard, A. (1981) Mutative Metaphors in Psychotherapy: The Aeolian Mode, p. 95. London: Jessica Kingsley.

Dawes, A., Tredoux, C. and Feinstein, A. (1992) Political violence in South Africa: some effects on children of the violent destruction of their community. International Journal of Mental Health 18, 16–43.

Dolan, Y. (1991) Resolving Sexual Abuse: Solution Focused Therapy and Ericksonian Hypnosis for Adult Survivors. New York: W. W. Norton.

Eastmond, M. (1989) The Dilemmas of Exile: Chilean Refugees in the United States. Ph.D. Thesis, Department of Social Anthropology, Gothenburg University, Sweden.

Eastmond, M. (1993) National conflict and refugees: re-creating Chilean identity in exile. In Lindholm, H. (ed.), Ethnicity and Nationalism: Formation of Identity and Dynamics of Conflict in the 1990s. Gothenborg: Nordnes.

Eastmond, M. (1998) Nationalist discourses and the construction of difference: Bosnian Muslim refugees in Sweden. Journal of Refugee Studies 11, 161–181.

Eisenbruch, M. (1991) From post-traumatic stress disorder to cultural bereavement: diagnosis of south-east Asian refugees. Social Science and Medicine 33(6), 673–680.

Englund, H. (1998) Death, trauma and ritual: Mozambican refugees in Malawi. Social Science and Medicine 46, 1165–1174.

Fernando, S. (1991) Mental Health, Race and Culture. London: Mind/Macmillan.

Foucault, M. (1972) The Archaeology of Knowledge. New York: Harper and Row.

Freud, A. (1965) Normality and Pathology in Childhood: Assessments of Development. London: Hogarth Press.

Gersie, A. (1997) Reflections on Therapeutic Storymaking: The Use of Stories in Groups. London: Jessica Kingsley.

Gorel-Barnes, G. (1998) Family Therapy in Changing Times. London: Macmillan.

Jones, E. (1993) Family Systems Therapy: Developments in the Milan-Systemic Therapies. Chichester: John Wiley.

Krause, I.-B. (1998) Therapy Across Culture. London: Sage.

Laub, D. and Auerhahn, N. (1993) Knowing and not knowing massive psychic trauma: forms of traumatic memory. International Journal of Psycho-Analysis 74, 287–302.

Loretti, A. (1997) Armed conflicts, health and health services in Africa: an epidemiological framework of reference. Medicine, Conflict and Survival 13, 219–228.

Main, M. (1991) Metacognitive knowledge, metacognitive monitoring, and singular (coherent) vs. multiple (incoherent) model of attachment: findings and directions for future research. In Parkes, C. M., Stevenson-Hinde, J. and Marris, P. (eds), Attachment across the Life Cycle. London: Routledge.

Melzak, S. (1993) You can't always see your reflection when the water is full of soap suds. In Van Willegan, L. (ed.), Health Hazards of Organised Violence in Children. Utrecht: Pharos Foundation.

Merton, R. (1973) The perspective of insiders and outsiders. In Storer, N. W. (ed.), The Sociology of Science: Theoretical and Empirical Investigations, pp. 99–136. Chicago: University of Chicago Press.

Myerhoff, B. (1986) Life not death in Venice: its second life. In Turner, V. W. and Bruner, E. M. (eds), The Anthropology of Experience. Chicago: University of Illinois Press.

Nazroo, J. (1997) Health and health services. In Modood, T. and Berthoud, R. (eds), Ethnic Minorities in Britain: Diversity and Disadvantage. London: Policy Studies Institute.

Papadopoulos, R. and Hildebrand, J. (1997) Is home where the heart is? Narratives of oppositional discourse in refugee families. In Papadopoulos, R. and Byng-Hall, J. (eds), Multiple Voices: Narrative in Systemic Family Psychotherapy. London: Duckworth.

Parkes, C. M. (1997) Normal and abnormal responses to stress: a developmental approach. In Black, D. et al. Psychological Trauma: A Developmental Approach. London: Gaskell.

Phillips, A. (1988) Winnicott. London: Fontana.

Punamaki, R.-J. (1990) Predictors and effectiveness of coping with political violence among Palestinian children. British Journal of Social Psychology 29, 67–77.

Punamaki, R.-J. (1993) Mental health function of war attitudes among Palestinian and Israeli children. In Van Willegen, L. (ed.), Health Hazards of Organised Violence in Children. Utrecht: Pharos Foundation.

Reynolds, P. (1996) Traditional Healers and Childhood in Zimbabwe. Athens, OH: Ohio University Press.

Richman, N. (1998) In the Midst of the Whirlwind: A Manual for Helping Refugee Children. Stoke on Trent: Trentham Books.

Rutter, M. (1985) Resilience in the face of adversity: protective factors and resistence to psychiatric disorder. British Journal of Psychiatry 147, 598–611.

Scarry, E. (1985) The Body in Pain: The Making and Unmaking of the World. New York: Oxford University Press.

Straker, G. (1994) Integrating African and western healing practices in South Africa. American Journal of Psychotherapy 48, 453–467.

Thomas, L. (1992) Racism and psychotherapy: working with racism in the consulting room – an analytic view. In Kareem, J. and Littlewood, R. (eds), Intercultural Therapy: Themes, Interpretation and Practice. Oxford: Blackwell.

UNICEF (1996) The State of the World's Children 1996. Oxford: Oxford University Press/UNICEF.

Van der Kolk, B. (1987) The separation cry and the trauma response: developmental issues in psychobiology of attachment and separation. In van der Kolk, B., Psychological Trauma. Washington: American Psychiatric Press.

White, M. and Epston, D. (1990) Narrative Means to Therapeutic Ends. New York: Norton.

Winnicott, D. (1971) Playing and Reality. London: Routledge.

Woodcock, J. (1995a) Healing rituals with families in exile. Journal of Family Therapy 17, 397–410.

Woodcock, J. (1995b) Family therapy and human rights: working with refugees. Mental Health Nursing 15, 20–22.

Zulueta, F. De (1993) From Pain to Violence: The Traumatic Roots of Destructiveness. London: Whurr.

Zwi, A. and Ugalde, A. (1989) Toward an epidemiology of political violence in the Third World. Social Science and Medicine 28, 633–642.

Index